TERRORISM POST 9/11

An Indian Perspective

IPCS Topical Series 3

Terrorism Post 9/11

An Indian Perspective

Edited by

P.R. CHARI
SUBA CHANDRAN

MANOHAR
2003

First published 2003

ISBN 81-7304-510-0

Published by
Ajay Kumar Jain for
Manohar Publishers & Distributors
4753/23 Ansari Road, Daryaganj
New Delhi 110002

Typeset at
A J Software Publishing Co. Pvt. Ltd.
New Delhi 110005

Printed at
Lordson Publishers Pvt. Ltd.
Delhi 110007

Contents

Preface

WHETHER OR NOT the cataclysm of 9/11 heralds an epochal change in the international system is disputable, although I believe that there are other threats to global peace and security that need equal attention. They include the threat from the proliferation of weapons of mass destruction, especially biological and radiological weapons; the inexorable spread of globalization, its downside subsumes international terrorism; and the crisis of governance, which afflicts different countries in South Asia differently, but should cause deep concern.

That said, the post 9/11 developments have profoundly affected the region. Pakistan became a frontline state in the US war against terrorism against Afghanistan, a status that India could not, obviously, have sought for conferral by the United States. It is evident that the aftermath of the war against terrorism has led to the spread of terrorism within Pakistan—witness the terrorist attacks in Islamabad and Karachi. A definite increase in cross-border terrorism in India was also witnessed, with spectacular attacks being made on India's icons of democracy like the J&K Assembly and Parliament, apart from the Army camp at Kaluchak and the Aksharadham temple in Gujarat. A fillip was provided thereby to the militarization of the two South Asian polities, larger spending on their internal security and defence apparatus, and the brutalization of their societies. A marked deterioration in the security of the region resulted.

Meanwhile, the US military presence has steadily encrusted in and around South Asia. Military bases have come up or been taken over by the United States in Pakistan, Uzbekistan, Tajikistan, and Afghanistan in addition to its subsisting bases in Saudi Arabia, Oman, Diego Garcia and the aircraft carriers positioned in the Northern Arabian Sea. It is doubtful if this military presence will be disestablished soon; indeed, it might be enhanced if the war against terrorism is extended by the United States into Iraq. That possibility could herald a rise in oil prices and add further to the energy security problems of South Asia.

The articles in this selection from the IPCS website were published at different points in time. They have consequently been dated to reflect the concerns that developed and have evolved in the post 9/11 period. This would become clear from the summary of discussions relating to the several seminars held in IPCS over the intervening months since 9/11 erupted. These articles/ seminar proceedings have been grouped together under seven headings that might be noticed in the table of contents. Apart from these articles and seminar proceedings the texts of several international conventions have been included in this volume, adopted by the international community over the last three decades. Unfortunately, the SAARC Convention on Terrorism is not being implemented in the region for reasons that are as recondite as they are tragic. It has also been included.

This issue of Topical Series is being published as a book in cooperation with M/s. Manohar Publishers & Distributors. Two earlier issues on *The Agra Summit* and *Kashmir* were brought out as IPCS publications. It is hoped to continue this Topical Series in future by focusing on further questions of significance to Indian security.

25.10.2002 P.R. CHARI

I. General

War against Terrorism: Some Anti-Thoughts

P.R. CHARI

IT IS ACCEPTED that the 9/11 cataclysm was traumatic for the United States. There is universal sympathy for the loss of lives suffered in New York and Washington on 9/11, although the US war against terrorism launched against Afghanistan, causing the loss of thousands of innocent civilians has been no less traumatic for that benighted country. This war speedily resolved itself into getting hold of Osama bin Laden and Mullah Omar "dead or alive". Hence, it has failed to achieve its war aims since both these worthies are widely believed to have escaped into the tribal region between Afghanistan and Pakistan along with large numbers of the Taliban and *Al-Qaeda* elements. Many of these latter warriors are believed to have slipped into Pakistan Occupied Kashmir (POK), where they present a cause for concern to India.

There are several questionable aspects of this war against terrorism. For one, using the term "war" is excessive. A war needs being fought against an identifiable enemy; terrorism is a faceless, inchoate phenomenon. War against a phenomenon introduces imprecision into the equation. Furthermore, "war" has a precise connotation in international law; consequently, prisoners of war are entitled to the protection of the Geneva Conventions. This creates problems as was witnessed in the inhumane treatment of Taliban/ *Al-Qaeda* soldiers captured in Afghanistan and incarcerated in Guantanamo. In truth, President Bush used the term "war" and expression "war against terrorism" essentially to conjure up evocative language to make it appear that the United States was doing something spectacular to avenge the outrage committed against it by the suicide pilots on September 11.

Bush's actions are comparable to those of Prime Minister Vajpayee after the terrorist attack on the Indian Parliament on December 13. High rhetoric followed to justify the need to proceed against cross-border terrorism by massively dispatching the Indian armed forces to the Indo-Pak border, where they remain deployed to this date. Terrorism in Kashmir, however, has not ceased; neither is this possible until a political solution is found to the Kashmir problem. Some proportion of this terrorism is obviously being perpetrated by locally based terrorists. Besides, foreign terrorists could be infiltrated through Nepal or Bangladesh or come via the sea route. It is not clear how stopping cross-border terrorism, assuming Pakistan is willing and able to effect this, would help eradicate terrorism in Kashmir. Indeed, the communal riots in Gujarat have created propitious conditions for hundreds of new recruits to join the terrorists.

There are further inconsistencies which can be framed in the question: is the war against terrorism contextual? Can terrorists become freedom fighters in one *avatar* and terrorists again in another *avatar*? This might appear impossible; apropos the Taliban, who were trained by the ISI in Pakistan, were transformed into freedom fighters when they were drafted against the Soviet occupation of Afghanistan, but have been re-converted into terrorists after 9/11. The United States had acquiesced in their training and utilization by the ISI and ignored their depredations and human rights violations in Afghanistan, especially against women. But, after September 11 they were hunted down as terrorists, responsible for the attacks on the WTC towers in New York and the Pentagon in Washington. No proof was adduced by the United States of their complicity in these attacks, and it is worth reiterating that fifteen of the nineteen terrorists responsible for hijacking the aircraft used in these crimes were Saudi citizens.

Which brings us to another aspect of the war against terrorism. Why was Afghanistan chosen as the culprit to atone for the sins of Osama bin Laden and Mullah Omar, and not Saudi Arabia. The list of charges against the "keeper of the holy places" is very long. It supported the Taliban and *Al-Qaeda* in their conflict against the

Soviets and later to seize the reins of power in Afghanistan. It is no surprise that Saudi Arabia recognized the Taliban government in Kabul, in the company of Pakistan and the United Arab Emirates. Besides, it is well known that the Saudis have financially supported the establishment of *madrasas* in South Asia, and bankrolled *jihadi* organizations all over the Muslim world. Why, then, has Saudi Arabia been exempted from either being attacked or even mildly censured for its stellar role in promoting international terrorism. Has its oil reserves, and American dependence on its manipulation of oil supplies and oil prices, stopped even censure of its nefarious role in promoting terrorism?

The short conclusion is possible that the war against terrorism cannot be contextual; it must be absolute. A pick and choose policy will not work. The problem is: who will cast the first stone with skeletons rattling away in various national cupboards. Cynicism, therefore, might remain the name of the game.

15 July 2002

War against Terrorism: Its Fuller Dimensions

P.R. CHARI

WHY DID THE United States stitch together an international coalition before launching its war against terrorism in Afghanistan? The short answer is that the US is aware that international terrorism reflects the downside of globalization, and the war against it cannot be waged unless the cooperation of the international community is procured.

The bombing of a church in Islamabad and the suicide attack upon the French technicians in Karachi dramatically testifies to the *Al-Qaeda* presence in Pakistan. Their network extends across 50-60 countries. Terrorist organizations are flourishing in several other parts of the world. It would be impossible to counter them unless the international community unites to address this problem. Some immediacy is therefore required to urgently address the draft Comprehensive International Convention Against Terrorism placed before the United Nations; hopefully, the compromises needed for its adoption will not eviscerate its basic content. The working document submitted by India enjoins State Parties to include the causing of death or serious bodily injury, and damage to State facilities, public transportation systems, communication facilities or infrastructure as criminal offences under their domestic laws, irrespective of their purported political, ideological, ethnic or religious nature. Significantly, if an aggrieved State Party makes such a request, the State Party in which the suspect is residing is obliged to weigh the evidence and prosecute offenders under its domestic laws, unless it decides to extradite them in terms of any prior agreement subsisting between two or more State Parties.

It bears reiteration that a convention to tackle international terrorism must be anchored on State Parties enacting domestic legislation to deal with the criminal offences listed therein, with additional provisions to either prosecute or extradite identified offenders against whom a prima facie case is made out. Thus far nations have not undertaken these seemingly non-controversial measures. On the contrary, the aiding and abetment of cross-border terrorism has become an instrument of foreign policy in South Asia, despite the fact that these countries have suffered grievous loss of lives and property due to terrorism—domestic, cross-border and international. Aware of its threat to national security, however, they had concluded the SAARC Regional Convention on Suppression of Terrorism in August 1988, which incorporated several of the general principles listed in a UN General Assembly Resolution passed as far back as December 1985. The SAARC Convention established a mutually accepted code for dealing with transnational political terrorism. But its failure to achieve any tangible results over the years is traceable to the lack of political will in the South Asian countries to act either unilaterally or bilaterally or multilaterally, despite the knowledge that cross-border terrorism can be greatly exacerbated by external manipulation. Several of these countries have yet to bring their domestic laws into conjunction with the provisions of the Convention although more than a decade has passed since it was adopted.

There are many other concrete steps that the South Asian countries could take at the declaratory and substantive levels to deal with the problem of terrorism in the region. This would include: unequivocal condemnation of terrorist activities; harmonization of domestic legislation dealing with terrorism; intelligence-sharing by exchanging "look-out lists" of wanted terrorists fleeing across national frontiers; and sharing experience about anti-terrorist operations and techniques. The recently concluded SAARC Summit declaration in Kathmandu has pledged them to fight terrorism "in all its forms and manifestations including by increased cooperation and full implementation of the relevant international conventions relating to terrorism", and "to prevent and suppress the financing of terrorist acts by criminalizing the collections of funds for such acts and refraining from organizing, instigating, assisting or participating in terrorist acts in States or acquiescing in organized activities within its territory directed towards the commission of such acts". These pious declarations will remain empty rhetoric unless credible steps are taken by the SAARC countries to implement them.

The history of the last decade has shown that, with the passage of time and availability of foreign assistance, a steady improvement has occurred in the competence of terrorist groups. This makes their suppression by State entities, acting individually, increasingly difficult. Besides, a nexus gets established between terrorism—national and international—and plainly criminal activity like human trafficking, extortion rackets, kidnapping for ransom and so on. International terrorism is also linked with, but also exacerbates, the allied transnational problems of small arms proliferation, drugs trafficking, money laundering and organized international crime. All these nefarious activities must be proceeded against if the war against terrorism is to succeed. The root causes underlying terrorism, however, lie in various protests against injustices in national and international polity. They need being seriously addressed in the war against terrorism, instead of dealing only with its outer manifestations.

21 May 2002

War against Terrorism: Can it be Compartmentalized?

P.R. CHARI

IS THE WAR AGAINST terrorism contextual? Is it premised on time and place, requiring a case-by-case determination? These uncomfortable questions need being raised about the current American, Pakistani and Indian approaches towards this war against terrorism.

No religious or political objectives can justify the horrendous attacks on the World Trade Centre Towers in New York and the Pentagon on September 11, causing a grievous loss of civilian lives. This led to the spouting of high rhetoric by President Bush to alleviate the American nation's unaccustomed sense of vulnerability and violability. But, the American war against terrorism soon transformed itself into a single-minded effort to capture Osama bin Laden and Mullah Omar, and the decimation of the Taliban/*Al-Qaeda* outfits. The United States has committed itself now to the daunting task of governing Afghanistan, whilst continuing to search for the elusive Osama bin Laden and Mullah Omar.

However, the painful question must be asked why the evils of terrorism, personified by this elusive duo, was undiscovered until 11 September 2001 by the United States. Neither was Pakistan earlier presented with the Hobson's choice of either supporting the Taliban/*Al-Qaeda* organizations or joining the global effort against international terrorism. Only the slightest reflection would inform that the ISI, Taliban and *Al-Qaeda* had formed an unholy alliance, bonding President Musharraf with Osama bin Laden and Mullah Omar. None of this was unknown to the ubiquitous CIA. The entirely contextual nature of the present US war against terrorism is patent; its past assistance to terrorist groups in Southern Africa and Central America might be usefully recollected in this regard.

Coming to Pakistan, the major problem confronting President Musharraf's participation in this war, despite the high rhetoric in his January 12 (2002) speech against the *Jihadists,* lies in reversing a policy assiduously pursued by his predecessors and himself for decades. Further, Pakistan's strategic goal in fomenting the proxy war in Kashmir was designed to turn that State into a modern-day version of the "Spanish ulcer" that defeated Napoleon. This objective could never have succeeded in detaching Kashmir from India. In truth, Pakistan's internal socio-political problems have greatly worsened instead; but its folly in continuing with this bankrupt policy exemplifies what Barbara Tuchmann said: "All misgovernance is contrary to self-interest in the long run, but may actually strengthen a regime. It qualifies as folly when it is perverse persistence in a policy demonstrably unworkable or counter-productive." Pakistan's present unenthusiastic support to the war against terrorism is entirely contextual; whilst supporting the US military campaign against the Taliban and *Al-Qaeda* in Afghanistan, it has continued to encourage their depredations in India.

That brings me to the Indian case. The NDA government's alacrity in supporting the American war against terrorism was conditioned by India's problems with cross-border terrorism dramatized by the brazen assaults on major symbols of Indian democracy, viz., the J&K Legislative Assembly on 1 October (2001) and Parliament House on 13 December (2001) last year. India has wisely chosen to unreservedly join the global war against terrorism in its best national self-interests. But its recent history would reveal the contextual nature of its present policy. India had encouraged, trained, armed, and financed the *Mukti Bahini* to excise East Bengal from Pakistan and create Bangladesh in 1971. Indeed, a proposal was made within the inner councils of the Government in 1986 that India might promote a joint statement pledging South Asian countries to eschew supporting terrorism in their neighbours. This was rejected as being "disastrous". The reason was clear; such a statement would have indicted India's covert support of the LTTE and other militant Tamil groups in Sri Lanka highlighting the contextual nature of India's perceptions of terrorism. The rest, as they say, is history.

What emerges from this dismal recital is that cant and hypocrisy must be abjured if the war against terrorism is to be credibly fought. Regrettably, it is viewed in South Asia only through the prism of national self-interests because, unsurprisingly, several bureaucratic constituencies are flourishing in the region that have a stake in not defeating terrorism. How committed the United States, Pakistan and India are to continuing the war against terrorism once the immediate problem of establishing a government with some minimal credibility in Afghanistan is achieved and the US turns its attention to some other troubled region in the world will soon become clear.

Meanwhile, by concentrating its troops on the border New Delhi has placed itself in limbo; opening hostilities with Pakistan could lead to unpredictable escalation. Withdrawing its troops, however, would resemble a similar exercise by the Duke of York in the Regency period who marched his troops up a hill and, thereafter, marched them down the hill.

21 May 2002

Terror Hunt: Hounding with Biometrics

MAJ. GEN. (RETD) YASHWANT DEVA

They will be brought to justice or justice will be brought to them.

GEORGE W. BUSH

How do we recognize Osama bin Laden or Masood Azhar to bring them to book? Does the answer lie in biometrics, the science of recognizing a person using distinguishing traits? Physiological and behavioural characteristics are unique to an individual and can be scanned, and scaled and scrutinized. The former include fingerprints, retinal and iris peculiarities, hand geometry, voice patterns, and facial recognition; the latter encompass gait, speech, handwriting, signatures, mannerisms, gestures; and traits that remain to be explored. Of greater scientific precision is the DNA test, of significance to verify the true identity of an individual, when boarding an aircraft, entering a high security zone, immigration control, police verification of suspects, security identification and collecting evidence to bring terrorists to justice. Passports, identity cards, personal identification numbers (PINs), photo identification and "tokens" are undoubtedly a help, but can be compromised. On the other hand, a digital biometric reader or identifier is distinctly more precise and cannot be easily duped. Sensor fusion is a natural cognitive attribute of the cerebrum and, if imitated artificially, can lead to functional integration of gadgetry.

Biometrics was a developed science during ancient times in India. References abound in the *Puranas* and *Mahabharata* of identification by physiological parameters. Elsewhere, too, there are records of it being practiced, though more as a 'black art' by some high priests. Later, in the nineteenth century, there was a marked spurt in research. During the days of the Raj, the science of criminology worked on the mistaken premise that physical features and characteristics were associated with criminal tendencies. This led to a variety of measuring devices and collection of data to detect latent tendencies that had the potential for legal abuse. However the idea of measuring individual physical characteristics was accepted. With the parallel development of fingerprinting, biometrics acquired international acceptance. Records of complexion, eye colour, height and so on were routinely kept to augment fingerprints and photographs.

Today biometrics is a frontier technology. Over the last decade the biometric industry has come a long way. Many devices are in the market, and some are reportedly used by hi-tech criminals.

Biometrics has many versatile but yet-to-mature applications. Of significance here is detection of bank frauds, Automatic Teller Machine (ATM) operations, workstation and network access, e-business transactions over the Internet, biometrics embedded credit card, key encryption security enhancement, digital water-marking, public identity smart cards and, above all, voice recognition for telephonic conversations. Biometrics can lend greater potency to digital signatures, which the country has adopted from 26 January 2001. The sky is the limit for possibilities that can be put to use for cyber intelligence operations, e.g. tracking *hawala* (money laundering) and illicit drug trails, monitoring Internet Relay Chats (IRC), e-mails, steganography and for counter-hacking and counter-terror operations.

There are undoubtedly many problems and gray areas in realizing the full potential of this technology, some technical, some commercial, but more psychological. The first problem lies in obtaining the sample or biometric template of the individual, whose identity is to be verified. Undoubtedly this is a Herculean task and often a sheer impossibility. However it would be folly if biometric samples have not been gathered and archived for example in respect of Osama bin Laden or Masood Azhar. The technology can work in controlled lab conditions or perhaps in a virtual environment, but not for real-time or large scale. The unit cost of gadgets is exorbitant and currently there is no demand for mass application.

The performance of a biometric device is measured in terms of its failure rate—"accept-fail" or the likelihood that an impostor may be accepted, and "reject-fail" or the likelihood of rejection of a *bonafide* person. The bias for either leaves scope for manipulation and spoofing, besides putting a question mark on its confidence level. Take for instance fingerprints, the absolute uniqueness of which is often debated. Recently a justice in the US has rejected the admissibility of fingerprint evidence, terming it subjective. Voice verification products also suffer because of variability of both transducers and environmental acoustics. Odour identification is an exciting domain of application, but is yet to acquire a viable character.

Much work continues to be undertaken and it will be interesting to watch its progress. Integration, scan-fusion and networking will achieve the desired quality and product reliability. Biometrics is a transition from science fiction to an over-the-horizon technology. Let us create public awareness about it and get down to some serious R&D.

10 April 2002

Terrorism and Tourism

Cdr. Vijay Sakhuja

Political and religious leaders across the world expressed indignation at the Taliban's decision to destroy the Buddhist statues in Bamiyan. Gen. Hamid Gul, former head of Pakistan's ISI, was quoted as saying: "This is their [the Taliban's] way of forcing the world to pay attention, to take them seriously." The recent threat to blow up the Taj Mahal by the *Lashkar-e-Taiba* (LeT) validates Gul's statement. The security around it and other major centers of tourism has now been tightened.

This is not the first time that tourism has become a target of terrorist attacks. In the early nineties, terrorists kidnapped five foreign tourists in Kashmir. There were several other incidents of pilgrims and even tourists being targeted by the terrorists. The LeT *fidayeen* (suicide) attack at the Red Fort clearly shows that the tourism industry is vulnerable to attacks.

Terrorists are well aware that the tourism industry is averse to uncertainty and sensitive to political and economic events, and have capitalized on these vulnerabilities for two reasons: first, this is seen as a way to influence political behaviour and, secondly, as a tool to destroy the state economy. These were the motives that triggered the actions of the *Al-gama'at al-Islamiya*, an Egyptian Islamic organisation that surfaced in 1997. It was responsible for several attacks in Egypt, including the assault on foreign tourists in Luxor in November 1997 in which 62 died. This brought Egyptian tourism to a grinding halt.

The impact of the events of September 11 on tourism is no different. According to the International Labour Organization, they severely affected the tourism sector and resulted in the loss of nearly nine million jobs worldwide and a 30-40 per cent drop in travel demands in the US, with revenues declining drastically. The impact on hotels was immediate with a drop-off in business of 40 to 50 per cent. The impact on the airline industry has been so damaging that it will take much time before it takes off.

While international attention has focused on the air and land components of the tourism industry, little attention has been paid to the disastrous effects on marine tourism. The September 11 attacks in the US have also taken a heavy toll of the sea cruise industry. Fewer passengers are embarking on liners. Renaissance Cruise filed for bankruptcy, stating that it was a victim of the terrorism fallout. Similarly, the London-based P&O Princess Cruises and the US-based Royal Caribbean announced a merger, noting that ships around the world were half empty. The declining revenue is due to companies struggling to pay more for security and insurance.

Terrorists have struck at cruise liners and merchant vessels to achieve their goals. In 1961, political insurgents embarked the Portuguese passenger liner *Santa Maria* as valid passengers. The ensuing scuffle resulted in several casualties, including one officer killed and eight crew members wounded.

But it was the Achille Lauro incident that sensitized the international community to the menace of terrorism at sea and the formulation of an international convention by the UN. This hijacking was a wake-up call that resulted in the introduction of several security measures such as the screening of all boarding passengers by metal detectors, hand baggage checks by X-Ray machines, surveillance and inspections of the ship's hull and added physical security of ships.

At the World Tourism Organization's 14th General Assembly and the Millennium Conference of Tourism Leaders in October 2001 held in Osaka, the participants were unanimous in their opinion that "terrorism is the direct enemy of tourism". Closer home, Prime Minister Vajpayee noted that terrorism is the foe of tourism. He said, "Whereas terrorism feeds on intolerance and arrogance, tourism breeds tolerance and empathy. Terrorism seeks to erect walls of hatred between faiths and communities. Tourism breaks such barriers. Terrorism detests pluralism, whereas tourism celebrates it. Terrorism has no respect for human life. Tourism pays tribute to all that is beautiful in nature and in human life."

According to experts, the tourism industry faces a major crisis and it will take some time for it to recover from the fallout of the September 11 attacks. If that be the case, the industry needs to face up to the fact that terrorism has become a component of modern day travel, and must develop strategies to counter its effect. Industry experts need to undertake a major overhaul of the security apparatus, building designs, staff-training, employ 'sea and air marshals' and use technology to improve security. There will always be risks, but a judicious employment of innovative security measures and guest management would add to the resilience of the industry.

17 February 2002

Terror Hunt: Warehousing and Mining Data

Maj. Gen. (Retd) Yashwant Deva

The official announcement of every terrorist attack invariably concludes with a stock phrase, "*Ghatna sthal ke nikat suraksha ke prabandh our kare kar diye gaye hain*" (security arrangements around the place of incident have been further strengthened). However each incident is succeeded by another attack, to be followed by a similar announcement. Terror strikes at the place and time of its choosing. Yet there is a pattern and that pattern essentially lies in the behaviour of the terrorist and *modus operandi* of the parent organization.

Future attacks cannot be predicted, but past ones can be catalogued, stored and retrieved in near real-time. "Data archiving" and "data mining" are scientific tools and methodologies, the former for gathering, sifting, hoarding and storehousing data, and the latter for displaying duly processed critical information to the decision-maker, whenever the need arises. Its hallmarks are virtuality and event-retrieval potential, and its purpose is to match, locate and track saboteurs, hijackers and terrorists.

In April 1999, Applied Systems Intelligence Inc was selected by the US Air Force to develop innovative information technology for a Global Information Base to "store global awareness information", besides providing information services for dynamic planning and execution of operations. The software developed by the firm is called KARNAC, short for Knowledge-Aided Retrieval in Activity Context. It is highly versatile, and is anchored in a group of technologies and decision support and database management systems. It is designed to detect and identify impending terrorist operations and similar missions.

It is well known that *Al-Qaeda* terrorists and others of their ilk hunt for information on the Internet, often leaving valuable clues while surfing and communicating. Therefore it is logical to look for and pursue them in their haunt rather than go on hunting missions. Adam Pasik writes in "Sifting through Data to Detect New Attacks", (infowar.com), "The problem is that intelligence and law-enforcement agencies are searching the world's biggest haystack—untold exabytes, or quintillions of bytes of data stored on computers across the globe—to uncover a few dangerous needles."

At the time of the September 11 attacks, there was a plethora of helpful scraps of information available e.g. e-mail intercepts, telephone calls, car rentals, airline reservations, financial transactions, casino winnings, immigration records and much more. During the attack on our Parliament, the terrorists left behind pertinent information such as a laptop, which has reportedly been sent to Microsoft for analysis, and vital information about the terrorists' *hawala* (money laundering) links and ISI connections garnered from cellular numbers called by the terrorists. Whereas security, intelligence and law-enforcement agencies work in tandem in the US and other Western democracies with common databases, in India, the right hand does not know what the left holds. Sharing information is the only way terrorists can be defeated at their own game and this sharing must occur within the security and law-enforcement agencies in the country, and also amongst all the countries fighting the global war against terrorism.

Critical event detection, information retrieval and knowledge-based technologies, products and systems are available off-the-shelf, and are widely used in the commercial world. Banking fraud detection, promotional mailing, market research, supply chain management, tracking stolen credit cards, and antecedent check by credit companies are some of these applications. The potential market for these products is estimated to be several hundred million dollars. Indian software companies are aware of its potential and have ventured into writing some useful software applications. The software is not infallible, but that should not detract from its merits, which essentially lies in integration, automation and embedded security.

The technology can bring to focus artificial intelligence and virtual reality to search large data repositories, identify events of interest and compare templates. Elsewhere, much work has been done to acquire this capability. The rub lies in matching wits, in which the terrorists have an edge. Making events appear unrelated, random and seemingly innocuous is their strong point. Archived information can help in timely detection by piecing together the pattern, and sounding the alert based on past acts of terror. It could thereby preempt attack on a government or commercial facility.

7 February 2002

Attack on American Centre, Kolkata

P.R. CHARI

THAT THE ATTACK ON the police personnel guarding the American Centre in Kolkata, was obviously carefully planned. It was timed around 6.30 a.m. when the guards were being changed. This was probably a daily routine, and has been studied by the assailants. Two motorcyclists mounted the attacks, one very shortly after the other, knowing that the second attack could take advantage of the confusion resulting from the first. Pillion riders armed with AK 47 rifles did the actual indiscriminate shooting. These terrorist tactics were extensively used during the Punjab militancy in the eighties.

The choice of victims, Indian security force personnel guarding the American Cenatre, although some civilians got caught in the indiscriminate shooting, was designed to serve a political end, viz., to show down the Indian state, and its growing cooperative relationship with the United States, in a spectacular manner. The symbolism of this terrorist act therefore cannot be missed. It has occurred when the Indian and American governments are discussing measures to increase their cooperation in counter-terrorism operations in New Delhi.

A Dubai-based mafia member, Farhan Malik alias Aftab Ansari, has claimed responsibility for this attack. He is associated with the *Harkat-ul-Jihadi-Islami* outfit, which, apparently, has intimate links with Pakistan's ISI organization. The Indian government has, wisely, not displayed a knee-jerk reaction by blaming Pakistan for this attack, which could vitiate the already existing tense relations between the two countries. Until credible evidence becomes available after a full and proper investigation, it would be unwise to blame any country or organization, lest an embarrassing retraction later become necessary.

Farhan Malik is a mafia element. His links with India-based criminals must also be properly investigated, and strict action taken against his local links. The internal and external dimensions of terrorism are equally important. So, of course, is cross-border terrorism.

Another point to be made here is the imperative need for a national consensus to unitedly fight the war against terrorism. The Opposition parties in West Bengal have criticized the government for its alleged security failure as a ritual, without appreciating that the terrorist always has the advantage of surprise. Such attacks, moreover, can never be totally anticipated or prevented from happening. Instead of criticizing the party in power for such alleged failures, it would be useful if all political parties and citizens cooperate with each other to deal with this menace of political terrorism.

25 January 2002

Challenging Terrorism at Sea

CDR. VIJAY SAKHUJA

MORE THAN EIGHTY naval ships including aircraft carriers and nuclear submarines are currently deployed in the Arabian Sea as part of the international coalition to support the US war on terrorism in Afghanistan. They include ships provided by the US, UK, Canada, France, Italy, Germany, the Netherlands, Australia and Japan. According to Rear Admiral Fitzgerald, Commander, US naval forces in the Arabian Sea, the coalition ships have "pretty much sealed the coast" of Pakistan to vessels that might attempt to smuggle *Al-Qaeda* operatives and Taliban leaders out of the region. According to intelligence agencies, the *Al-Qaeda* is reported to own about twenty merchant vessels capable of ocean passage. These vessels are operated or chartered through front companies in Liberia, Panama and the Isle of Man.

The terrorist groups appear to be extending their land attack capabilities to the maritime domain. Maritime assets (commercial ships, liners, ferries, ports and maritime infrastructures) are vulnerable to attack by terrorist groups. But what is most worrisome is the ability of the terrorists to challenge and attack naval vessels. The *Al-Qaeda* attack on USS Cole in Yemen, Tamil Sea Tigers attack on Sri Lankan naval ships and the attempted *Hamas* attack on Israeli naval craft are pointers to the fact that even warships are not safe. The recent arrest in Singapore of twelve *Al-Qaeda* operatives planning to attack the island nation's deep water naval port has added to the risk of attack.

Terrorist tactics involve attacking ships both in harbour and at sea. They are known to use improvised explosive devices, submersibles, mini submarines and high-speed boats. Dual-use technologies such as the Global Positioning Systems (GPS), satellite communication systems, sea sport scooters and scuba diving equipment are found in their inventories. At sea, these terrorist groups have used rocket-propelled grenades, explosive-loaded speedboats and even armour piercing weapons. The terrorist networks have kept pace with changing technologies and have adapted themselves to counter maritime forces. It is therefore essential to understand the contemporary and emerging tactics and technologies employed by terrorist groups.

Although it is too early to determine trends or patterns in maritime terrorism, terrorists have struck in Latin America, Europe, Middle East, and in South and South East Asia. Among the two dozen odd terrorist groups identified to have engaged in maritime terrorism, at least nine are currently active and five operate in the Asia Pacific region. Notable among them are the (*Liberation Tigers of Tamil Eelam*) LTTE in Sri Lanka and the *Moro Islamic Liberation Front* (MLF) in the Philippines. The recent capture by the Israeli navy of *Karine–A*, a Palestinian ship, carrying 50 tons of lethal ammunition has added to this growing list.

With the center of gravity of international terrorism shifting from the Middle East to Pakistan and Afghanistan, there appears to be a confluence between groups located in the Asia Pacific region and those in the Middle East. These groups have built sophisticated organizations that run an efficient network of commercial as also terrorist activities pursuing their business with total impunity.

Like terrorism, piracy at sea is an international crime. It is also a form of terrorism that affects the crew, passengers and shipowners. Its perpetrators engage in violence for both political objectives and commercial profit. An aircraft hijacking makes sensational news and attracts media attention, but piracy at sea remains a non-issue for the world. The International Maritime Bureau reported a total of 469 attacks on ships in 2000. They resulted in 72 seafarers being killed and 99 injured, up from 3 killed and 24 injured in 1999. There is an alarming rise in piracy and robbery in Indonesia, Bangladesh, Malacca Straits, India, Ecuador and the Red Sea. The center of gravity of piracy appears to have shifted to the Bay of Bengal-Malacca Straits region.

Terrorism has come to stalk the maritime environment. Terrorists recognize that maritime infrastructure is the soft underbelly of states that can be attacked with little effort. They have the capacity and capability to disrupt maritime enterprise and threaten the peaceful use of the seas. It is a wakeup call for all naval forces and coast guards to reinforce their capabilities to challenge this menace of terrorism at sea.

19 January 2002

International Terrorism: The Pakistan Connection

DR. SUBHASH KAPILA

INTERNATIONAL TERRORISM in its most diabolical manifestation found expression on 11 September 2001 when *jihadis* wreaked vengeance and terror in New York and Washington. Their vicious attacks were aimed at two symbolic targets of the mightiest nation in the world, namely the seats of American global military and financial power.

Regrettably for the Islamic world, which may not be largely associated with it, international terrorism is associated with *jihadi* terrorism from Algeria to Chechenya to India, Israel and the United States. Islamic terrorism in earlier periods was left wing in nature and confined to the Middle East. The decades of the 1980s and 1990s witnessed the transformation of Islamic terrorism into *jihadi* terrorism, generated and dictated by Islamic fundamentalists, under the guidance of Pakistan.

The loci of Islamic *jihadi* terrorism shifted from the Middle East to Pakistan and Afghanistan. Pakistan became its chief proponent and adopted it as an instrument of state policy to achieve its strategic gains. Today, with Pakistan declaring that it would join the American campaign against international terrorism terrorism, it would be pertinent to highlight Pakistan's connections with Osama bin Laden, the Taliban and international terrorist organizations.

Pakistan's active links with Osama bin Laden spans the premiership of Benazir Bhutto to President Musharraf. It is strange that while General Bashir, under US pressure, forced him to leave Sudan in May 1996, Osama bin Laden found sanctuary in

Afghanistan under the tutelage and control of Pakistan. Benazir Bhutto was then the Prime Minister. Pakistan's Inter-Services Intelligence (ISI) consolidated the *jihadi* terrorist camps in Afghanistan. Pakistan also shifted many of its own Kashmiri terrorist camps to the Afghan side to evade global censure.

Osama bin Laden did not have to set up a terrorist infrastructure on arrival in Afghanistan. It was ready for him in the network of training camps established by Pakistan's ISI and Qazi Hussain Ahmed's (Chief, *Jamaat-e-Islam*) followers in the Pakistani defence establishment. Osama bin Laden's logistics, communications, training camps, weapons, equipment and explosives were provided by the Pakistan Army.

The Taliban have imposed a medieval Islamic society upon Afghanistan. Terror has been the chief weapon to continue their hold on Afghanistan. The Taliban was also created, organized and assisted by Pakistan to take control of Afghanistan during the tenure of Benazir Bhutto as Prime Minister. Her Interior Minister, Major General Naseerullah Babar was its architect.

Pakistan's aim was to have a regime in Afghanistan, which would be Islamic fundamentalist in character and hence immune to Western pressures. Such regime, under Pakistani tutelage, would serve two aims: (a) Provide strategic depth to Pakistan, and (b) Host the network of Islamic *jihadi* organizations; their being in Afghanistan would provide Pakistan an exit route for deniability of involvement.

The Taliban has been propped up by Pakistan. Even Pakistani authors like Ahmed Rashid have documented Pakistan's financial grants to Taliban despite its own insolvency. These grants find no reflection in Pakistan's budget figures. Obviously, the money came from Pakistan Army's state-sponsored drug-trafficking.

Peshwar in Pakistan emerged as the centre of the pan-Islamic international *jihadi* organizations. The first bureau was opened by Dr. Ayman-al-Zawahiri in 1984. He has since emerged as a top aide of bin Laden. In 1993, former Pakistan Army Chief Gen. Mirza Aslam Beg and Lt Gen. Hamid Gul attended the Popular Arab and Islamic Conference (PAIC) in Khartoum. This conference discussed Pakistan's role in the Armed Islamic Movement and international terrorism. ISI's front organizations like the *Markaz-Dawat-al-Arshad* and others have been boasting of their international Islamic terrorist connections and the successes they have had. Today, with the consolidation of pan-Islamic terrorists from all over the Islamic world in these Pakistan-based or Pakistani-sponsored organizations, it would be fair to say that all of them are involved in international terrorism.

The United States had long ignored Islamic *jihadi* terrorism, because it felt invulnerable to it. The myth was broken on September 11. The US needs to pay heed to what Brigadier S.K. Malik of the Pakistan Army wrote in his book *The Quranic Concept of War* in 1979: "Terror is not a means of imposing decision upon the enemy; it is the decision we impose on him." The US has now to decide whether Pakistan provides both the support and the means to eliminate global terrorism.

10 October 2001

A Border Guards Organization for Anti-Terrorist Operations

BRIG. (RETD) S.S. CHANDEL

INDIAN INTELLIGENCE HAS chosen to remain myopic, both in terms of space (neighbours, relevant nations and superpowers) and time (present and future); all our wars in 1947, 1962, 1965, 1971 and 1999 bear testimony of this statement. We did not have foreknowledge of the Pakistani nuclear capability. Our infirmities regarding anti-terrorist operations have caused consternation and led to increase in the central paramilitary forces—Central Reserve Police Force (CRPF), Border Security Force (BSF), Indo-Tibetan Border Police Force (ITBF) and the various provincial armed constabularies. These forces are ineffective and incompetent to tackle the motivated, skilled and hardy Afghan, Pakistani, Naga and other terrorists.

The BSF cannot effectively guard our border for the following three reasons: Firstly, the BSF is not knowledgeable about the terrain, people, language, and local sensitivities. Secondly, its personnel keep getting rotated, thus losing the expertise gained and contacts cultivated. Thirdly, they stand apart as outsiders, inhibiting trust from likely sources and agents. The CRPF and provincial armed constabularies are basically a *lathi* (stick) wielding and physically unfit force who are killed and have their weapons taken away with sickening regularity in Nagaland, Manipur and Jammu & Kashmir.

Border guards should be recruited from the region nearest to the area of operations; the Ladakh Scouts have been recruited for operations in Ladakh and they have performed very well in all the

Indo-Pak wars. There is a need for raising Kargil Scouts, Doda and Kishtwar Scouts, Punjab Rangers and Rajasthan Rangers. Similarly, Western and Eastern Sea Guards and Andaman Sea Guards should be raised from coastal and island fishermen. The usual physical and educational standards should be modified to suit the local standards as in the case of Gorkhas and Assam Regiments. The terms of engagement should be up to the age of 45 years for all ranks, and they should remain located in the same region for the duration of their service. Many advantages will accrue out of these arrangements. For instance, a ready reserve of personnel will be available in times of need. They could disrupt the enemy's lines of communication if he penetrates the border in depth. The population will also get employment resulting in economic prosperity; buying them for providing intelligence to the enemy will then become very difficult.

The men should be equipped only with small and held signal sets like cellular phones. Their training should be organized by a regular unit posted in the neighbourhood. This will obviate the requirement of raising expensive training centres. The duration of training should not exceed three months. Emphasis should be laid on weapons training, field craft, mines and explosives. Drill and ceremonials should be pruned. Commanding officer, second in command, adjutant and quartermaster should be from the regular army on deputation. Company commanders and other officers should be promoted from the ranks on the basis of their field performance.

These border guards should be tasked to patrol the land borders and coastal waters on foot, local ponies or yaks or local boats/ trawlers to identify and report any intrusion or hostile act to which the appropriate service—Army, Navy or Air Force—can react.

28 August 2001

II. The WTC Attacks and After

Shifts in American Anti-Terrorist Policy

R. VENKATA RAMANI

IT IS WELL KNOWN that international terrorism is a threat to the safety and security of Americans. In 2001 around 63 per cent of terrorist incidents worldwide were committed against American citizens or their properties, the worst being the September 11 attack on the World Trade Centre, New York, which changed the perception that America is immune to terrorist attacks by foreign nationals on its own soil. Till then, attacks by foreign terrorists on Americans were on foreign soil. September 11 rang an alarm bell in the United States that it was the most vulnerable in the world.

Till that date, US government was talking about protecting Americans from foreign state or terrorist missile attacks with the National Missile Defense (NMD). The attack on 9/11 proved that the NMD was helpless in protecting them from outside attacks, and exposed the vulnerability of NMD to guarantee their safety. When the attack took place, the US lacked an anti-terrorist policy.

From the late 1970s to mid-1990s, the basic American anti-terrorism policy was to target the regimes that supported terrorist organizations or allowed them to operate from their soil, by economic sanctions, covert action, economic inducement, use of military force, diplomacy/constructive engagement and so on. This was like attacking the oceans when the real target was the ship in the ocean. The policy of targeting the regimes enabled the real targets—the terrorists and their organizations—to carry on their activities undeterred.

This negative approach was realized by the Americans only in mid-1996. This year witnessed a shift in American anti-terrorism policy from targeting regimes to targeting terrorist organizations and individual terrorists itself. This led to enactment of the Anti-Terrorism and Effective Death Penalty Act of 1996, under which a legal category of Foreign Terrorist Organizations (FTOs) was created; funding, granting of visas and other material support to such organizations was banned. This American policy is clearly visible in its campaign against *Al-Qaeda*, and through its global diplomatic, military and economic onslaught against the *Al-Qaeda*.

This shift in American anti-terrorism policy has meshed with a change in its approach towards the states which sponsor terrorism. Thus, *Patterns of Terrorism 2001* highlighted that countries like Sudan and Libya have made progress towards renouncing terrorism. But terrorists too, have changed their policy of attacking America from outside to attacking it from within, exposing the vulnerability of American homeland security. Due to this, the US has undertaken unprecedented changes in their administrative structure. Scholars compare the 2001 World Trade Centre attack with the 1945 attack on Pearl Harbor, which forced Americans to integrate their War and Navy departments into a single Department of Defense; the National Security Act of 1947 established this unified Department of Defense during the Presidency of Truman. Similarly, the attack on the WTC has compelled Americans to establish a new department called Department of Homeland Security (DHS). President Bush called on Congress to set up a cabinet-level homeland defense agency to protect the nation from "a titanic struggle against terror", which encompasses around twenty-two separate federal agencies, offices and research centres. The new DHS would provide the unified structure with a mission to prevent terrorist attacks within America, reducing its vulnerability to terrorists and finally, to minimize the damage and recover from attacks that do occur.

Thus another shift in American anti-terrorism policy has occurred from 'national security' to 'homeland security'. Although, the DHS is still in the process of being established, the office of Homeland Security had been already established to oversee national security emergency preparedness "with respect to terrorist threats and attacks *within* the United States". It would be the "principal forum for consideration of policy" related to such threats and attacks.

Thus, it is evident that the US policy towards fighting terrorism is dynamic and responds to the needs of the hour. The establishment of the Department of Homeland Security would increase its vigilance over anti-terrorist agencies but whether it succeeds or not, only time will reveal.

15 July 2002

Pakistan's Role in War against Terrorism: Costs and Benefits

PROF. CHINTAMANI MAHAPATRA

THE US-LED international coalition's war efforts against terrorism have destroyed the military machine of the Taliban forces in Afghanistan, but the ouster of the Taliban from the seat of power has raised several questions about the country's future.

In this complex war against terrorism, Pakistan was able to make some gains, economically and diplomatically, but appears to have lost its control over Afghan affairs. Pakistan, which created, nurtured and sustained the Taliban Government, had no choice but to join the US against the Taliban.

By doing that, Musharraf was able to keep Pakistan outside the potential targets of the coalition war. Pakistan came close to being declared as a state sponsor of terrorism with US intelligence fully aware of Pakistan's role in training terrorists. It was therefore probable that Pakistan could be targeted by the US campaign against terrorism.

Secondly, Pakistan was averse to any Indo-US joint war efforts against terrorism. Pakistani fears were reflected in its response to the terror attacks in the US. When Indian Prime Minister offered India's unconditional support to the US, President Musharraf announced his country's "unstinted support". By making this announcement, Musharraf cleared the road for closer US-Pakistan ties to prevent closer Indo-US cooperation from developing.

Thirdly, the events of September 11 brought some economic relief for Pakistan which was in the throes of a massive economic crisis, having accumulated a massive $40 billion foreign debt. Pakistan got a new lease of life as America prepared for a sustained, prolonged and all-out war against terrorism. Washington lifted its sanctions against Pakistan and wrote off, along with Japan, US $1 billion of in loans. Concerned about the illicit supply of arms and ammunition to the Taliban from Pakistan, the US announced in early November (2001) US $73 million in emergency aid to Islamabad to strengthen security on the country's porous borders with Afghanistan.

Pakistan was also promised helicopters, fixed-wing aircraft, night vision goggles, and communication equipment. A few days later, on the eve of President Pervez Musharraf's meeting with the US President in New York, Washington pledged US $1 billion in aid to Pakistan—doubling the earlier proposal to give US $500 million. The Asian Development Bank (ADB) decided around the same time to increase assistance to the country from the planned US $626 million to US $950 million. The President of ADB said that the Bank would substantially enhance its assistance to Pakistan for various projects to cope with the Afghan refugee crisis. And now the UNDP has joined the ADB for enhancing its economic assistance to Islamabad.

The fourth gain for Pakistan came in ending the country's international isolation. The Chagai series of nuclear tests, Kargil misadventure and military coup had led to Pakistan's international isolation. The various Commonwealth Committees had kept Pakistan out of its meetings. Pakistan had also lost sympathy in the US Congress, which was to lift some of the sanctions against only India before the terrorists struck the World Trade Centre and Pentagon.

When the US bombing of Afghanistan began, Pakistan found itself as a frontline state in the war against terrorism. The isolation of the country ended with visits to Islamabad by Japanese, British, Australian and American leaders and high officials. During his recent six-nation trip abroad, Musharraf received praise for his role in the war against terrorism at every stop.

While Pakistan gained these benefits, the fall of the Taliban regime in Kabul and the entry of the Northern Alliance forces into the Afghan capital came as a shock. This happened hours after President George Bush had assured Musharraf against such a possibility. It is clear that the US is no longer taking Pakistani advice on Afghan affairs. Its role in the formation of the next government in Kabul will be limited. Islamabad is yet to come to terms with this new development, which is reflected in Foreign Minister Abdus Sattar's statement that Islamabad has not yet de-recognized the Taliban Government; Pakistan's recognition or de-recognition hardly matters.

Given the fluidity of the ground situation, it is premature to draw any conclusion on the long-term consequences of the current developments. But the fact remains that while Pakistan had made some economic and diplomatic gains, its political and security interests have been adversely affected.

26 November 2001

War on Terrorism: Coalition Sans Commitment

Maj. Gen. (Retd) Yashwant Deva

The grand alliance that the US has rigged up to shadow box terrorism is a collage of disparate interests with a marked absence of commitment to the cause. It smacks more of crass opportunism rather than a willing cooperation to take on the evil of naked terror.

Every country that has promised to go along with America has done so for a price—something in return for the active or passive efforts that they may make in pursuance of anti-terrorism agenda. Even the US, for all its rhetoric, is looking at the problem in the narrow ambit of its own interests. In their rabidity to assemble a coalition against Osama bin Laden, the Americans have sacrificed their avowed commitments to root out globally the evil of terror.

The Arabs have laid down their own conditions, seeking more active role for the US in the Middle East in meeting the Palestinian aspirations. Musharraf has made the best of adversity and cunningly extracted a pound of flesh that inter alia includes the end of sanctions, debt relief, millions of dollars in aid for refugees, a role in post-Taliban dispensation and above all legitimacy for the regime. One marvels at his balancing acumen of realpolitik with faith, and ingenuity at image building, media manipulation and of course, India baiting, in which he excels par excellence.

When it came to terrorism in Jammu and Kashmir, the US administration has made it abundantly clear to India that its priorities lie elsewhere. Its harp on phasing the operations is neither ethical nor pragmatic, particularly in view of the overwhelming evidence of involvement of the notorious terrorist Masood Azhar, of hijack fame and the founder of *Jaish-e-Mohammed* (JeM) with spider web of connections on the money trail. Washington has yet to give a convincing proof of bin Laden's involvement, on the other hand, JeM has owned responsibility cocking a snook and daring the civilized. Whereas India has fallen head over heels in its unqualified support to the US, convincingly construed by its detractors as abject placation, Israeli Prime Minister Ariel Sharon has been blunt to the point of effrontery, admonishing Washington, "Do not try to appease the Arabs at our expense."

Like India, Russia too stands vindicated. Chechnya and J&K were proving grounds for *jihad*—a prologue to WTC. Russians however are far from being naïve. It is apparent that they have bargained prudently. Criticism of Chechnya has been muted, even doings legitimized in what was earlier denounced as "atrocities". Besides, Russians could now bank on Western help in developing their economy and infrastructure.

China has joined the coalition because it perceives an opportunity to put down Muslim insurgency in the western region of Xinjiang province. China prefers to go alone and eschew publicity to its efforts. It is believed that after the attack on America, China quietly intensified counter insurgency operations and executed at least seven persons and arrested dozens more. In other times the US would have been leading China badgers in crying foul and would have called it yet another evidence of repression *a la* Tiananmen Square. Following Jiang Zemin's offer of condolences and support to Bush, a Chinese foreign office spokesman sought *quid pro quo* in dealing with Uighur separatists and independence seekers in Tibet and Taiwan.

Japan has shed its pretence and is willing to provide logistic support to the US, its scope undefined. Ironically, the Japanese are questioning the status of their own military which was relegated after World War II. Prime Minister Junichiro Koizumi has increased diplomatic efforts in backing the coalition with visits to China and South Korea. Indonesia, the most populous Muslim country, has given the endorsement to America's war on terrorism in return for an aid package worth US $600 million. Malaysia, Thailand and Philippines have likewise tried to balance economic and diplomatic pressures with internal fissures and threats from the extremists.

There is a lesson for us. The asymmetric attacks on the most powerful nation in the world has shown how tenuous the world order is and how skin deep is the commitment to coalition. Let us therefore stand on our own and not look elsewhere to fight our wars against violence and terror. Besides, there is no virtue in being taken for granted.

10 October 2001

Terror in America: US Military Options

P.R. CHARI

THE UNITED STATES will never be the same after Black Tuesday; its sense of invulnerability, sheltering between the Atlantic and Pacific Oceans, has disappeared after the World Trade Centre towers in New York and the Pentagon in Washington were attacked. They were/are the symbols of American economic and military power. Had the airplane that crashed in Pennsylvania succeeded in attacking the White House, the symbol of American political power would also have been assaulted.

We share the grief at the fate of innocents killed and maimed in these attacks. Terrorism is part theatre, theatre of the macabre if you will, designed to focus attention of the intended audience—the global community in this case—to the terrorist's cause. And what could that cause be apart from highlighting the vulnerability of the American homeland? All of America's wars in the last century were fought on foreign soil; whilst it accepted the economic costs and the deaths of its soldiers in those wars, the horrors of conflict occurred elsewhere, in Europe and Asia and Africa and Latin America. The United States remained inviolate until Black Tuesday. The psychological dimension of this rude awakening cannot be underestimated. It has created a heightened sense of insecurity in the American government, a fear of crowded places and air transportation afflicts its people. A hint of xenophobia is also creeping in with citizens having stereotypical features of Arabs and Muslims being singled out for attack. This feeling could increase as the economic downturn in the United States gains momentum with falling car sales and rising layoffs adding to the recessionary trends already visible in the American economy before Black Tuesday occurred.

The immediate response of the Bush administration to assuage the enormous sense of outrage in the American people is understandable. Osama bin Laden was identified as the hate object, and the *Al-Qaeda* organization as the instrument of his malevolence; the Taliban was targeted as his patron. No thought was given to the root causes underlying the phenomenon of Osama bin Laden, his acceptance in the Muslim world, and ability to enlist large numbers of recruits willing to sacrifice their lives. They cannot be dismissed as religious fanatics. The Bush administration should reflect on the desperation imbuing these suicide squads of Osama bin Laden. Why is this happening? Could it be the result of the unilateralism of the United States in the last decade? Has its bombing of Iraq, attacks on Sudan and Afghanistan created this sense of hopelessness and desperation?

These events placed Pakistan in the difficult position of either supporting its creation, the Taliban and, by extension, the Taliban's actions in providing sanctuary to Osama bin Laden in Afghanistan. The alternative of supporting the Taliban and obstructing the US would have proved extremely costly in political and economic terms, given Pakistan's isolation in the world and its staggering economy. Naturally Pakistan is seeking to gain as much as it can out of the American compulsion to capture Osama bin Laden "dead or alive"; so it has abandoned, temporarily at least, the Taliban, *Al-Qaeda*, and Osama bin Laden to support the Americans.

The US military response is still evolving. Aircraft carriers have been moved into the northern Indian Ocean, and aircraft positioned in the Gulf region; they are poised to launch air and missile strikes on Afghanistan over-flying Pakistani territory. Both US Secretary of Defence Rumsfeld and British Prime Minister Blair are touring the region to strengthen political support for the coalition's military action against Afghanistan. But, what shape and form could that take?

The most desirable outcome would be for the Taliban to deliver Osama bin Laden "dead or alive". So far Pakistan has been unable to deliver. Whether this will happen in future is uncertain, but the

Pathan adage is worth recollecting, "every head has its price". A variant would be for the Northern Alliance to undertake this enterprise. Ironically, the erstwhile combatants in Afghanistan, the United States and Russia, are cooperating in this venture. The next best option would be for the coalition forces to undertake a "surgical operation", by a missile or bomb attack to kill Osama bin Laden. Or capture or kill him in a commando operation. The problem would be to acquire pinpoint information about Osama's whereabouts; this would be very difficult given the nature of the Afghan terrain. The worst possible option would be bombing of locations in which he is suspected to be hiding—the collateral damage to its population, already suffering the ravages of starvation would alienate world opinion. The creation of larger numbers of desperate people who willingly contemplate suicide attacks can hardly be the end objective of US policy.

What then can or will the coalition forces do in the coming days? The world waits and watches.

9 October 2001

Telling Flaws in Understanding Rubrics of Terror

MAJ. GEN. (RETD) YASHWANT DEVA

PROFESSOR SAMUEL HUNTINGTON'S thesis on "Clash of Civilizations" argues that the root of global conflict is cultural; this is too simplistic, if not totally flawed. How else can one explain the Taliban, a creation of the unholy alliance between the US and Pakistan, or Osama bin Laden, America's own Frankenstein, and the reported collusion between the LTTE and *Al-Qaeda*? Terror is no civilized act and its perpetrators, collaborators and sponsors are no crusaders or holy men. The clash is truly between the civilized and the uncivilized.

Terrorism poses a host of grim challenges to democracies, secular regimes and countries in conflict with religious and racial minorities, Eastern or Western states alike. This is a defining moment for the Americans. Let them understand that neither is Islam their enemy nor opportunist states who change sides their friends.

The first problem that America faces is intelligence-sharing and cooperation among the intelligence agencies. That CIA and ISI had close links during the Cold War days is well known. That Taliban and ISI had and continue to have close links too is well known. That Taliban and *Al-Qaeda* had and continue to have close relations is also well known. Therefore the Americans cannot claim ignorance of the ISI's role in spreading the terrorist network. Pakistan was and continues to be an intelligence window for the Taliban. Abdullah Abdullah, the Foreign Minister of Afghanistan (Northern Alliance), has a word of caution about America trusting ISI again. Our reservations about this organization are, of course, well known.

The second problem is absence of an institutionalized and centralized system to penetrate terrorist outfits and foil their nefarious activities before they can inflict catastrophes like Mumbai and New York-Washington. This makes international cooperation in intelligence operations between civilized regimes and countries that are imminent victims of terror, both critical and pressing. The purpose of such cooperation should be to create a database and monitor the movements of terrorists throughout the world. This includes the development of intelligence potential, bilateral and multilateral agreements, planning and execution of joint intelligence missions, training, information and propaganda and seeking media support.

It is with the Taliban regime that Pakistan had gloated over finding "Strategic Depth". Further, Musharraf revealed in the Kargil Tapes that he was keeping the so-called *Mujahideen* from Afghanistan in grip of their peak by the scruff (he called it *tooti*). The latest news that Osama bin Laden has vanished and that Pakistan is opposed to ousting the Taliban offers ample proof of their close linkages.

The third problem is the effectiveness of political and economic sanctions. These cannot be applied by an individual country or the international community against countries helping terrorists. Pakistan has unequivocally refused to sever its ties with the Taliban but it has been the greater beneficiary of the sanctions being lifted. Pakistan undertook the Kargil adventure unmindful of its adverse effect on its economy. Obviously, the money came from sources, which the Americans are hard put to find out. The very purpose of introduction of military sanctions to destroy support to Talibans has been defeated. Pakistan has been and continues to be the recipient of Islamic charities, the *jihad* fund, besides being involved with the drug cartel.

Given the intricate nature of the problem, only broad-based and vigorous international cooperation can achieve any significant results in the war against terror. It is for the international comity of the civilized to understand the psyche of terror, before they formulate a strategy to contain it. Terrorism is a pastime of the wealthy and has nothing to do with deprivations and discontent born of social, economic and political inequalities, particularly in a democratic polity.

27 September 2001

Terrorism in America

(Report of the IPCS Panel Discussion held on 21 September 2001)

PANELISTS: T. ANANTHA CHARI, ANAND VERMA AND P.R. CHARI

LIEUTENANT GENERAL NAYYAR initiated the seminar by highlighting the following discussion points regarding the September 11 terrorist attacks on the World Trade Centre and the Pentagon in the US. The magnitude of this tragedy is unsurpassed in the history of terrorism. The US response to the tragedy has been two-fold. Firstly, amidst the anguish and the anger there is a controlled reaction on the ground in trying to build a global coalition against terrorism. And, secondly, the US says for the first time, it will not distinguish between the perpetrators of the outrage and those who harbour them.

Despite the declared support of a large number of countries, some reservation to the US fight against terrorism must be appreciated. A military strike on Afghanistan would result in increasing anti-American sentiments in many parts of the world. Though there is a massive show of force by the US in moving its aircraft carriers and destroyers to the Gulf and surrounding regions, action on the ground is still awaited. Intelligence gathering about Osama bin Laden and the terrorist camps in Afghanistan is on; but this information will obviously not be made public. If the US had intended to strike against Osama, they should have done so immediately after the terrorist attacks in the US when the terrorist camps were still operating. At present Osama bin Laden and members of his organization have had ample time to disperse and go underground; hence US military action does not seem imminent.

Operationally, the proposed US military action needs to be assessed in the light of past US operations like the *Delta Force* operation in Iran. The aversion of the US public to body bags coming back must also be borne in mind. There are discordant notes also within the US establishment; the defence forces want to go for an immediate strike but the Congress is advocating a more cautious approach.

Fallout in South Asia

Pakistan has once again become a frontline state for the US in South Asia, and is making full use of this opportunity to garner support for its stand on Kashmir. India has fought *jihadi* violence in Kashmir for the past twelve years, and feels concerned about this issue. Pakistan has made the demand that neither India nor Israel should be part of an offensive against the Taliban regime. So far the US has not asked for help from India and, even if the need arises, India's role, limited to logistical support, will be marginal.

Though the *jihadis* have been asked by the Taliban to return from Kashmir to fight against the US in Afghanistan, India should not be complacent about this and expect a de-escalation in violence in Kashmir. India tends to overemphasize the international element of the Kashmir conflict, without concentrating on the local problems. The present crisis will have ramifications on Indo-Pak and Indo-US relations, and will once again push the local conflict issues into the background. India needs to address the local Kashmiris to tackle the root cause of terrorism in Kashmir. Finally, the theory of civilizational conflict regarding terrorism needs to be debunked as it will have impact on India. Whilst cracking down on all fundamentalist organizations in the country, the branding of an entire community as fundamentalist must be discouraged and needs to be fought against.

The panel raised the following issues in their presentations:

- The September 11 attacks have shattered the myth of American inviolability. Though there has been a lot of tall talk in the US, the actual response is a considered and cautious one, with attempts to build a global coalition before launching a military operation. This is a positive development as the Bush administzration's penchant for unilateralism resulted in the US walking out of many international treaties and commitments. These include the CTBT, Protocol to the Biological Weapons Convention, the Kyoto Protocol, hindering the formation of an International Criminal Court and an international agreement on small arms transfers. The US proposal for National Missile Defence was the high point of the Bush administration's arrogance in international affairs.

- The present crisis has proved that terrorism has no territorial limits. It is a low cost war to which all countries are vulnerable. Further, no country is in a position to deal with this phenomenon alone, and global cooperation against terrorism is required.
- The September 11 attacks highlight the failure of human intelligence. In the fight against terrorism, the need for intelligence sharing between like-minded nations should be stressed.
- Does the current US-Pakistan cooperation against the Taliban signify the beginning of a long term relationship between the two countries? Or, is this an issue based cooperation that will not have any bearing on the South Asian politics in the long run? This is an open-ended question at present.
- In the event of a US military strike on Afghanistan, India should be prepared for a refugee influx from Afghanistan.
- Osama bin Laden's relation with different fundamentalist organizations around the world needs to be investigated. Does bin Laden control the different fundamentalism groups directly or is there some loose organization to which he provides encouragement and support, but who are independent for all practical purposes? It is essential to determine this relationship if the global fight against terrorism is to succeed.
- There must be a realization that even the highest levels of security cannot deter a suicide bomber or *fidayeen*, and hence this chink in the armour of security will have to be accepted.
- Quite apart from terrorist organizations, various cult groups like the Japanese *Aum Shinrikyo* that threaten mass destruction

to promote a new social order, need to be watched and researched.

- An overemphasis on the use of nuclear weapons to ensure national security needs to be re-examined. The dangers from chemical and biological weapons must be appreciated.
- The actual military operation against Afghanistan needs to be discussed while talking about the "war against terrorism".
- Pakistan is playing for high stakes that includes the removal of all sanctions, loans from the IMF and World Bank, and arms transfers from the US. The resentment of the *jihadi* elements in Pakistan against cooperation with the US is not likely to derail Musharraf's efforts to strengthen his ties with the US.
- India can only play a peripheral role in the present situation, unless the government is ready to raise the stakes. India could join hands with the Russians and the Northern Alliance in Afghanistan to ensure that a friendly government replaces the Taliban.
- The Indian reaction to the terrorist attacks and its offer of help to the US was an over eager gesture that has earned us the hostility of the Islamic world without any tangible benefits. The same could have been conveyed quietly to the US through diplomatic channels.

The discussion after the presentations centred on the following issues:

- The economic dimension of the fight against terrorism should not be ignored. The links of the narcotics trade in Pakistan and Afghanistan with terrorism must be identified and dealt with.
- The show of force by the US is mainly aimed at satisfying its domestic constituency that wants revenge against the terrorists. Actual ground operations against the Taliban in Afghanistan will need acquiring more intelligence and preparation.
- India must watch its borders vigilantly, and not be complacent about the possibility of an escalation of violence in the Kashmir valley.

- India must educate the world community about terrorism in Kashmir, and its links with Pakistan and the Taliban.
- The "war against terrorism" must be fought under the auspices of the UN rather than a global US led coalition with narrow objectives. This is the right time to revive the blocked UN convention against terrorism and take advantage of the global support for dealing comprehensively with it.

27 September 2001

Pakistan's Response to America's War against Terrorism

PROF. CHINTAMANI MAHAPATRA

As TERRORISM STRUCK the symbol of power—the Pentagon, and the symbol of wealth—the World Trade Centre, in Washington DC and New York on September 11, it heralded a new type of war in the twenty-first century between democracies and terrorist outfits.

However, democracies can easily be identified but not terrorism, which does not represent a country, nor an individual or a group. One man's terrorist is someone else's freedom fighter. Thus all democracies may not unite in a war against terrorism. Non-democracies may also not cooperate in the war against terrorism, especially when some of them have been promoting terrorism themselves. Pakistan is a quintessential example. But they may have to be pressurized to play ball. This is what the Bush White House has done. It came up with a set of demands and asked Pakistan to spell out whether it is with the US or the terrorist outfits.

Pakistan, which has aided, abetted, trained and equipped the terrorist groups involved in atrocities in Kashmir, has only paid lip service to the dead in the recent terrorist attacks against America. President Pervez Musharraf had declared "unstinted support" to the US fight against terrorism, but when the Bush Administration actually sought Islamabad's assistance, he asked for more time to take a decision.

Pakistan has been a long-standing ally of the US. It assisted the US during the prolonged warfare in Afghanistan in the 1980s. It also offered its support during the Gulf War. But in a war, which has taken a toll of thousands of American lives and has cost that country billions of dollars in financial losses, Musharraf wanted more time to decide. The Pakistani hesitation derived from its years of involvement in promoting terrorism in its neighbourhood as well as distant places, such as Chechnya. Siding with the US would mean creating enemies among the terrorist groups. It would also lead to destruction of Pakistan's own creation—the Taliban Government in Afghanistan. Denying cooperation could lead to retaliatory US action against terrorist hideouts and training camps in Pakistan, and its further isolation in the international community.

The military government in Islamabad found, after deliberations, that antagonizing the injured lion—the United States—would be more costly to Pakistan. It would increase Pakistan's international isolation, make the terrorist training camps in Pakistan a target of US retaliatory attacks, turn the country into a bankrupt nuclear power and, more significantly, bring India and the US closer together. Sandwiched between the devil and the deep blue sea, Pervez Musharraf, in a televised address, sought to promise different things to different constituencies. He promised all assistance to the US. He told his people that the struggle for Kashmir would continue and siding with the US at this juncture would facilitate that struggle. He told the Islamic hardliners that he was joining the war against terrorism and not Islam. He also sent an indirect message to New Delhi that it was Pakistan, and not India, which could best serve as a frontline state in America's wars.

Bush was apparently pleased with Musharraf's "bold speech". But he knew that Pakistan's help was needed, not because of that country's strategic location but because of its Islamic credentials. The war against terrorism would not be like the war against the Soviet troops in Afghanistan. The US would not require a conduit. It would need the support of Islamic countries to tell Muslims around the world that America's war is against terrorism and not Islam. Given Pakistan's close links with the Taliban Government, it could become the frontline Islamic State in the war against terrorism.

While the military ruler could please the US President, the supporters of the Taliban and Saudi dissident Osama bin Laden in Pakistan were not impressed by Musharraf's argument. Quite a few military officers in his own junta remained unconvinced as well.

The Afghan opposition leaders of the Northern Alliance have asked the US not to believe the Pakistanis. The Taliban has vowed to wage war against those who support US military action against the Taliban. India must remain resolute in its own war against cross-border terrorism.

It remains to be seen how the US would fight an expected long drawn out war against terrorism without disrupting the links between terrorists and those who harbour them. It also remains to be seen how Islamabad fights one kind of terrorism but promotes another.

27 September 2001

Changing Equations in the War against Terrorism

ARPIT RAJAIN

THE DELIBERATE ATTACKS on the World Trade Centre and Pentagon on 11 September 2001 have re-emphasized the issue of supreme national interests if international responses are any indication. As President Bush and his team of advisors set about the task of forging a broad coalition against an enemy that has no defined borders, other countries are likely to position themselves keeping their supreme national interests in mind.

In a world of opposing interests and conflicts, moral principles can only be realized by the balancing of interests and resolution of conflicts. Increasing power and prestige is manifested in the conduct of foreign policy. All states work within the same problematique: states define the same goals (survival), identify the same threats (power imbalances), and choose between similar courses of action (internal and external balancing).

The US has no option but to involve other states since there is a growing conviction that the US should not do it alone. Moreover, the US needs to legitimize any military action. Hence it is in dialogue with NATO, Australia, Britain, Canada, Israel, Kuwait, France, Germany, Indonesia, Japan, Russia, Turkey, Iran, Sweden and the countries in the neighbourhood—Pakistan, Afghanistan, China and India.

Some of the countries that are US allies have offered strong support. Britain, the closest US ally, has pledged to work "shoulder to shoulder" with Bush and has also brought less enthusiastic European states on board. Canadian Foreign Minister John Manley has said that Canada would "unambiguously" join US military action. The US says Israel is providing vital intelligence inputs on Islamic militants, although US Secretary of State, Colin Powell, said that the US sees no role for Israel in any military response. Spain has offered its air bases for retaliatory air strikes and promised to act "without any reservations".

Such manoeuvring is also underway in countries that are most likely to be affected by a military strike—China, Pakistan and India. India has offered to allow US military forces to use its facilities, if needed. The reason underlying the policies of these countries is governed either by their traditional support of the US or their hope to support the US and come on board to, as the US says, "be counted". The other Indian interest lies in the US warning to states that harbour the terrorists. India firmly believes this is a veiled warning to Pakistan. India is of the considered opinion that military strikes on Afghanistan ought to be the "last resort" and that a "large concert of democracies" should be mobilized before launching "extensively-prepared" military strikes. India has already offered location sites maps of militant training camps both in Pakistan administered Kashmir and Afghanistan. It is unlikely that the US would involve India in a military action. With both China and Pakistan sealing their borders with Afghanistan, the possibility of Afghan mercenaries sneaking into India has not escaped the Indian Government's attention. What bothers India is the thought that US might end up focusing on Osama bin Laden and not addressing the real issues involved. India does expect action being taken against the militant training camps in Pakistan administered Kashmir.

On the other hand, there are reports of hard bargaining by Pakistan as well. Pakistan, apart from being one of the three states to have recognized the Taliban, has also nurtured and helped it over the last two decades. With Washington promising rewards to Pakistan for its decision to back US military action against Afghanistan, General Musharraf has to walk a tightrope between the *jihadis* supporting Osama's actions and the US response. There is great unhappiness in many Pakistanis towards the United States which is threatening to sour or, at worst, disrupt any agreement reached over the American use of airspace and deployment of ground troops in Pakistan but it was left with no option except to side with the US.

President Musharraf has chosen to use this opportunity to extract concessions from the US by hard negotiations.

China has said it is ready to join the US in fighting "terrorism", but has warned that military action should be based on concrete proof and should not harm innocents. China has also made it clear that any military action must comply with the objectives and principles of the UN Charter and the recognized norms of international laws. China has further said that it would not link its commitment to other issues like Taiwan. China, fearing Muslim separatist violence in its westernmost provinces of Sinkiang has also expressed concern about the intensity of the likely strike, and the nature of the anti-terrorism coalition. Soon after the September 11 attacks, General Musharraf expressed a desire to visit China for consultations. Beijing has carefully avoided the international spotlight by persuading General Musharraf not to rush to Beijing, and instead sent Vice Foreign Minister Wang Yi to Islamabad for consultations.

The struggle between a liberal order and collective sectarian frenzy is likely to reveal itself at different times in different parts of the world; the supreme international interest at this moment is to forge a common alliance against a common foe.

27 September 2001

A Coalition against Terrorism?

SONIKA GUPTA

THE ATTACKS ON THE World Trade Centre and the Pentagon in the US raise many questions pertaining to terrorism. The outcome of a terrorist attack is the same worldwide; the loss of innocent lives and a serious disruption of normal life. However, different countries perceive terrorism in different ways. And till perceptions of terrorism are linked solely to different national interests, there may not be any effective solution for it.

While violence in all its forms must be condemned, it is imperative to keep in mind that terrorist violence is an armed expression of discontent. This discontent may be born of social, economic and political inequalities in a society, a nation state, or the community of nations. When the channels for political expression of this discontent are perceived to be either hijacked by the dominant parties or suppressed, terrorist violence erupts. The eruption of violence, however, is not intended to solve problems but to coerce a solution favourable to the party indulging in terrorism. Ironically, the state then has a legitimate reason to crush any popular revolt against its policies. This cycle of violence only perpetuate more violence and takes both parties further from any solution. Until the futility of violence is recognized by both sides in a conflict, there can be no solution to the conflict. This fact must be kept in mind while discussing policy options for responding to the terrorist attacks in the New York and Washington.

The Bush administration has made contradictory statements regarding its response to these attacks. While on the one hand, George Bush has declared that the US will make no distinction between those who perpetrated the attacks and those who harbour them, the fact that it is reviving its old alliance with Pakistan contradicts its intention to address the issue of terrorism. In fact, in a bid for revenge, the US is focusing narrowly on the capture of Osama bin Laden. This may assuage the feeling for revenge in the US, but it will not go very far in combating terrorism. Pakistan's symbiotic relationship with the *jihadi* forces in Afghanistan is well established. However, by condemning the attacks and complying with US demands in the event of a military operation against Afghanistan, Pakistan is making a distinction between terrorist attacks in the US and the "freedom struggle" in Kashmir. And if the US does not make a clear statement against this distinction, it will contribute to legitimizing the use of violence to achieve political ends. Further, an attack against the Taliban regime is bound to inflame the *jihadi* forces in Pakistan and the Middle East. The *jihadi* forces in Pakistan have made clear their displeasure with General Musharraf selling out the Taliban to the US. A scenario of heightened violence in Pakistan cannot be ruled out. Though Pakistan may bear the brunt of their anger, the US too would not be immune to it. Even if the US succeeds in replacing the Taliban with a favourable government, would that guarantee the end of the anti-American *jihad* that inspired the attacks in New York and Washington?

Despite his support to the militants in Kashmir, General Musharraf has been trying to clamp down on the fundamentalist forces in Pakistan. His motive is to release Pakistani society and politics from the regressive influence of these forces. Pakistani investment in the Taliban has boomeranged with a threat of war against itself. A recognition of this fact should make Pakistan realize that this crisis can prove to be an opportunity to sever its ties with a regressive regime like the Taliban and deal comprehensively with the *jihadi* forces at home. The people of Pakistan would welcome this more than conflict with Afghanistan and the growing fundamentalism at home.

As far as Kashmir is concerned, India and Pakistan have to get their act together before they jockey for securing US support on Kashmir. A clear understanding is required that the US will broker a peace between India and Pakistan for its own national interests and legitimately so. It is mystifying what inspires a faith in the US eschewing any vested interests in this regard. No amount of mediation is likely to produce any result as long as violence does not stop. India needs to recognize that the people of Kashmir need to be represented in any final solution being negotiated, while Pakistan needs to recognize that trans-border terrorism is only making matters worse for the Kashmiris while bleeding Pakistan of its resources. They may sound idealistic but minus this idealism, both governments will only seek a military solution of the conflict, which in any case will not be permanent.

Finally, though there has been widespread support for the US forming a coalition against terrorism, is it really directed against terrorism? And as long as the objectives of this coalition remain narrow, the problem will not go away though it might be suppressed by brute force for a limited period of time. The philosophy that inspires suicide attacks is not likely to disintegrate because of the threat of violence. It will only get strengthened.

19 September 2001

11 September 2001: Terrorism and After

SHABNAM MALLICK
RAJARSHI SEN

THE SENSE OF SHOCK at the unprecedented tragedy befalling one of the greatest nations of this world on 11 September 2001 is matched only by a feeling of numbing bewilderment. Official responses and policy matched the fractiousness of information on the perpetrators of today's incidents of terrorism. Whether or not Osama bin Laden is responsible and how to punish him if he was is unclear, notwithstanding assertions of the inevitability of US's retaliatory response. There is no general consensus or even idea, let alone specifics, on any vital question in the nature of when, where and how, beyond the immediate emergency attentions and evacuations.

Those of us who are devoted to the esoteric branch of national security dealing with asymmetric threats, on any given day, find us in the minority in terms of attention, influence, or understanding. Coming to light of the resource scarcity in the American human intelligence community is indication of that minority status. Yet, even if we concede that terrorism, at least, has been in the process of establishing its niche in policy space of late, particularly since the end of the Cold War, those of us who analyse the realms of roots and causes of terrorism are an endangered species indeed. This is significant because tied closely to the correct analyses of the emergence of terrorism, is the factor of correct response to that threat.

Since the roots of terrorism are slow and ever emergent, so

should be the analyses and response to that—patient. Our lifestyle has mutated in modern time to an extent that patience is a luxury we do not have today, leading to slam-dunk responses to threats. Such attitude creates an asociological bias in the study of terrorism, which remains an inexact science, as are most of its cohorts, like the one of intelligence, on whom it traditionally depends.

The roots of terrorism are often more prosaic, more ordinary, more commonplace than is usually understood. Poverty, deprivation, being socio-culturally dominated, and other everyday causes, often, give rise to the frustration-aggression syndrome. As the name suggests, if one's aspirations are prevented from being realized for sufficiently long, one may get aggressive beyond the canons of civility; once that feeling is put in a context of socio-economic deprivation beyond a certain threshold, it mutates to a collective sense of victimization. Throw in a handful of already highly mutated zealots fanatic enough to act as leaders of any cause—religious, ideological, self-serving or whatever—then we also have a terrorist group, complete with a constituency or pool from where to draw cadres ready to become martyrs for a cause, however repulsive. Terrorism, thus, remains a weapon of the weak; their way of getting at the strong by attacking the weaknesses of the strong—the logic of asymmetry. And the strong can never be strong enough that they will have no weaknesses.

Retaliatory strikes against such a situation may perpetuate the cycle of violence. (The comparison of 11 September's events to Pearl Harbor ends here.) Not retaliating may elicit criticism of the Hamlet syndrome—the feeling of not being able to do anything for want of a perfect solution. Lost amidst it all, is the price of freedom—eternal vigilance.

The crude fact is that as long as vast disparities remain among populations who cohabit one world, the threat of terrorism may not be erased. They can, nevertheless, be reduced to a minority. That, above all, requires moral sanction; and moral sanction is unfortunately even more elusive than the terrorists who have perpetrated the events of 11 September. Moral sanction can come, however, by a change in our lifestyle. The change will have to come through patient sacrifice, not of the type that is now worrying America: that freedom will have to be sacrificed at the altar of heightened security in air travel, for instance. But, sacrifice in America's surprising innocence that while one must have their own way of life, it is not enough to only not interfere in others' ways of life elsewhere, but to actively aspire to fulfil that those "others" receive what they too want as theirs. The immediate response, then, must come in the form of a genuine sharing of common security concerns that threaten the collective interests of freedom around the world.

Unlike in Cold War days of manifest threats, America no longer retains the readymade clout to create "an empire by invitation". In keeping with lessons of history, if we examine America's peculiar situation (a powerful nation facing an indeterminate strategic climate) we begin to wonder if, despite its military might, America will remain invulnerable, after all. Further, if we take a cue from the emerging threats to international security, asymmetric or otherwise, our wonder widens to the point of asking if we do not require a major shift in paradigms so that it is of collective benefit to America and rest of the world.

Today, America is having to argue more persuasively than ever that the moral component of its foreign policy is both necessary and sufficient safeguard against what the rest of the world, most notably its most trusted allies, views as hegemonic aspirations. Such a public image, as it were, is not conducive in the fight against such phenomena as terrorism.

It is important to note that political order often does not pertain to the social economy. It is said that politics is often not the rational adjuvant of social change. If politics is often not the rational adjuvant of social change, then political change itself, it may be argued, is contingent on the factor of political order. It is, therefore, the duty of an appropriate political order to underwrite conditions from which desirable political change obtains.

In other words, it is prudent on the part of governments to be responsive to social pressures on behalf of political change, for the sake of their own safety and stability. On the one hand, those social pressures require a functional unity of nation states to counter sub-state threats like terrorism confronting them; on the other hand, Hobbesian political disunity between nation-states is precluding congealing of that necessary wide-ranging functional unity.

Only a continuing and prevailing government or political order will, therefore, be in any position to underwrite the dynamics of change. It is thus expected that America explore beyond the Hobbesian paradigm to the direction of an evolving cooperative security regime. Cooperative security may manifest in many varieties, but should engage the minimum common denominator: political will to think "out of the box" in line with an expansive paradigm that does not view national security in zero-sum terms.

Admittedly, many loose ends will have to be tightened in due course. But what remains clear, however, is that at least in today's peculiar operational situations, when increasingly sophisticated terrorists may one day have access to nuclear weapons, defenders of freedom if operating within a dedicated rubric of cooperative security-based counterterrorism doctrine, will not remain hamstrung by issues of national sovereignty and similar jurisdictional restrictions, even as the moral sanction accruing of a collective involvement of the world community will be brought to bear in, say, "hot pursuits" of terrorists across international borders into hostile territory in counterterrorism operations; or, in fishing out masterminds of terror from their safe havens.

Recruiting foreign human intelligence assets, too, will conceivably pose less of a problem in the domain of collective security. For example, the Central Intelligence Agency (CIA) uncomfortably grapples with its current policy of having to pre-screen such potential recruits and discard those with less than impeccable background. A multilateral counter-terrorism regime will entail institutionalized intelligence sharing of a more robust nature than what is in place now, and intelligence agencies that are not constrained by "background checks" may surrogate when recruiting those whom the CIA, for instance, will ordinarily reject.

Collective security may also be our lasting protection, by virtue of a demonstration of multilateral cooperative unity, against what may well turn out to be a misdirected backlash of Caucasians against other races/ethnic minorities (as is evident from reports of selective aggressiveness in parts of America directed against Muslim and Sikh communities, etc., in the aftermath of 11 September), and serve to underwrite against the worst Huntingtonian nightmares of a clash of civilizations.

International legitimacy of a cooperative security-based anti-terrorism force may not only conveniently offer a pool of resources in terms of security apparatus, it could also allow circumventing domestic criticism against possible over commitment when one's country is not directly in the line of fire; or, other criticisms against foreign intervention in the country where intervention is actually taking place. The United States is poised to cooperate with Israel and India, for instance, drawing on terrorism/counter-terrorism experience of these two terrorism-afflicted countries, especially in the wake of India's recent anti-terrorism cooperation with Israel and also in view of its lead in the last two years to have the United Nations adopt the Comprehensive Convention Against Terrorism.

And the US is today poised better than any other nation to take a lead in that direction; because despite the terrorist attack America still retains the most powerful resources that are now stirred and focused to ensure what may yet be one of America's enduring contributions to the world. That is, to paraphrase Franklin Delano Roosevelt: More than an end to terrorism, we want an end to the beginnings of all terrorism.

19 September 2001

Jihad against America

BRIG. (RETD) D. SHARMA

THE DRAMATIC AND nerve-shattering terrorist attack on New York and Washington on September 11 have once again established the ability and the freedom of terrorists to strike at will in any part of the world. By targeting the might of the sole superpower, both economic and military, they have exposed the vulnerability of even a state as powerful and advanced as the US to ruthless and determined terrorists. The attacks also exposed the serious laxity in the functioning of intelligence agencies. Aircrafts were hijacked and commandeered away from their flying lanes for nearly forty minutes without arousing any suspicion. This goes to show that there can never be an impregnable ring of security. Precision, meticulousness and audacity of assaults indicate that terrorists or the group backing them up, are highly skilled and superbly motivated. The "Attack on America" has reportedly left more than 5,000 dead almost twice the number seriously injured. The sheer magnitude of destruction has sent ominous reverberations throughout the world. The UK, European Union and even Russia have decided to join hands to combat this rising menace. President George W. Bush has said that the US will hunt the terrorists and not only punish them but also punish those who harbour and shelter them. Afghanistan and Pakistan are already on the defensive and are making placatory overtures to the world.

It may sound sadistic and uncharitable to say that it is just as well that terrorists chose the US and its most visible symbols of economic and military power for their attack. The Western world led by the US has so far followed a policy of ambivalence and indifference as they were not directly affected by this evil, despite an attempt on the World Trade Centre in 1993. It may be recalled that during the Soviet occupation of Afghanistan, the US was obsessed with the Afghan war, giving financial and material support to Afghanistan via Pakistan. Osama bin Laden was thus the creation of the US. It was also guilty of fuelling Islamic fundamentalism since it suited her short term interests. In the process, it propped up dictatorship in Pakistan giving disproportionately higher status to Pakistan as a country in South Asia. Despite warnings from India and the incontrovertible evidence of Pakistan's complicity in terrorism, the US chose to treat these as inanities.

There is absolutely no doubt that "Islamic Fundamentalism" has its fertile nurseries in Afghanistan and Pakistan. Pakistan has more than 120 training camps in POK and on the Afghan-Pakistan border. Each of these camps is equipped to train 100-250 militants. Pakistan thus trains approximately 12,000 militants in a year. These militants have the entire world as their battlefield. Besides Pakistan takes pride in providing shelter to high profile criminals like Dawood Ibrahim and possibly Osama bin Laden and his ilk. Pentagon's own studies have indicted Pakistan as a "rogue state". Some studies have also suggested that Pakistan is selling nuclear technology to the Arab countries—a small contribution to the "Muslim Bomb". In the gory decade of violence from 1990 till July 2001, 13,237 militants, more than 30,000 civilians and 3,000 security personnel have been killed in J&K. Pakistan has been pursuing a policy of self-destruction in attempting to wrest the Kashmir Valley, an integral part of India, by using terrorists in its proxy war against India.

There is a discernible similarity between what has happened in New York and Washington and what has been happening in India, particularly the Mumbai explosions of March 1993. It is an open secret that Talibans could not have occupied nearly 90 per cent of Afghanistan without the active support of Pakistan. Similarly, the dreaded billionaire Osama bin Laden could not operate with impunity from Afghanistan without the connivance of Pakistan. Pakistan thus gets inexorably linked to international terrorism and the horrendous crimes against humanity.

Now that America has been rocked by terrorism in its most

insidious form, President Bush and his administration should take steps to quarantine those states, such as Afghanistan and Pakistan, which support *jihadi* terrorism or shelter terrorists. Punitive action against suspected terrorist outfits must be swift and pulverising. There is a requirement of a global and effective mechanism to monitor international terrorism. The US must take the lead. As far as India is concerned, it needs to fight *jihadis* more aggressively and destroy these areas which breed terrorism. We must also review our security and intelligence set-ups and tone up disaster management procedures to cope up with air borne terrorism.

19 September 2001

III. Religion, Fundamentalism and Terrorism

Jihad: Its Two Facets

BRIG. (RETD) CHANDRA B. KHANDURI

JIHAD, A WORD RARELY found in the holy *Quran*, has gained coinage and its importance has gained salience as an Islamic symbol of holy war against the unbelievers. The American military offensive against Afghanistan, following the carnage of September 11, is being regarded by Islamic fundamentalists as a war against the Islamic civilization, and its clash with the West.

This question revolves around fundamentalism, which represents a deliberate effort by the clerics to superimpose the percepts of the holy *Quran* without taking into account socio-political and contemporary realities. In its fundamentalist fervour, the basic tenets of democracy such as individual rights, social homogeneity and national integration have all been ignored.

The divine message of the *Quran*, written in the seventh century AD, could not have predicated the changed needs of the twentieth and twenty-first centuries. There is none the less, incredible foresight and vision in the book. The spirit of Islam, propagated by Prophet Muhammad, was liberal and humanist. It accommodated enquiry and hence spiritual fulfilment. Its pristine beauty lay—and continues to lie—in providing a practical code of human conduct. It became a law for the common man and woman, virtually from womb to tomb, by adopting a simple but strict monotheism of one God (Allah) and of Muhammad being His apostle, charged with disseminating His commandments to a people steeped in superstition, prejudice and idolatory. Those messages became the literal and infallible words of God conveyed through the *Quran*. It became the unchallenged source of the new religion, beliefs and practices with a law (*sharia*) providing "a straight path".

The basic message of Islam of brotherhood and observance of righteousness is universal. It shuns compulsion, best demonstrated by the Arabic lexicon, "*La ikra fi idadin*" meaning, "your religion is yours, mine my own". Islam, thus forces no proselytization. The Prophet allowed autonomy in the observance of their faith to Christians and Jews albeit imposing a *zajiya* or a tax on them as a measure of political control.

And while Islam perpetuates piety and righteousness, it equally stresses *jihad* and terror as stratagem, for the presentation of faith. "Evil is the end of the evildoer," says the *Quran* (30:9). To enjoin good and forbid evil so that there is no mischief and corruption in the world, the *Quran* exhorts *jihad. Jihadis*, or the army of God, was designated a place of honour; it aided and abetted the Prophet throughout his ten year struggle against his enemies with fidelity and sacrifice. The Prophet had stressed that the *jihadis* should observe the "cause of truth" (one God, one religion and one book). Persuasion to win over the "insincere and hypocrites" was also a part of *jihad* (9.73 and 66:9). In an earlier *Sura*, he asks all to give "courage to the believers". The *jihadis* were required to be steadfast; for, "twenty steadfast men shall vanquish two hundreds". So they were required to stand and fight and withdraw only if such a withdrawal could provide greater tactical advantage.

The *Quran* also sees *jihad* in its spiritual divinity as a way of God, expressed in the holy book as *Jihad-fi-Sabilaallah*. Also known as the "Great *Jihad*", it aims at cleansing oneself of evils within. Control of the satanic evils of lust, greed, anger, desire and passion is the objective. Vainglory and arrogance are unrighteous and pride is the cardinal sin of human beings—both being impediments to obtaining God's grace.

This form of *jihad*, which most Islamic leaders, intellectuals and clerics hold is the true meaning of the word, epitomizes a condition of emancipation from all cravings and indulgence of the body, and is intended towards achieving righteousness. At 13:49 the *Quran* urges all men to "excel one another in piety (as) the noblest of you in Allah's sight is the most righteous". It is salvation by faith, achieved through one's own acts and God's mercy. It aims at dispelling ignorance and spiritual blindness. *Sura* 28:15 is poignant: "Forgive me my Lord; I have sinned against my soul."

Jihad, therefore, is like a coin with two faces—both originating from the same fountainhead Islam, the religion of peace. The temporal and the spiritual are like the body and the mind or soul. Both were meant to strengthen the faith and the resolve of believers. It is this universal appeal of Islam—its virtue of universal brotherhood, that has created the second largest religion of the world.

15 December 2001

Understanding *Jihad* and Fundamentalism in South Asia

(Report of the IPCS Panel Discussion held on 23 November 2001 at India International Centre)

PANELISTS: PROF. RIYAZ PUNJABI, PROF. KALIM BAHADUR AND SULTAN SHAIN

ON HIS WELCOME remarks, Mr Chari emphasized the importance of conceptual clarity especially on words like "*jihad*" and "fundamentalism" as they connote different meanings in different contexts.

Introducing the topic, the Chair, Mr Anand Verma, pointed out its importance in the present context. Fundamentalism in the sub-continent is a product of the Reformist Movement during the colonial period not a century ago. There are three types of Islamic followers today:

- Those who believe in the "restoration" of the present civilization to an idealized form.
- Those who emphasize the combination of both tradition and modernity.
- Those who take a pragmatic approach of keeping out religion from governance.

Fundamentalism belongs to the first trend: it refuses to accept any modern political system—neither any debate nor discussion is permissible. Only the fundamentalists' interpretation of the *Quran* and other Islamic scriptures is acceptable. Though less intensive, its influence is felt in India too. In this regard, the important questions that need to be addressed are:

- Is the average Indian Muslim clear about the difference between religion and nationalism, given the fact that religion and nation are one and the same for the fundamentalists?
- Whose responsibility is it to guide the Muslim community, and how?
- Why are Muslims inert over important national issues like Kashmir's accession to India, Pakistan's efforts to sabotage and subterfuge India, and consequences of *madrasas* and *jihad*?
- Why is *jihad* not attempting to positively reform the society?

Prof. Kalim Bahadur began his speech by providing a definition for the various terms such as "communalism", "fundamentalism" and "revivalism". Fundamentalism means going back to the fundamentals, where there is a text. There are two kinds of fundamentalists—creative and conservative. The first creatively interprets the fundamentals, whereas the second strictly follows the text.

Taliban fundamentalism is a mixture of tribalism and *mullahism* in Afghanistan. It is doubtful whether Mullah Omar, the supreme leader of the Taliban, has ever attended any seminary.

The Muslim writers, in general, have misunderstood the concept of *jihad*. *Jihad* literally means struggle. It calls for fight against oppression but not to propagate Islam. *Jihad* also includes the fight against the self – the vices of an individual. Only an Islamic state can declare a *jihad* and there can be no subterfuge in its declaration. It should be overt and not covert. *Jihadi* organizations' claim that *jihad* can be declared by individuals is incorrect. Most of these organizations use *jihad* to achieve an Islamic state. Neither Mullah Omar nor Osama bin Laden can declare *jihad*, as they are individuals. *Jihadi* groups consider *jihad* as the sixth pillar of Islam.

The Arab concept of *jihad* is totally different. For them, *jihad* is not a means to end, but an end in itself. They prefer to keep fighting, whether or not they achieve anything. For them, *jihad* is not territorial.

Sultan Shahin, the second panelist, focused on the role of *madrasas* in India and traced the history of the Islamic fundamentalist movement. *Madrasas* in India do not teach *jihad* in their curriculum and one of the main reasons for their popularity is the failure of government-run schools to provide effective education. It is wrong to presume that the fundamentalists are uneducated.

One of the main factors that contribute to the growth of fundamentalism is the pride among the Muslim community regarding the vast Islamic empires of the previous centuries and the desire to achieve that lost glory. The second factor for the growth of fundamentalism, especially their hostility towards the West, is that they feel the ideals of Islam, are represented, in fact, by the West. For example, the idea of Human Rights, introduced to the West by Islam, is now being used against them.

According to Prof Riaz Punjabi, as Islam transformed into a state system, *Ahadis*, certain sayings attributed to The Prophet, proliferated. It is the *Ahadis* from which contemporary fundamentalist groups like the Taliban and the *Al-Qaeda* draw inspiration. Along with this, misinterpretation of the *Quran* contributes to the ideology of violence that these groups follow. Secondly, a myth has been created that the door has been closed on *Ishtehad* as this would lead to the reconstruction of religious thought. Mohammed Iqbal had given a series of lectures in Madras (Chennai) on this issue and its importance in dealing with fundamentalism. It must be noted that these lectures were in English and this has been a continuing problem with the Muslim intellectuals in India. Liberal Muslim opinion in India is expressed mostly in English and hence fails to reach the majority of the Muslim people who do not understand it.

The Islamic concept of *Haqmat-ullah* or "Sovereignty of God" is another concept that the fundamentalists interpret for narrow gains. It also works as a form of mental block in the minds of the people. Though the Organization of Islamic Countries (OIC) talks about self determination, Islam rejects the concept. Maulana Mehdudi condemned the formation of Pakistan on the basis of this principle. However, he later changed his position on the issue and migrated to Pakistan.

Fundamentalism is being used as a mechanism of grievance redressal. There are geographical areas in the world where the Muslims are faced with different kinds of problems ranging from unequal representation to territorial conflicts. In these areas the bogey of fundamentalism has been raised to fight the existing power structure. Earlier, in many countries, Islamic idiom was used in the fight against colonial oppression. However, it needs to be debated whether it is still relevant today.

Finally, fundamentalism is being used as a strategic weapon. The US-Pak axis used the ideology of fundamentalism to push the Soviets out of Afghanistan. At that time, "*jihad*" and "*mujahideen*" were revered words in the American press. Even after the exit of the USSR, the use of Islamic fundamentalism as a strategic weapon continues. Between 1990-8, the US turned a blind eye to the growth and spread of fundamentalism in Central Asia, Afghanistan, Xinjiang and Kashmir. In fact, the West pleaded for a dialogue with the fundamentalists and objected to the Taliban being referred to as "fundamentalists". Even after the September 11 attacks, fundamentalism is being used as a strategic weapon, with the US differentiating between different types of political violence in Kabul, Kandahar and Kashmir. India must devise its own means and strategies to deal with it.

What are the implications of Islamic fundamentalism for Indian foreign policy? India is fighting a war in Kashmir and should not mince words in describing it as such. Political patronage to people like the Shahi Imam must stop. Narrow political goals are endangering the internal security of the country. There is a need to evolve a mechanism to see what is happening in the *madrasas* without offending their sensibilities. The government should also show greater urgency in instituting a Hindu-Muslim dialogue. More attempts need to be made to integrate the voices advocating peace from both communities and for this, space should be created at different fora for the expression of moderate opinion. Better governance in Kashmir and other areas where communal tension prevails is essential to prevent the alienation of the population from the government. Finally, India must call the bluff of the US in differentiating between different types of fundamentalism. This principle must not change on the basis of political exigencies.

Discussion

The discussion highlighted the following key points:

- Liberal Muslim opinion does not get percolated down to every section of the Muslim population in India because of extensive use of English by the intellectuals.
- Muslims in India are not a monolithic entity. They can be

differentiated on the basis of adherence to a religious doctrine, language, region and political affiliation.

- The explicitness inherent in the *Quran* does not restrict the space for interpretation and adaptation because the principle of "free will" established very well in the *Quran* endows enough space both for interpretation and adaptation.

5 December 2001

Terrorism: A Messiah Needed in the Arab World

Lt. Gen. (Retd) A.M. Vohra

The September 11 attacks on the World Trade Centre and the Pentagon were heinous, fiendish and abhorrent. The reaction to punish the perpetrators who threaten to repeat their performance is natural. The demand that Osama bin Laden and his *Al-Qaeda* compatriots be handed over to face retribution is unlikely to be met. Military action to "hound" them and destroy the Taliban forces is, therefore, justifiable. The intense air bombardment and cruise missile attacks will effectively downgrade their military potential. Some collateral damage by way of civilian casualties is unavoidable. The commitment of the US and coalition ground forces to a *Desert Storm* type role is unlikely. Employment of special forces and commandos in strike and snatch raids against *Al-Qaeda* cadres are required. Intelligence is of the essence for such tasks.

The Northern Alliance will need support by way of armaments, logistics and air support. The US air and missile operations have eased the Alliance task. The objective is obviously to weaken the Taliban to the extent that they accept a new political dispensation in Afghanistan. Efforts are afoot to hold a *Loya Jirga* under the stewardship of the 86 year old King Zahir Shah, whose emissaries arrived in Islamabad around mid-October for discussion with the Pakistan government. The support to the Alliance appears to be restricted to facilitating the capture of Mazar-i-Sharif, but not Kabul. Both the Taliban and the Northern Alliance would be amenable to a compromise if the former is weakened and the latter is not too strong.

Expectedly, there are voices being raised against the military action, although most Arab and other Muslim countries including Pakistan have vowed support to the "coalition" led by the US despite their own reservations. In many countries there have been large-scale protests, particularly in Pakistan, Indonesia and Algeria and a display of religious sympathy, overlooking the gravity of the acts of terrorism. Nevertheless, to deal with terrorism one has to deal with its basic causes.

Despotic monarchies in West Asia impose values and a way of life that promotes protest by violent means. The *Wahabi* creed is intolerant. Fundamentalism flourishes in these circumstances. US policy in this region is also questionable. Religious fundamentalism spawns terrorism but geopolitics precipitates violent acts. However, nothing can justify the acts committed on September 11. The perpetrators must be brought to justice. This would only be the start of the war against terrorism to be followed by dealing with its causes, be they despotic regimes, intolerant beliefs or, the flawed policies of the US. The continuing threats of more *fidayeen* attacks or bio-terrorism necessitate urgent action on all fronts.

Islam is a religion of peace. Islam means "peace". The Islamic greeting, *Aslam-e-lekum*, means "Peace be upon you". Collin Powell is right when he says in a *Newsweek* column on 15 October (2001) that, "the millions of our fellow Americans of the Islamic faith, and the 10 Muslim nations that lost citizens in the September 11 attacks, need no convincing that the killers and their accomplices pervert Islam when they use it to justify their appalling crimes". On 28 September (2001), the FBI released the text of identical letters in Arabic, found in three different places in the United States, that link together the hijackers of three of the four airlines. Commenting on these letters, Nehad Awad, the Director of the Council on American Islamic Relations, recalled his horror at the twisted use of Islam in the text and said, "I felt sick to my stomach. Then I consulted with other scholars, and they had the same reaction. The terrorists are sick individuals and they have no knowledge of their religion. Whoever wrote these letters was just trying to deform the *Quran* to justify what the terrorists were about to do." Truly, the Arab world needs a Messiah to preach the true Islam.

India has been suffering from cross border terrorism for over a decade. Its pleadings with the international community to tackle the problem of global terrorism drew little attention. Naturally, it was among the first to join the "coalition" against terrorism in the hope that action would be taken to end it everywhere and, in particular, the *jihadi* organizations and training camps in Pakistan and Pakistan Occupied Kashmir. Action against terrorism, both at the perceptual and physical levels, cannot be taken simultaneously and has to be phased. It is clear that Osama bin Laden, his *Al-Qaeda* set-up and the Taliban must be the US's first objectives; it is also evident that Pakistan is geographically so situated that its support is vital for US operations. In these circumstances, US condemnation of the 1 October 2001 terrorist attack on the Legislature in Srinagar and the statement that terrorism against India is also on the coalition agenda should be accepted at face value, and built upon in due course of time.

31 October 2001

Banning SIMI: A 'Right' Beginning, But...

SUBA CHANDRAN

THE CENTRAL GOVERNMENT finally decided to ban the Students Islamic Movement of India (SIMI), under the Unlawful Activities (Prevention) Act, 1967, after considering the issue for a long time. The ban was justified on at least four accounts—its linkages with militant organizations that are operating in Jammu & Kashmir; its pan-Islamic connections with organizations known to be funding "*jihadi*" organizations worldwide; its network at the national level, which has been used for subversive purposes; and, finally, the objectives and policies it supports.

Firstly, what makes the SIMI dangerous is its network. The SIMI was established in Aligarh in 1977 and ever since it has set up an extensive network nation-wide. It has cells in various parts of the country and is especially active in Madhya Pradesh, Gujarat, Maharashtra and Kerala. Besides, the SIMI has close links with other fundamentalist Muslim organizations in various states. The Chief Ministers of these states and the intelligence agencies have repeatedly been demanding a ban on the SIMI for the last few years. It has a cell for young children aged between 7 and 11 called *Shaheen Force,* sympathizers called *Ikhwans* and full-time workers called *Ansars*. There are around 400 *Ansars* and 20,000 *Ikhwans*. The SIMI also has a *Dawah Cell*, whose main objective is to re-convert those who "were misguided by the *Shuddhikaran* movement". It brings out several magazines all over India—*Islamic Movement* (in Urdu, Hindi, and English), *Vivekam* (Malayalam), *Sedi Malar* (Tamil), *Rupantar* (Bengali) and *Iqraa* (Gujrati).

Secondly, the ban on SIMI is justified for its role in creating communal disharmony and its disruptive policies. The SIMI was responsible for inciting communal violence in Gujarat, Maharashtra and Madhya Pradesh, by its inflammatory speeches and posters. In 2001 alone, the SIMI was responsible for the communal riots in Pune and Kanpur in March and for the bomb blast in the Sabarmati Express on Independence Day.

The SIMI believes the parliamentary system is unsuitable for bringing about an Islamic Revolution and is against democracy, socialism, secularism and nationalism. At its conferences conducted all over India, the SIMI praised Osama bin Laden as the ideal *mujahid,* pasted his posters, and supported Taliban policies including the destruction of the Buddha statues in Bamiyan. In one of the interviews, Dr Shahid Badr, President of the SIMI, when asked whether he believes in nationalism answered "Nationalism causes war and hatred among people" (*The Week*, 9 September 2001).

Thirdly, the SIMI has extensive linkages with pan-Islamic organizations and groups and gets most of its moral and monetary support from them. Though the SIMI claims that it is not receiving "contribution from abroad either from individuals or from institutions" but is only collecting "funds through personal contributions of its members and collection of *Zakah* from its well-wishers within the country", it is reported to be getting funds from the World Assembly of Muslim Youth (WAMY) and the International Islamic Federation of Students Organization in Kuwait. The WAMY has organized anti-India meetings on Kashmir and funded the construction of new mosques and *madrasas* in Jammu & Kashmir. Besides, these pan-Islamic organizations which liberally fund for Muslim causes, the SIMI has extensive linkages with other fundamentalist and militant Islamic organizations in South Asia. For example, it has links with the *Jamaat-e-Islami* in Pakistan, Bangladesh and Nepal.

Fourthly, the SIMI's ban is justified due to its links with some of the militant organizations. The SIMI has ties with the *Hizbul Mujahideen* which came to light this year when the Maharashtra Police arrested nine members who attempted to bomb the RSS and the VHP offices in Nagpur in May 2001. Eight of the nine arrested were part of the SIMI and four of them were trained by the *Hizbul*

Mujahideen; the *Hizbul* had trained the SIMI cadres in handling arms and explosives.

While banning the SIMI, some questions also need to be addressed. First, how was the SIMI able to gain support on such a wide scale. Any organization with a membership of over 20,000 should not be treated casually. What makes a community join such a fundamentalist organization? The social, economic and political conditions that drive it to support fundamentalism need to be addressed. Secondly, it is essential to look into the objectives and actions of all fundamentalist groups irrespective of the religion to which they belong to. If the reason for banning the SIMI is that it was involved in creating communal violence, then groups like the *Bajrang Dal* and *Vishwa Hindu Parishad* (VHP), which also spread communal hatred, need to be banned. The fundamentalist groups belonging to the Muslim community became violent only after the demolition of the Babri Masjid in 1991. The violent activities of the *Bajrang Dal* and the VHP against the Christian and Muslim communities and their role in inciting communal violence have been proved beyond doubt. Dig Vijay Singh, Chief Minister of Madhya Pradesh, has called for banning the *Bajrang Dal*. These Hindu fundamentalist organizations also have a wide network and impart arms training to their cadres. The only difference between the SIMI and these Hindu fundamentalist groups is that they are not trained by any militant organization. Is this reason good enough not to ban the VHP and *Bajrang Dal*?

Banning the SIMI has been a step in the right direction. However, it will have little credibility if other organizations fanning communal tensions are not banned.

9 October 2001

Islamic Fundamentalism and Terrorism

(Report of the IPCS seminar held on 16 February 2000)

SPEAKER: DR. JOSEPH KOSTINER

DR. JOSEPH KOSTINER outlined the essential reasons for the rise of Islamic Fundamentalism. One is the tendency within Islamic civilization to scrutinize its early origins and scriptures for clues to return to its golden eras. Islamic scriptures have sanctioned no political institution that has arisen in the Middle East since Prophet Muhammad did not clearly designate a successor. Since no particular system of government is prescribed by the *Quran*, a strong tradition of scriptural scrutiny has been embedded in the Middle East. Added to this is the fact that the *Quran* was disclosed in the full bloom of history, unlike say, Christianity, whose origins are obscured by the turbulence of the Roman occupation of Judea. The Muslim perception that the *Quran* is eternal besides being a miracle creates an aspiration of looking for political solutions to contemporary problems within the principles of a text that was conditioned by medieval life.

The rise of Islamic fundamentalism is also linked to the problems of the Arab world over the last several centuries, wherein Islamic revivalism has stalled soon after its territorial expansionism ceased. The Ottoman Empire is an exception though, but it did not reach the level of sophistication that the Abbasids attained in the eleventh century. Over the last two centuries, Arab leaders have been trying religious reforms to galvanize Islam somewhat unsuccessfully. Islamic proponents have been overwhelmed by the bureaucratization of their societies through the introduction of Western mechanics such as the army and secular education. The import of liberalism and parliamentarianism in Egypt, Syria has bred cultural anxieties that political Islam has capitalized on. The failure of pan-Arabism and Arab nationalism has created a political space for fundamentalism. Islamists have insisted that imported influences and ideologies have failed to deliver genuine development while fostering illegitimate values, and therefore a return to traditional Islamic concepts of governance is the only way to redeem crisis-ridden societies. Hence, a combination of existential frustration and disenchantment with the West has created the conditions for Islamic fundamentalism.

Kostiner clarified that Islamic fundamentalism should not be considered as tantamount to Islamic orthodoxy. In fact, fundamentalism could imply the rebellion against an existing orthodoxy just as Saudi Wahhabism was a rebellion against the regnant practices of its day. Fundamentalism is a move to return to the fundamentals of the Islamic faith. An Islamic fundamentalist is an extremist but not a terrorist. Islamic Fundamentalism is an impulse to reconcile the pristine morality of the days of the Prophet with the challenges of modernity.

Terrorism is the violent manifestation of a frustration that modernity induces in Islamic groupings. Organizations that employ terror inveigh against the existing social order and attempt to annihilate it completely. Most Islamic thinkers have not reached such extreme conclusions but a few are very vocal. There are two main streams of Islamic terrorism prevalent: one is the Iranian Shii stream inspired by Ayatollah Khomeini which is practiced by the *Hizbollah* in Lebanon at the behest of its leader Fadlallah. The other is the Sunni stream inspired by Sayyid Qutb and is observed in Egypt and Gaza. The Shii leadership grew out of the seminary in Najaf in southern Iraq. Khomeini entirely overturned the traditional Shii attitude to state power that was pietistic and almost fatalistic. Khomeini argued that corrupt regimes can be violently opposed and toppled if Islam was under attack. Militant Shiism has not been very successful by hindsight though it threatened to spread to Iraq and the Gulf. Its success is most evident in southern Lebanon where the *Hizbollah* has managed to create a state within a state—a feat none too difficult in Lebanon which has always been a disorganized state. *Hizbollah* is funded by Iran and receives arms via Syria; it is opposed to the peace process.

The Sunni proponents of terror tactics do not originate from the Wahhabi trend but project themselves as a kind of an Islamic vanguard who impose traditional lifestyle patterns and attack symbols of foreign influence like tourists in Egypt. Qutb is their patron thinker, who interestingly studied in the United States. He preached that Middle Eastern regimes were corrupt and was eventually executed by President Gamal Abdel Nasser in 1965. The Muslim Brotherhood that he inspired eventually assassinated Egyptian President Anwar Sadat. The Brothers have not had much success elsewhere besides Jordan where they have been ruthlessly dealt with or been coopted. President Hafez al-Asad of Syria too ruthlessly destroyed the Brotherhood stronghold of Hama in 1984 where an estimated 25,000 people were killed.

The Islamization of the Arab-Israeli conflict is of recent vintage. The physical absence of the PLO leadership prior to 1993 created a vacuum of political opposition to Israeli rule in West Bank and Gaza that was filled by the Islamic Resistance Movement commonly known as the *Hamas*. It garnered support from professionals like doctors, engineers, teachers and trade unionists and is led by the blind cleric Sheikh Ahmed Yassin. Their socio-political message is directed against Chairman Yassir Arafat's regime which is supposedly neither ameliorating Palestinian discontent nor extracting adequate concessions from the Israelis. The *Hamas* could command the loyalty of up to 20 per cent of the Palestinians. It aims at qualitative terrorism intending to send a message by conducting blasts in Israeli cities that the Jewish nation is vulnerable even at its core. There have been many psychological studies into the psyche of suicide bombers. The belief that heaven is the reward for a martyr may be a compelling reason as also the fact that large sums of money are promised to the families of suicide bombers.

Kostiner concluded with the note that Islamic fundamentalism has not had much political success in the world with the exception of Iran which is an autocratic regime. Sudan is another example that has an Islamic regime prone to violence but it does not rank as an important country like Iran does. There is a stalemate in Algeria while Islamists have failed to capture power in Jordan, Egypt or any of the Gulf states.

Discussion

COMMENT: Pakistan has a sizable population of Shias who are largely politically dormant. Pakistan believes not in a reinterpretation of fundamental Islamic principle, rather it believes in exporting *jihad* to different parts of the subcontinent.

RESPONSE: The politically inferior situation of Shias is common to many Muslim country's with sizable population of Shias like Lebanon. In fact, in Iraq, despite being in a majority, they were politically weak. It has to do with a historical sense of neglect of the community. Until the rise of Ayatollah Khomeini in Iran, the Shia did not assert themselves politically. The doctrine of *jihad* as practised in Pakistan, may have political motives. Gen. Musharraf seems to use this to ensure his survival. There are a number of schools in Pakistan that teach fundamentalism. Further, recruitment of *jihadis* is done from the lower economic strata with promises of monetary benefits for their families. In fact, the action of the *jihadis* especially their involvement in suicide missions cannot be explained rationally. As for export of *jihad* by Pakistan to different parts of South Asia, it is a particularly murderous brand of fundamentalism that caters to the campaigns of revenge and vendetta as well as an anti-West propaganda.

COMMENT: Fundamentalism is the political face of Islam. Akin to Marxism, it has a certain ideology, a revolutionary aim and a cellular structure. The line between fundamentalism and fanaticism is very thin. There is no gentle face of Islamic fundamentalism. This should be kept in mind while dealing with fundamentalism elements.

RESPONSE: All movements in Islamic history have been political movements. The Prophet Muhammad established a political order and the Caliph was a religious and political leader. However, not every manifestation of Islamic fundamentalism leads to terrorism. Fundamentalism also aims at merging tradition with modernity in a reinterpretation of the fundamentals of Islam. The call to rebel against the existing regimes or to annihilate existing orders has not been very widely accepted in the Islamic world.

QUESTION: Kindly provide a comparative analysis of Arabism and Islamism?

RESPONSE: Arabism is a trend in decline. Arab national identity based on secular criteria like language, geography, ethnicity and common history did not work very well in the Arab world as it led to no socio-economic changes. In the 1960s Marxism emerged as an option to Arabism. It was in 1967 that South Yemen gained independence and became Marxist. However, because of the decline of Marxism as an ideology in other parts of the world, it did not cut much ice in the Arab world. Hence in the late 1970s the Arab world turned to Islamism. This was prompted by a reinterpretation of fundamentals of Islam. The rise of Khomeini was a manifestation of this phenomenon. Khomeini crowned himself as the source of all law and Islamic belief in Iran.

QUESTION: How are the suicide missions of the fundamentalism groups any different from serving in a national army?

RESPONSE: The situation in an Army is different because armies are not indoctrinated to commit suicide. Psychologists have enumerated thirty different reasons for people opting for suicide missions. Some of these are, a religious desire to ascend heaven, personal failure in life, revenge, etc. Rational choice depends on the definition of rationalism adhered to by different people. This is not to say that Muslims are irrational but suicide missions are. It cannot be likened to taking a job in the army.

QUESTION: How does the creation of Israel and the occupation of South Lebanon by Israel contribute to the rise in Islamic fundamentalism?

RESPONSE: Israel does not aim to dominate or colonize Lebanon. Though in 1982 Israel did invade Lebanon, it withdrew its forces from all parts of Lebanon including Beirut. In fact, it has created a security zone in South Lebanon as a buffer zone. This region is populated by Christians who are more comfortable with Israel than Lebanon and also keen to avoid the *Hizbollah.* The alternative for Israel is to withdraw from South Lebanon. The current Israeli Prime Minister is offering this solution. Compared to Syria, which despite an agreement of friendship between it and Lebanon continues to sit in Lebanese territory, Israel has only created a security zone as a peaceful way to deal with the situation. Israel is not a source of fundamentalism. Fundamentalism emerges in countries like Sudan, Egypt, Iran without having any thing to do with Israel. The Arab Israeli conflict has been Islamized. It was not a religious conflict to begin.

COMMENT: Any Islamic movement is condemned as fundamentalist. The Wahabbi movement in Saudi Arabia and the Taliban movement in Afghanistan can be condemned as fundamentalist, however, there are other aspects to it. Ideologizing of Islamic belief to reach certain goals like in Iran cannot be condemned as fundamentalist. The slogan for the Islamic revolution in Iran was "Freedom, Independence and Republic". Further, the Israeli are making the Arabs pay for the sins of the Europeans against the Jewish community by rendering Arabs homeless in Palestine. These Palestinians, who are struggling to save their homes cannot be branded terrorists.

RESPONSE: In the Arab-Isreali conflict there is no one side which is right. In fact, it is in the interest of both sides to come to a peaceful compromise to the situation. As for Khomeini, he was fundamentalist in that he posited himself as the chief interpreter of Islam.

QUESTION: Can you represent *Hamas* and the rise of Osama bin Laden as a unified threat of Islamic terrorism?

RESPONSE: At present, Islamic revolution is the only one in the world that offers any hope and the *Hamas* has place within the Islamic ideology. As for Osama bin Laden, he is not the only source of the *jihadi* threat. It probably has a number of actors under working on similar ideological lines.

QUESTION: Comment on the succession race in Palestine after Yasser Arafat.

RESPONSE: Arafat is not openly grooming any one successor. However, there are echelons within the PLO where the struggle for succession to Arafat is being waged. Some of the prominent names in this race are those of Mahmoud Abbas and Abu Ala. Abbas is perceived by the Israelis to be the best bet as he comes across as balanced person. Abu Ala, the minister for finance and the head of the Parliament, is another contender in the race for succession. Of the younger people, the new security establishment seems set to play an important role. They are knowledgeable, well informed people used to the ground realities of the situation. Secondly there are groups of academicians and business people who have local constituencies like youth movements in Palestine. Some of these people like Hannah Ashrawi and Jonathan Qutab are Christians. They argue for democracy and have influence among the intellectuals. Any future government in Palestine shall be composed of these different groups.

QUESTION: What is the future of Islamic terrorism?

RESPONSE: There may be a single idea that guides Islamic movement all over the world but there can be no single authority that controls all activity. The reason is the conflicts within the Islamic world, and at some point some of these movements may turn hostile towards each other. However, in the lack of any other revolutionary idea, Islamic revolution does hold a certain legitimacy and shall give rise to corresponding movements.

COMMENT: The various state-funded Islamic fundamentalist organizations such as the *Hamas* and the *Hizbollah* are increasingly becoming independent of their supporters. They generate their own funding through drug trade and are consequently becoming independent in their operations. This is a very dangerous trend. The Taliban was created by vested American interests in Afghanistan to fight against the Soviet influence. However, after the end of the Cold War, it has come into its own as an independent organization operating from a largely lawless state like Afghanistan. One can deal with state terrorism but to deal with amorphous entities like these is more difficult and more dangerous.

Lashkar-e-Shivba: Do We Really Need It?

MALLIKA JOSEPH A.

THE *LASHKAR-E-SHIVBA* has been formed by youth in Pune and Sangli in reaction to the *Lashkar-e-Taiba's* anti-Indian activities. It is designed to be a people's force against the *Tayyaba* and *Hizbul Mujahideen.* When youth in Maharashtra launched the *Lashkar-e-Shivba* with these objectives one could view it as mere vigilantism. In developed societies, vigilantism is part of a community-policing programme. In others, it emerges whenever the need arises and the local security apparatus is unable to meet the demands of policing. Can *Shivba* be seen in this light?

Firstly, the agenda. Many members of the group are Shiv Sainiks, and the group was launched "with the blessings of Shiv Sena chief Balasaheb Thackerey"; it "draws its inspiration from Shivaji Maharaj and Balasaheb's militant Hindutva". Though the immediate objective of the group is to check the spread of the *Lashkar-e-Taiba* (LeT) in various parts of Maharashtra, the founders are clear that they do not want to limit their operations to Maharashtra. With utterances like, "Kashmiri Hindus have been thrown out of their state. Their land and rights have to be restored immediately...", it is obvious that the agenda is more communal than just vigilantism.

Secondly, the logistics. LeT is the militant wing of the *Markaz Dawa-wal-Arshad* located near Lahore in Pakistan. Its finances are drawn from Pakistan and other Middle Eastern countries. It has some 600 hardcore militants fighting in the Kashmir valley, with hundreds of others getting trained in Pakistan. With a constant source of manpower and sophisticated weapons, the LeT has proved to be a deadly force, even when pitted against the Indian Army and Paramilitary Forces operating in Kashmir. That the *Shivba* should contemplate confronting LeT, not only in Maharashtra but also in other areas including Kashmir, is intriguing. Obviously, to confront the LeT requires similar, if not more resources, especially in the area of sophisticated arms. And, the founders' optimism that they would be able to quickly acquire the necessary resources, manpower and intelligence network needs to be noted with concern, particularly the implications of such an armed group operating in the region.

Maharashtra has been the hotbed of communal tensions in the recent past and the last thing wanted is an armed group with a "militant Hindutva" ideology and communal agenda. The Shiv Sena has already played a role in increasing the level of communal intolerance in the region, and Mumbai has still not healed from the riots following the demolition of the Babri Masjid. Any move towards making the *Shivba* operational would only lead to the mushrooming of other groups based on communal lines. The caste armies in Bihar, operating outside the control of the police machinery in the state, highlights why forming armed groups against militants, secessionists or criminals needs to be nipped at the bud. In democracies there is an established machinery for handling issues of national security. They should be left to do their job without interference from organizations like the *Lashkar-e-Shivba.*

23 October 2000

IV: Weapons of Mass Destruction and Terrorism

International Terrorism: Osama bin Laden and Weapons of Mass Destruction

DR. SUBHASH KAPILA

THE UNITED STATES and Western countries have been haunted ever since the disintegration of the Soviet Union with the prospect of Weapons of Mass Destruction (WMD) falling into the hands of terrorist groups. Their fears have turned out true with information now available that *jihadi* groups led by Osama bin Laden have indeed acquired WMD. In the hands of Islamic fundamentalist terrorists fortified with the spirit of martyrdom and imbued with the frenzy of expelling the United States from the Islamic world or Islamization of countries with sizeable Muslim population, these weapons indeed become frightening weapons of terror.

Indications of possession of WMD by Osama bin Laden are amplified below.

Chemical and Biological Weapons

Islamist terrorists, both Afghan and Arab Afghans under the guidance of Osama bin Laden and supervision of Pakistan's ISI have established well fortified facilities in Kandahar in Afghanistan for production of chemical, bacteriological and radiological weapons (perhaps) too. This set-up was established in May 1998 with the acquisition of plant and machinery from Yugoslavia. This plant arrived via Pakistan with assistance of the ISI.

The first WMD base at Kandahar commenced training of terrorist operatives for biological and chemical weapons from Pakistan, Bangladesh, Afghanistan, Egypt and the Gulf states thereafter.

The second WMD base is reported to have been established at Zenica in Bosnia-Herzegovina. Terrorist operative training here is being imparted to first generation European Muslims convertees and second generation emigres from the Muslim world.

Sources from which chemical and biological weapons materials/ samples have been obtained or purchased for relatively small amounts of money are as follows:

- Russia: Viruses causing deadly diseases such as Ebola and Salmonella.
- Czech Republic: Samples of botulism bio-toxin.
- North Korea: Samples of deadly anthrax.
- Unknown Source: Sarin.

The production facilities are being supervised by a group of Ukrainian experts (chemists and biologists).

Nuclear Suitcase Bombs and Tactical Nuclear Weapons

Osama bin Laden's quest for nuclear weapons commenced in 1996 and he is reported to have spent millions of dollars on this project. The focus has been an acquisition of nuclear suitcase bombs. Arab intelligence sources indicate acquisition of tactical nuclear weapons also.

Corroborative evidence has reached United States from Russian, Arab countries and from confessions by captured Islamic terrorists worldwide. The estimates of Osama bin Laden acquisitions are as follows.

- Russian estimates—Few nuclear suitcase bombs.
- Arab intelligence sources—More than 20 nuclear suitcase bombs.

The nuclear suitcase bombs have been acquired from Central Asian Republics (CAR) Islamic countries with the active assistance of Chechen Muslim rebels. Laden's agents are reported to have paid US $ 30 million cash and two tons of Afghan heroin worth US $ 700 million in Western markets, to Chechen mafia for this purpose.

The suitcase nuclear bombs are reported to be stored at two locations in Afghanistan:

- Khowst: In deep tunnels
- Kandahar: In deep caves

This nuclear programme is being run by a Western educated Arab nuclear scientist, (turned *jihadi*) and assisted by five Turkoman Muslims. Others too have been brought from CAR countries.

The nuclear suitcase bombs could only be operated by SPETZNAZ (Russian Special Forces) personnel. Some Ukrainian and Baltic region SPETZNAZ troopers are reported to have been recruited, not for operating the bombs but as escorts/protection for these bombs and the technicians.

However the operational use of suitcase nuclear bombs will be entrusted only to *jihadis*. To overcome the technical problems of coded transmissions for activation of these nuclear suitcase bombs (Russian technique), it is reported that Laden's nuclear experts could "hot-wire" them and these can be used by human-bomb volunteers from amongst the *jihadis* seeking martyrdom.

That nuclear suitcase bombs could have reached Osama bin Laden stand corroborated by General Lebed's (former Security chief of Russia) statement in 1997 that a number of such bombs stood missing from Russian arsenals.

Combating terrorism is itself a very complex and frustrating task. The task of combating *jihadi* terrorism of the Osama bin Laden variety imposes new challenges for countries being targeted by *jihadis*. The WMD threat so posed can only be effectively met by intelligence of a very high order which could facilitate pre-emptive actions.

If the current record of Taliban's attitudes to intentional criticism over the Bamiyan episode is an indicator, Osama bin Laden will have nothing but contempt for any overtures to give up the WMD as a tool of *jihad*. WMD give the Islamic Jehadis an unprecedented power to indulge in political blackmail of Western and other targeted countries. Aware of the vulnerability of civilized societies to political terror and panic, the WMD provides a heady intoxication of unrivalled power to the *jihadis*.

Technical means for long distance disablement of such weapons do not seem to be in existence. Devoid of these, the United States as the primary target has no choice but to keep strict and effective surveillance of Osama bin Laden's activities, the Taliban in Afghanistan and Pakistan as the main conduit of both westward and eastward movement of the *jihadi's* WMD. India too, as one of the targets identified by bin Laden, needs to ponder seriously as to how combat this menace.

12 April 2001

Weapons of Mass Destruction and Terrorism

(Report of the IPCS Panel Discussion held on 9 November 2001)

PANELISTS: G. BALACHANDRAN AND P.R. CHARI

THE SEMINAR BEGAN with introductory comments by ACM Mehra who emphasized the fact that in an atmosphere dominated by concerns regarding nuclear weapons, the threat from chemical and biological weapons had not been appreciated. This thinking needs change. Following the World Trade Centre (WTC) attack in the United States and the anthrax scare, the world community has woken up to the possibility of a chemical and biological weapons attack by a terrorist group.

G. BALACHANDRAN: The possibility of nuclear weapons being used as a terrorist weapon is not very high. The reason is that though nuclear weapons may be easy to assemble, the technology required to deliver and detonate it is very complex and requires a high degree of expertise and sophisticated infrastructure. However, the terrorists could use radiological weapons that are much simpler to use and the material needed to make them is available as spent fuel in reactors and nuclear research centres around the world. The use of a radiological weapon may not cause mass destruction but will cause much panic and confusion, which is the prime objective of terrorists.

Biological and chemical weapons can be considered Weapons of Mass Destruction (WMD), but not when used by terrorists. Chemical weapons are easy to make but their use involves other requirements like stability and potency of the agents over a period of time. The manufacture of lethal WMD also requires them to possess weapons-grade chemicals that are for restricted use in most countries and not easily available. Further, storage of biological agents requires special containers which, again, are only available on a restricted basis. Attempts to buy either the chemicals or their storage infrastructure in the open market would arouse suspicions. The dispersion of these weapons over a large area requires equipment like crop-dusters. Ground dispersal is easier to detect. Finally, heat, humidity, oxidation and climatic conditions change the behaviour of the agents, and users need to possess the expertise to factor these changes while making a weapon. Hence a crude device can be made by terrorists but it will not have the same impact as a WMD.

There is no protection against these weapons though vaccines are available for protection against bacteriological weapons. However, vaccines too have side effects and logistically speaking, entire populations cannot be vaccinated. The only way to guard against the use of chemical and biological weapons is to increase safeguards. Protocols should be strengthened and there should be stringent control over the manufacture and distribution of weapons-grade material. For chemical agents, markers like those used for plastic explosives to identify the country of manufacture, permit tracing the movement of these chemicals. Technological surveillance needs to be increased over the purchase of storage equipment and precursors. However, no amount of prevention will eliminate the threat of use of these weapons, but if they are used by terrorists, the fatalities could be minimized using preventive measures.

P.R. CHARI: The history of WMD is largely the history of nuclear weapons. The threats from chemical and biological weapons had receded into the background because no state can really deter these threats. It was believed that WMD were not terrorist weapons because of the technological hurdles involved in their manufacture, delivery and use. The earliest threats included an attack on a nuclear weapons facility to release radiation and creating terror in the surrounding areas or the theft of a nuclear weapon or getting hold of a fissile material and its subsequent use for making a nuclear weapon. Alternately, the terrorist could steal spent fuel from a nuclear facility and manufacture a radiological weapon. That, however, would not result in mass destruction but definitely succeed in creating terror and panic.

After the break up of the Soviet Union, there was a tangible threat of loose nukes and fissile materials falling into the wrong hands. Further there was a danger of terrorists utilizing the expertise of the unemployed nuclear scientists and engineers from the new republics. There was a sanguine belief, however, that chemical and biological weapons would not be used and was hardly any interest in the academic and policy community. The Institute of Peace and Conflict Studies (IPCS) has initiated a debate and research on the issue of biological and chemical weapons, held seminars and published a recent book, *Verification Protocol for the Biological Weapons Convention*. After the September 11 attacks on the WTC and the anthrax scare in the United States, people are sensitized to the threat from biological and chemical weapons. In the US, the National Guard has been trained to handle attacks of this kind.

The possibility of chemical and biological weapons attacks by non-state actors needs to be debated. Though these weapons are easier to manufacture, their storage and use presents problems for their use as WMD. However, they are potent weapons and can be used to create panic. In fact, more hoaxes, like in the recent anthrax scare, are possible in the future. Hoaxes cannot be treated complacently and must be responded to, keeping the threat perception in mind.

Certain remedial measures can be suggested. An effective public health system, the stockpiling of medicines and vaccines, better policing, intelligence gathering, physical protection of chem-bio facilities and psychological evaluation of the people who work in them along with international cooperation and education of the population are necessary steps in this regard. However, it also needs recognition that there can be no foolproof contingency plan to deal with a possible attack, because of the logistical problems involved in such an exercise.

Traditional counter-terrorism activities including political and diplomatic efforts to safeguard against these threats need to be strengthened. For the last six years the world has been struggling to finalize the Verification Protocol for the Biological Weapons

Convention. However, this effort was sabotaged in August 2001 by the US. The upcoming Review Conference of the Biological Weapons Convention may result in the Protocol being passed as it is being held against the background of the threat of anthrax in the US.

Discussion

- There are logistical problem in using nuclear weapons as WMD by terrorists.
- The sabotage angle in the Bhopal gas tragedy and the Surat plague cannot be ignored.
- India's response to a chem-bio attack by a hostile country needs to be debated at the highest levels in the government.
- There must be a concerted effort to educate the public for responding to and dealing with a chem-bio attack.
- The definition of WMD needs to be re-examined in the light of the use of aircraft as WMD in the WTC attacks.
- Links between terrorists and states providing them with logistical and technical assistance to manufacture or use WMD is a serious possibility and needs to be focused upon.
- Greater vigilance is required by states by adopting mechanisms like preparing lists of the institutions that store and use chemical and biological agents.

17 November 2001

Biological Weapons: Most Preferred WMD

ANIMESH ROUL

COINCIDING WITH THE "strike against terror" by the US led coalition, the terrorists have unleashed the germs of terror against the "civilized" world. A biological weapons (BWs) strike by terrorists has become part of the international debate in the US during the last decade. Opinion is divided between the alarmists and those holding the threat to be unrealistic. But within the last twenty days there have been 45 cases of exposure to anthrax (16 confirmed cases of anthrax with 4 deaths); this has started a new trend in recent terrorist activities. They choose to deliver fear and death through the postal services, leading to a "mail phobia" all over the world.

Why did the terrorists choose anthrax spores instead of other conventional or unconventional weapons? What if the terrorists use the more lethal ebola, tularemia or small-pox; or designer viruses instead of anthrax? These questions will haunt us in future.

In biological war, living organisms like bacteria, virus, fungi and rickettsiae, and their natural byproducts (toxins) are used to cause death or disability on a large scale in human beings, animals, and plants. The military and economic advantages in their production and use make biological weapons the weapons of choice for states. They kill people but cause no harm to buildings, factories, etc. Their detection and identification is difficult. These weapons can be produced in an antibiotic factory or in a brewery and can be disseminated by letters, packets, crop-dusters or agricultural sprayers. One can contaminate water supplies or pour agents into a ventilator.

More importantly, the difficulties of acquiring nuclear weapons capabilities due to technical and fiscal costs has stimulated interest in developing chemical and biological weapons capability by States and non-State actors, comprising terrorists group, religious cults, mafia syndicates and deranged individuals. Also, chemical weapons as compared to BWs require a moderately advanced facility. The availability and accessibility of ingredients for BWs makes them more attractive.

There are many factors that attract a terrorist group towards biological weapons and biological weapons attack. Most important is their toxicity. It is estimated that one ounce of botulinum toxin can kill 60 million people if dispersed properly. Another estimation by the World Health Organization's Expert Committee is that 50 kgs of tularemia bacteria, dispersed in aerosol form over a city with a population of 5 million, would cause an estimated 19,000 deaths and a total of 2,50,000 incapacitating casualties. According to an Office of Technology Assessment (OTA) study, very few tularemia organisms are required to cause the onset of symptoms. Unlike anthrax, however, plague and small-pox pose a different problem. They can spread from person to person and lead to epidemics. Another study noted that four tons of nerve agents and 50 kgs of anthrax spores would cause the same number of casualities in a crowded urban center. Some scientists claimed that the mortality levels from a biological weapons attack could exceed that of a large nuclear explosion. Besides the toxicity factors, their undetectability and capacity to reproduce rapidly make BWs a prime choice.

But the drawbacks are many. They seldom inflict casualties instantly and take time to injure or kill depending upon the incubation period of the pathogen. This process cannot be expedited and the results are often uncertain. More importantly, BWs are double edged weapons and do not discriminate between friends and foes. Looking at these drawbacks experts termed BWs as strategic weapons which can cover a large area if dispersed properly, but they have underestimated the likelihood of a BW attack in the past. The prevailing situation is proving them wrong.

However, one vital question which has galvanized the defense and scientific communities all over the world, including India, is how to counter a large-scale biological weapons attack? A future attack on India is not remote. Hoax calls and false alarms are taking their toll in India. Till now, one letter has tested positive. If a sudden outbreak occurs, it will definitely cause mass casualties. Ironically, India is not prepared even for a natural outbreak of diseases. The disease currently in the news, in its natural outbreak, has never been contained in India. Statistics shows that there are some 35 cases of human anthrax documented during the last decade and since 1953 some 182 cases of human anthrax have been documented.

Looking at the possible emerging scenarios, an effective surveillance mechanism for detection and identification, physical protection and decontamination, and medical countermeasures are some of the steps India should undertake. Recently India has started working on a surveillance mechanism under the auspices of National Institute of Communicable Diseases (NICD). It is vitally important that India maintains effective protective measures for both the armed forces and civilians against potential biological threats.

15 November 2001

C&BWs: Panic Poisons

Lt. Col. (Retd) A.K. Sharma

The horrendous effects of gas attacks in trench-warfare during the First World War had a lasting effect on the conscience of nations. This led to chemical and biological weapons (CBWs) being proscribed under the Geneva Protocol of 1925. Nations abhor their employment, yet undertake clandestine research and development as this is not prohibited under any international convention; the Biological & Toxin Weapons Convention only prohibits research into offensive biological agents. Thus countries have no qualms in maintaining secret military arsenals. Iraq and the US are two cases in point, which show that these weapons continue to remain a viable and cost effective means of mass annihilation.

This aspect is not lost either on terrorist organizations who could use CB munitions to spectacular effect. This is evident from the recent anthrax attacks. For terrorists, they are an easy means of propaganda, blackmail and coercion. The law enforcing agencies face great difficulties because of the specialist nature of the counter operation entailed.

Some cases have been referred to in scholastic writings on terrorism; others made the headlines in their time; they include cases involving religious cults, right and leftwing terrorist outfits who have used CBW agents with some effect. They are:

- The Weather Underground—a radical leftist Vietnam era group, which tried to pilfer one of US Army's biological centers (1970).
- RISE—who were on the verge of releasing the typhoid bacteria into Chicago's water supply (1972).

- The Alphabet Bomber—one Muharem Kurbegovic, who threatened to release nerve agents in populated areas (1974).
- The Baader-Meinhof Gang—who stole 53 canisters of mustard gas from a US bunker in West Germany and threatened to use them in Stuttgart (1975).
- The Red Army Faction—who sought to acquire BWs in West Germany (1980).
- The Rajneeshis—a religious cult originating in India that employed biological agents in Oregon sickening 751 pecple (1984).
- The Covenant, the Sword, and the Arm of the Lord—that acquired a large drum of potassium cyanide for poisoning water supply in major US cities (1985).
- The Minnesota Patriots Council—which got hold of ricin, a deadly protein toxin (1991).
- The World Trade Centre Bombers—(1993).
- Aum Shinkriyo's sarin nerve gas attack in the Tokyo subway station in 1995 that transformed the threat of use of CBWs into a risk to national security.
- Larry Wayne Harris—who possessed military grade anthrax (1998).
- US/World Scare and Fatal Cases of Anthrax in the wake of the *Al-Qaeda* terrorist attack on the twin towers of the WTC on September 11. Eight fatal cases in the United States due to military grade anthrax spores being delivered through US Mail and inhaled; and one in Pakistan. A serious scare in Japan (and Argentina, UK, USA, Canada, Belgium and France; amongst others).
- Worldwide Small Pox warning issued by WHO in late October 2001.

A study of these cases, except the recent postal-anthrax cases, reveals, that:

- the use of CBWs has been conspicuously few;
- a lone terrorist or a small group can acquire them with ease;
- hoaxes should not be treated non-seriously;
- it is important to distinguish between isolated and blanket attacks;

and lastly, the choice of agents and modes of delivery differ significantly.

A comparison based on motivation/objective, ideology, targets, delivery and outcome provides a thumbnail profile of the CBW terrorists and of their motivations, the prime ones are charismatic leadership and a sense of paranoia. Propagation of beliefs is another aspect of relevance. The ease with which it can be done in this age of the internet revolution can be fathomed from the fact that there are thirty terrorist's web sites on the net! People are susceptible to this propaganda, as the written word retains its sanctity.

The greatest threat of CBW terrorism comes from religious fundamentalists and rightwing extremists. The redeeming factor however is one: their resource constraint inhibits mass-casualty attacks; and two, the unpredictable damage possible by ambient weather conditions like wind direction, rainfall, temperature, water currents, difficulty in ingesting biological agents, and the incubation time involved, that makes the use of CBWs dicey. They are potent nevertheless, due to the panic and insecurity they can wreak in the populace at large.

10 November 2001

The Spectre of Chem-Bio Terrorism

ARPIT RAJAIN

FOLLOWING THE EVENTS of September 11 there is an emerging concern of terrorist use of chemical and biological weapons. There is a large assortment of chem-bio weapons with diverse characteristics that are suitable for terrorist use. There are many advantages in using these weapons rather than conventional arms and their disadvantages are quite insignificant; hence they could become a key element in the terrorist arsenal.

The first distinct advantage of chem-bio weapons is the terrifying effects of using such weapons in the minds of common citizens. Second, a cost-benefit analysis reveals the difficulty of anti-terrorist groups detecting such weapons, and the low expense and expertise required to develop them. Chem-bio weapons have long been considered "the poor man's atomic bomb". The cost argument is supported by experts who contend that a large-scale operation against a potential civilian target might cost US $2,000 per square kilometre with conventional weapons, US $800 with nuclear weapons, US $600 with nerve-gas weapons, and a mere US $1 with biological weapons.

Like other weapons, there are some disadvantages that the terrorists will encounter in the use of chem-bio weapons. Due to their nature, the use of chem-bio weapons could have two repercussions. The first would be retaliation by anti-terrorist squads, and the second is that it could damage the image of the terrorist groups, unless these groups are not concerned about their image and the collateral damage caused. Following such an assessment terrorist groups are likely to renew their efforts to procure and eventually use chem-bio weapons. After getting these agents the terrorists would have to determine how they can disperse the agent effectively, given the potential risk it poses to those who handle it.

The choice of lethal chemical agents is large. There are several approaches to classifying them but the most useful is to group them by their effects: blister agents, blood agents, choking agents, and nerve agents. Blister agents are intended to "cause incapacitation rather than death". These agents were used during World War I and their use by a terrorist group depends on the objectives of the group. Mustard gas, Nitrogen Mustard, Phosgene Oxime and Ethyldichloroarsine (ED) are examples of blister agents. Cyanide based compounds are the key components of blood agents. Hydrogen Cyanide (HC) is a blood agent that has a lethal dose, which is slightly higher than that of Phosgene, but is less effective due to its rapid rate of evaporation. Other agents are Arsine (SA), Cyanogen Chloride (CK), and Hydrogen Chloride. Choking agents were used during World War I and also in Nazi concentration camps. With the advent of nerve agents they have lost much of their value. These substances can cause death and their greatest danger arises from is their easy availability. Phosgene, Chlorine, Diphosgene (DP), Nitrogen Oxide and Perflurorisobutylene (PHIB) are examples of choking agents. The recent developments in chemical weapons has been in nerve agents. Its latest use by a non-state actor was at the 1995 Tokyo subway attack by the *Aum Shinrikyo* using Sarin. Nerve Cyclohexyl Sarin (GF), Sarin (GB), Soman (GD) and Tabun (GA) are other nerve agents. These chemicals are difficult to obtain.

The Geneva Protocol 1925 and the Chemical Weapons Convention (CWC) of 1993 (entered into force 1997) are the only international instruments that govern chemical weapons. Presently 174 states have signed the CWC or acceded to it, while 143 States have deposited instruments of ratification or accession. The CWC is the product of more than twenty years of negotiations at the Conference on Disarmament in Geneva. It is one of the most complex international conventions ever negotiated. It contains a Preamble, twenty-four Articles and three Annexes. It also incorporates a highly intrusive verification mechanism.

Biological weapons have been used in war since antiquity. The Persians, Romans and Greeks poisoned the drinking water wells of their adversaries by throwing corpses into them, while the British and French infected North American Indians by giving them small-pox infected blankets. Biological agents were employed in military conflicts in the twentieth century too (Japanese experiments on prisoners killed some 3000 people at unit 731, its main facility for biological warfare research, and trichothecene mycotoxins or "yellow rain" was used in South-East Asia).

Biological warfare agents that spread disease include bacteria (anthrax, plague), virus (small-pox, ebola), fungus (potato blight, wheat rust) rickettsiae (resembling bacteria, but grown in living tissue, e.g. typhus), and toxins (non-living products of micro-organisms, e.g. botulinum, ricin, saxitoxin). There is a likelihood of non-state actors using a tested micro-organism for an offensive biological weapons programme. Pathogenic micro-organisms have the property of multiplying rapidly within their host; hence quantities of biological agents dispersed as an aerosol can cause widespread casualties over a large area, if meteorological conditions are suitable. There is a complex interrelationship and balance between the host, the parasite (or pathogen) and the environment.

Hypothetically, non-state actors could carry out three types of biological attacks. First, the pathogen or toxin could be injected. This method is suitable when the need is to cause injury (or death) to a single individual. Second, pathogens could be used to contaminate or poison foods and beverages. This method has the potential to cause hundreds of casualties. Third, pathogens or toxins may be suspended in a wet or dry formulation and dispersed over the target area as aerosolized particles. This manner of attack has the potential to produce thousands of casualties. It needs three key conditions to operate in tandem (a) the formulation to be designed for aerosol dispersal; (b) the aerosol particles produced by the dispersal mechanism should have the capability to withstand environmental stresses; and (c) meteorological conditions (sunshine, humidity, temperature) at the time of dispersal should be conducive for the pathogen to have the maximum effect.

The prospect of non-state actors carrying out an airborne attack with pathogens is possible. Nevertheless, there are technical difficulties in formulating pathogens and toxins for airborne dispersal, successfully developing dispersal mechanisms and ensuring that meteorological conditions are suitable for effective aerosol dispersal.

For these reasons, this type of attack is very difficult for terrorist and criminal groups to attempt. Additionally, after they have been produced, pathogens and toxins have to be preserved in a storage facility before dispersal, or they might lose their potency. This could involve developing methodologies necessary for suspending or dissolving weaponized pathogens and toxins in special solutions containing preservatives, adjuvants and anti-static chemicals. Hence an airborne attack is unlikely; besides it could be detected. A more likely scenario is using pathogens or toxins to contaminate food and beverages or livestock. Another route could be contaminating the water supply of a city. Given the poor health standards in the developing world such contamination may go unnoticed for a long time.

The Geneva Protocol 1925 and the Biological and Toxin Weapons Convention (BTWC) of 1972 remain the only international instruments governing biological weapons. The BTWC has been signed by 162 countries, while 144 countries have submitted their instruments of ratification. A major limitation of the BTWC is the absence of provisions for the verification of its compliance. It remains a matter of faith whether the BTWC signatories are complying with its provisions. To overcome this lacuna the State Parties to the Convention had constituted an Ad Hoc Group in 1991 to devise adequate verification measures from a scientific and technical standpoint. The Ad Hoc Group, which has spent some six and a half years attempting to negotiate a legally binding document to enhance confidence in compliance with the BWC, received a shock when the US in July 2001 announced that it could not support the draft protocol, as this would not improve the ability to verify BWC compliance.

An effective implementation of the chem-bio conventions would greatly contribute to diminishing the threat of chem-bio terrorism, and support the global efforts to combat all forms of terrorism. A cooperative approach would be imperative to detect any chem-bio proliferation-relevant activities. This could best be undertaken in an institutional setting. It remains therefore in the national interest of all States to strengthen these conventions.

18 October 2001

The Looming Threat of Bioterrorism

MAJ. GEN. (RETD) YASHWANT DEVA

A TWO-DAY WORKSHOP was organized last week under the aegis of Indian Institute of Communicable Diseases on developing "surveillance mechanisms for pathogens with biological warfare potential". It is encouraging that the medical communities, particularly those in the defence services, are concerned with the looming threat of bio-terrorism. Earlier in March this year a US D.A. Henderson, Director of the Centre for Civilian Biodefence Studies (US) and expert in bio-warfare was in India. He warned about bio-warfare and social degenerates unleashing bio-terror against the civilized. Whereas the US Administration is conscious of the likelihood of this happening and is bracing itself up, we in India are indifferent, even oblivious the threat.

Biological weapons are cheap to produce. The NATO Handbook on the Medical Aspects of NBC Defensive Operations published in 1996 gives comparative figures of the costs involved. It suggests that whereas the cost (in 1969 figures) of conventional weapons is US \$2000, nuclear armaments US \$800, and chemical agents US \$600, the bargain-basement price of biological weapons is US \$1 to cause 50 per cent casualties per square kilometre. The *inter se* comparison has tilted further over the years to emphasise this point. The logistics requirements also are the least sophisticated. A laboratory that produces pharmaceuticals, with readily available instrumentation and testing facilities, is all that is needed and it is well nigh impossible to discover the existence of such a factory, say in Afghanistan, under the control of Osama bin Laden.

As for delivery system, the organisms only have to be packed in an aerosol can and sprayed around. Perpetrators can escape long before biological weapon agents cause casualties, due to the incubation lag of the agents. They neither have to undertake elaborate planning, nor take on suicide missions.

Research is not prohibited by the Biological Weapons Convention. It is difficult to differentiate between an offensive and defensive research programme; hence any motivated group can easily advance to development and production stages from basic research.

In the US, research on offensive use is not inhibited. In a recent discussion at an IETE Forum, one of the participants suggested that we too should permit countermeasures and offensive related research if we wish to evolve and work out defensive strategies. There is much force in this argument.

Research on biological agents for offensive purposes would be characterized by activities such as the selection for growth, virulence, and toxin production; improving stability under varying environmental conditions; and selection of strains that might overcome existing means of prophylaxis and treatment. Knowledge about these matters is essential for evolving suitable protective strategies and treatment of diseases. However, intent is often misconstrued. Yet when it comes to US's own research programmes, these are justified on the basis of the strength of their laws and scrupulous adherence to them by the military and the scientific community.

If a country was to initiate a biological weapons research programme, and was willing to risk worldwide condemnation, there is nothing stopping it to initiate one and reach a fairly high level of competence in development and production capabilities. If even those who have signed the Convention and swear by it cannot be trusted, what to talk of terrorist groups who are beyond the pale of the Convention and civilized behaviour. Talibans and *Al-Qaeda* prove the point. And what if the vile act is perpetrated by a third party and linked on Osama bin Laden? None would be wiser in the prevailing ambience of suspicion and mistrust, when opportunities and motives are aplenty.

Herein lies the rub and the agenda for our intelligence, security and civil defence agencies.

27 September 2001

V: Suicide Terrorism

An Inquiry into Suicide Terrorism: Sociological Perspectives

SUBA CHANDRAN

SUICIDE TERRORISM has assumed greater significance after the attack on the US in September 2001. In South Asia, Sri Lanka and Kashmir have been witnessing this phenomenon. The background of the suicide terrorists reveals that they are neither fanatics nor mentally deranged or uneducated; instead they seem to have come from a higher economic and educational background.

What makes them willing to make the supreme sacrifice? The sociological and psychological causes for committing suicide must be analysed to understand suicide terrorism.

According to Emile Durkheim (1856-1919) the French sociological thinker who propounded a theory on suicide, suicides are of three basic types. First, "egoistic suicide", in which an individual commits suicide if he fails to integrate himself with his family and society. The individual's beliefs and value systems are not approved by societal values and belief systems (which includes one's own family) or the individual does not approve of the society, which results in his alienation from the society and results in "egoistic suicide".

The second form of suicide is "anomic", in which the individual commits suicide due to anarchy in society. If there is a breakdown of regular life, especially in economic matters, due to industrial, financial and social insecurity, the individual feels helpless commits suicide. Here, the suicide is out of frustration, which differentiates it from the third form of suicide.

The third category of suicide is "altruistic", in which the individual commits suicide due to his integration with prevailing social values and belief systems. An analysis of suicide terrorism and motivations of the suicide bombers reveals that it falls in the third category. The individual feels a part of a whole and believes that there is no hope for the individual, if the society is under threat. The individual is therefore ready to give up his life, so that his "whole" might survive. The society to which the suicide bomber belongs makes him believe that the "collective whole" is under social, cultural, economic or political dominance by an external force, which drives him to self-sacrifice himself for the sake of society. This belief is generated within individuals by various means—both intentional and unintentional. An understanding of the linkages between the society, its value and belief systems and the phenomenon of suicide bombers is essential.

First, the role of the family. Factors vary from the loss of prestige and employment to the loss of lives due to the policies pursued by the government and its security forces; they have a negative effect on the perception of the families, especially the younger generation. Both in Kashmir and Sri Lanka, the policies pursued by the state, have resulted in the loss of family business, unemployment, killings and related violence. The views of the family of the state as evil has a great bearing on the younger generation, which is willing to defend the honour of the family and society.

Secondly, education largely shapes the values and belief systems of the individual, and imposes these values and beliefs on individuals. If the education system is not under the control of the State, then the possibility of non-state actors using education to impose their version of history becomes easier. In the Kashmir valley, a number of *madrasas* have proliferated in the last two decades which inculcate a particular value and belief system. When mis-interpretation of history to suit the political objectives of religious and political organizations is imposed through these *madrasas,* it results in raising the level of violence among the current generation, who are its products. In northern Sri Lanka, which is under the control of the LTTE, the education system is controlled by this organization.

Thirdly, society imposes its values on individuals and demands more from them through charismatic leaders, who define the history, objectives and future of the society. Prabhakaran, leader of the LTTE, decides what constitutes the "Tamil Eelam" and how to achieve it. Prabhakaran is worshipped in the Tamil society and there are many LTTE cadres who are ready to become Black Tigers, since this would ensure an exclusive meeting and dinner with him. There is a direct linkage between the leadership and suicide bombings, as seen in the case of the PKK Kurdistan Workers Party. After the arrest of its leader, Abdullah Oclan, in March 1999, there have been no suicide attacks by the PKK. There were around twenty suicide attacks carried out by the PKK between 1966 and 1999 killing nineteen persons and wounding more than hundred persons, but there have been no suicide attacks since 1999.

Thus the assimilation of the individual into society, especially in a conflict environment, assists the birth of suicide bombers. The society seems to approve their acts as they increase its cohesiveness. This approval is apparent from the fact that suicide bombers are glorified as martyrs to their common cause. In the case of the LTTE, July 5 is celebrated as the day of the Black Tigers, when a number of ceremonies are performed: the families of the suicide bombers are honoured and the brave deeds of the Black Tigers are publicized. The societal approval and admiration of these suicide bombers inspires others to carry out such terrorist suicide attacks.

28 February 2002

Fighting the *Fidayeens*: Combating Suicide Terrorism in Kashmir

SUBA CHANDRAN

SUICIDE TERRORISM IN Kashmir is bound to increase in the coming days given the internal dynamics and objectives of the various militant groups operating there.

Besides the *Lashkar-e-Taiba*, *Hizbul Mujahideen*, *Jaish-e-Mohammed* and *Harkat-ul-Mujahideen*, there are a number of minor militant groups comprising of Kashmiris, Pakistanis and Afghans. The *Hizbul* is considered the most indigenous militant group and its objective is very limited: it fights for an independent Kashmir and does not support the merger of Kashmir with Pakistan. The *Lashkar-e-Taiba*, comprising mainly of Pakistanis, is well organized and is independent (especially financially) of the ISI (Pakistan's Inter Services Intelligence) when compared to other militant organizations. For the *Lashkar*, Kashmir is a means to achieve its pan-Islamic objectives.

Understanding the objectives of these two organizations and their limitations, the ISI created the *Jaish* with Maulana Masood Azhar as its chief. *Jaish* has been involved in all suicide attacks carried out in Kashmir. The first ever suicide attack took place when a student rammed his car at the gate of the Badamibagh cantonment in April 2000. A similar second attack took place in the same spot in December 2000. The *Jaish*, coming into being much later than other militant groups, is attempting desperately to find some "space" for itself through spectacular acts aimed at capturing the attention of people both inside and outside Kashmir.

Second, suicide terrorism results in a lot of publicity for the militant group that perpetrates the attack. In Kashmir, this publicity is very essential as militant groups need to compete with each other to gain popular support and/or prove their invincibility to their mentors and clientele. Publicity is crucial to attract more funds, especially from abroad, and boost up recruitment drive inside Kashmir; the more Kashmiris in its fold, the more support the group can garner in terms of logistics, planning and escape.

Third, Kashmiri participation in militancy has been on the decline in recent years. The suicide attack at the Srinagar Legislative Assembly complex was carried out by a Pakistani; and, the *Jaish* and the *Lashkar* have been regularly carrying out the so-called *fidayeen* attacks with Pakistanis. The main reason for these *fidayeen* attacks is to keep the hopes of the Kashmiris alive reminding them that Pakistan will "liberate" Kashmir.

Fourth, there exists close linkages between the militant groups, especially the above-mentioned three groups and the rightist political groups of Pakistan who patronize and/or run the *madrasas*. Continuous indoctrination in these *madrasas* has produced a number of "*jihadi* robots", who could be used as human bombs.

How to combat suicide terrorism in Kashmir? What are the options before India?

The first option is to strike the roots of terror, through hot pursuit or surgical strike. Though this option sounds easier, it would be extremely difficult in practical terms. A hot pursuit involves chasing the militants inside POK (Pakistan Occupied Kashmir). There are a number of Pakistani military posts along the Line of Control that would have to be dealt with militarily. A surgical strike, on the other hand, involves wiping out the terrorist camps in POK, based on intelligence regarding their accurate location. Besides, such a strike needs to be undertaken with missiles based on Indian soil or from air violating Pakistani airspace. There is every possibility that such strikes could hit other targets, resulting in loss of innocent lives. Both hot pursuit and surgical strikes are bound to escalate the conflict between India and Pakistan and the possibility of an all-out war cannot be ruled out. Whereas the Indian military establishment would be eager to exercise this option, it is doubtful whether the ruling BJP, rhetorically impressive but politically spineless, would resort to it.

The second option is to send specialized ground teams to physically annihilate the leaders and the camps. This requires precise information. Israel used this option in tracking the militants even in other countries and assassinating them. Such counter-attacks would, in the short run, increase militant attacks but in the long run, yield better results.

On the policy front, India should take concrete steps at the national and international levels. Instead of merely accusing Pakistan and the militant groups for the violence in Jammu & Kashmir, it is very essential that the much talked about "White Paper on ISI activities in India" be tabled in the Parliament. This should be followed by diplomatic pressure, instead of media statements, both at national and international levels.

Unnecessary criticism of the security forces in the Valley dampening their morale should be checked. Little understanding the hostile environment in which they operate, the security forces, along with their planning, intelligence and alertness, have come under unfair criticism. Given the nature of suicide bombing, it is tough for any security force to tackle a bomb, which can think, move, dodge and be ready to destroy itself.

28 November 2001

Born to Die: The Black Tigers of the LTTE

SUBA CHANDRAN

THE *LIBERATION TIGERS of Tamil Eelam* (LTTE) is one of the few groups in the world along with the *Hizbollah*, the *Hamas* and the *Kurdistan Workers Party* (*PKK*) of Turkey to have an elite suicide squad. A comparative analysis of the Black Tigers with other terrorist organizations will reveal its significance. Ever since the first suicide attack by the *Hizbollah* in 1983 in Beirut, in which more than 150 American and French Peace Keepers were killed, there have been more than 250 suicide attacks by various groups all over the world. Of these attacks the Black Tigers alone had carried out 150; more than those carried out by all other groups put together. They are the only group which succeeded in assassinating two former Prime Ministers—Rajiv Gandhi and Premadaṣa.

Known as *Karumpuligal* (Black Tigers), they form the elite section of the LTTE. What makes the Black Tigers unique? How is it that the LTTE has succeeded in continuously sustaining its suicide wing? What makes the cadres of the LTTE opt for becoming Black Tigers? Why is there such glorification of the Black Tigers in the LTTE?

First, though the entire LTTE cadre can be argued to be a suicide squad, considering each and every cadre carries a cyanide capsule garlanded by the local commando leader in the "passing out parade", and does not hesitate to use it when captured or faced with an adverse situation, the Black Tigers are considered far more significant. The mission of a Black Tiger is to give up his or her life, which provides them elite status inside the LTTE and makes other cadres to aspire for that status.

Second, the glorification of the Black Tigers by the LTTE makes it prestigious. Every year July 5 is celebrated by the LTTE as the day of the Black Tigers. (It was on 5 July 1987 that the first suicide attack was perpetrated by the LTTE, when its "Captain" Millar drove a truck full of explosives into a Sri Lankan Army camp, killing nearly forty soldiers.) On this particular day, an eternal lamp is lighted in front of the tombstone of every Black Tiger, who had lost his or her life. The LTTE flag is hoisted and the parents of the Black Tigers, who had sacrificed their lives, are honoured. The LTTE radio broadcasts the brave deeds of the Black Tigers with their operational details. When Jaffna was under the LTTE's control, the *Maveerar Thuyilum Illam* (Resting Home of the Brave) was cleaned and lighted and the day celebrated in such an emotional way, that it made other cadres to aspire for becoming Black Tigers. When the Sri Lankan Army took over Jaffna from the LTTE, the first thing it did was to bulldoze this cemetery which eulogized the Black Tigers.

Third, the Black Tigers lead most of the military operations of the LTTE, especially its attack on the Sri Lankan Army camps. The Black Tigers, armed with explosives, drive directly into the army camp, catching the Sri Lankan Army totally by surprise and causing maximum damage. Before the Army recovers from its initial shock, the regular cadres of the LTTE attack, making maximum use of the sacrifice by the Black Tigers. The Black Tigers, being the "Leading Force" of any military operation, have an extra attraction for the cadres.

Fourth, the success rate of the Black Tigers make them very popular. In most of the cases, except on a couple of rare occasions, the Black Tigers have succeeded in achieving their mission. Chandrika Kumaratunga was one of the few targets who escaped the Black Tigers. Their ability to penetrate the tough security not only in Colombo, but in other places also and carry out its mission, make the Black Tigers invincible in their mission.

Fifth, the Black Tigers have an additional advantage—they can meet the leader of the LTTE, Prabhakaran; the LTTE considers Prabhakaran to be a demi-god. Since his public appearances are limited, meeting Prabhakaran is a lifetime goal for many of the young cadres of the LTTE. In fact, Prabhakaran has very carefully cultivated this image. Besides, before the mission, the Black Tigers have their "Last Supper" with their leader, which is considered a lifetime honour for its cadres.

Sixth, women cadres as Black Tigers is a distinct phenomenon. Other than the LTTE, only the PKK has women cadres in its suicide wing; nearly one-third of the Black Tigers are women. The presence of women in the suicide squad asserts the gender equality that the LTTE preaches.

Finally, the LTTE does not have an ideology that could impress and motivate its cadres. There were a number of other Tamil militant groups which had a Marxist ideology and even the LTTE, initially, did have a socialist framework; this can be seen from the work of Anton Balasingam, *Socialist Tamil Eelam*. But, at a later stage, Prabhakaran gave up this ideological orientation. The Black Tigers, to a great extent, motivate the cadres by their action and sacrifice.

The Black Tigers, thus, form the backbone of the LTTE, which in turn eulogizes the former and this overt glorification ensures the continuous inflow Black Tigers have.

7 October 2001

The Uniqueness of LTTE's Suicide Bombers

SABIL FRANCIS

IT IS AN IRONY that those on death row for the Rajiv Gandhi assassination had a peripheral role in the act. It was carried out by the Black Tigers, the suicide squads of the LTTE, a shadowy group within the terrorist organization. Other organization, like *Hamas,* which is fighting Israel, have induldged in suicide bombings; but the LTTE has made suicide bombing an article of faith, with the Black Tigers (*Karum Puligal*), the most honoured members of the organization, entitled to one last meal with Prabhakaran himself before setting out on their missions.

On 21 May 1991, the LTTE adopted suicide bombing to assassinate Rajiv Gandhi at an election rally in Sriperumbudur near Chennai. Since then, suicide bombers have killed Sri Lankan President Ranasinghe Premadasa (1 May 1993) and Presidential candidate Gamini Dissanayake (23 October 1995). This tactic has also been used to attack army convoys and to overrun army bases. For example, in the assault on the Jaffna Fort in the early nineties, the LTTE used a 14-year-old cadre wrapped in explosives to defeat a 200-strong garrison and capture the fort. The LTTE also used this tactic to indiscriminately truck bomb the Central Bank on President's street in Jaffna in January 1996. Over a hundred innocent civilians were killed and more than 1,000 injured.

Though the LTTE was founded in 1974, suicide bombing was only accepted as a tactic in the late 1980s. The first instance of a suicide bombing was on 5 July 1987, when "Captain" Miller of the LTTE Black Tigers drove a van full of explosives into a military camp at Nelliaddy. More than 128 soldiers were killed.

What are the motivations of the Black Tigers, who regularly indulge in "Dry Runs" that could terrify a normal person? None of the classical theorists on guerrilla warfare like Mao, Lenin, or Che have advocated suicide bombing. The only comparable instance are Islamic militants in the Middle East. Their ideology believes that they will go straight to heaven. The LTTE is officially atheist and the cadre, being Hindus, believe in reincarnation of the soul. The LTTE ideologue Anton Balasingham made a speech in Jaffna in November 1995, claiming that *karma* was the reason for the untimely and unnatural deaths of Sinhala leaders who had "tormented the Tamils".

In the LTTE's case, the motivation for suicide attacks seems to be a kind of *en masse* cult hysteria that the LTTE consciously cultivates by rituals like Martyr's Week promoting a cult of martyrdom, building of special cemeteries, naming of weapons after Black Tigers and, in short, the promise of honour after death. In fact, the "dry runs" of the Black Tigers, recorded on videotape, are enough to terrify the most courageous. Clearly, something more than courage is involved and the promise of honour beyond death is attractive to those who have nothing to gain in this life. This becomes significant as most of the LTTE cadre now come from lower middle class backgrounds and easily accept such propaganda.

Another powerful motivation for the LTTE's suicide cadre is that the LTTE connects its ideology with a judicious use of symbols rooted in Tamil myth such as the tiger, the symbol of one of the most favourite Tamil gods, Murugan. It was the emblem of the ancient Chola emperors, the concept of *maram* (wrath), the concept of the (brave mother) *vira tayar* and the *vira pen* (brave woman) who sacrifice their loved ones for the war. This is a recurring theme in *Purananuru* (poetry of the Sangam period between 500 BC and AD 200). The LTTE cadre are expected to conform to the ideals of the past. A failure is not that of an individual letting down the organization, it is failure to live up to the ideals of a glorious past.

The motivation of the LTTE Black Tiger cadre is similar to that of the *Kamikaze* pilots of the Japanese airforce in the Second World War. They would crash their explosive laden planes against American warships crying "I die for the Emperor". They were deluded into believing that they were carrying on the ancient

Samurai tradition, that they were living up to ancient warrior ideals, that they were fulfilling a sacrifice demanded by the Emperor, and would face tremendous shame and humiliation if they surrendered. The same is true for the LTTE.

4 February 2000

VI: Tools of Terror

Tools of Terror: The Art and Science of Steganography

Maj. Gen. (Retd) Yashwant Deva

Even the communication cognoscenti were unaware of the meaning and importance of steganography until recently when the term made headlines, thanks to *Al-Qaeda*. It is a marvel how this ancient branch of knowledge has been exploited for running a network of terror and a fail-proof system of covert communications.

The word *steganography* is derived from the Greek word *steganos*, which means secret or concealed, and *graphy*, which means writing or drawing. State of art steganography is anchored on digitized imagery and sound. It works on the principle that such files contain bits and bytes that can be altered without affecting their function, quality or meaning. These alterations are not easily discernible by human sensory system and this is true of a 16-bit sound or 24-bit imagery. This knowledge was effectively put to use by bin Laden's outfit to send photographs, maps and sketches of targets with orders and instructions to the operatives spread over thirty countries around the globe. What could be better than to hide imagery in pornography and what could be a more suitable medium than the Internet? Besides pornographic sites, other popular sites for posting terrorist instructions are sports and technology chat rooms, and bulletin boards.

There is no dearth of knowledge—historical, popular, or technical, on the Internet. Volumes can be downloaded if one has the desire and inclination to learn. Bin Laden has shown the world the merits of virtual learning. It is widely known that steganography is more abused than used. It is like watermarking, which has become a must for copywriting, particularly in the case of music. In the commercial world, the main driving force for steganography is protecting copyright, especially when audio, video and text have become digital, facilitating the making of near-perfect illicit copies of music, book or software. There is a sudden spurt of defence-related applications also.

Equally significant is the usage of *steganalysis*, which is the art of discovering and rendering *steganos* useless. Wet Stone's *Detection and Recovery Toolkit* which is being developed for the USAF by the Air Force Research Laboratory in New York is a case in point. They are working on evolving a set of statistical tests capable of detecting covert messages in files and transmissions. The laboratory is also engaged in development of blind *stegano*-detection for algorithms.

Steganodress primarily shows up on hacker, *hawala* (money laundering), drug trafficking and terrorist websites. But there are cases of it appearing on commercial and news sites too, e.g. Amazon, Bay, Dow Jones, and Technology News. Although a matter of conjecture, bin Laden's broadcasts over *Al Jazeera* may contain "hidden messages", "killer codes" or "*anonymizers*", indicative of the prolific terminology that the art and science of steganography has spawned. These broadcasts have raised a storm of indignant protests, "Can media be a megaphone for anyone inciting murder and mayhem?" (Raja Menon in *Economic Times* Plainspeak, 18 November 2001).

Steganography is similar to cryptography, but not entirely. The former goes much beyond encryption by hiding a secret message within an ordinary message. An encrypted message is inserted into an innocuous file, like an image, by using a special algorithm. This obviates scanning and interception of the data. A code is needed to identify the secret message. There are several ways to communicate it, e.g. timestamp on the message, an uncommon word in the subject or a phrase in the header. They call it a "dead drop".

Many products are available online. S-Tools is one of the free-ware spread-*steganography* variety which combines both *crypto* and *stegano* attributes. The encryption is done using one of the symmetric algorithms, e.g. Data Encryption Standard (DES), Triple

DES or International Data Encryption Algorithm (IDEA). The *all-nettools* site describes the working with S-Tools—it states: "You just drag the carrier file into the programme window, then you drag the file you want to hide, choose an algorithm and a password, and here we go!"

19 January 2002

RDX & IEDs: The Deadly Duet

SUBA CHANDRAN AND MALLIKA JOSEPH A.

THOUGH VARIOUS militant groups in the subcontinent have been using IEDs (Improvised Explosive Devices) for the last few years with increasing regularity, recent killings have highlighted their deadly impact. Of all the weapons that the militants possess, IEDs, coupled with explosives like RDX, pose the greatest danger to human and material security due to the ease with which they can be made, planted and blasted. The IED is a simple weapon containing some explosive, fuse, detonators and wires, shrapnel and pieces of metal, and a container to pack the explosives and shrapnel.

IEDs have assumed great importance for militants and Naxalite groups for various reasons. Despite the possession of sophisticated arms, including machine guns—light and heavy, an encounter can probably result in the death or injury of one or more security personnel and also kill or injure a few cadres; but IEDs can cause in the death or injury to an entire security convoy or all the personnel in a vehicle with no harm to the militants. Besides, IEDs are target-specific, in the sense that they can be detonated by the user at the right moment and at the right spot. By being able to target only security personnel, the militants avoid getting alienated from the people they claim to represent. Thus, IEDs provide maximum flexibility to the militants and Naxalites.

Secondly, IEDs are simple to carry and assemble. Using a grenade or ammunition, which are relatively easy to locate during search by the security forces, the fuse, wires, batteries and detonators used in IEDs can be carried by different persons and assembled later with little risk of being detected.

Thirdly, IEDs are effectively used as booby traps by militants to lure the security forces into the area. The Naxalites in Andhra Pradesh and the militants in Kashmir have used IEDs as bait to get the security forces out to the particular spot where they are subsequently ambushed. There are multiple blasts with the second explosion occurring a few minutes after the first one, timed for the security forces when they reach the spot for investigation. The militants also use a mechanism similar to a conventional "double impulse fuse", where the same IED initiates both blasts, the first one to bait and the following one to target the investigating team.

Fourthly, IEDs are very easy to plant. They can be placed under a culvert or under a road by digging and then camouflaging the spot. Given the conditions of roads in militancy prone areas, it is very difficult to detect IEDs despite the employment of road-opening parties.

What makes the IED lethal is the explosive used for assembling it. The types of explosives used range from those available for commercial use to those meant specifically for military use. The commonly used commercial explosive in India is the gelatine stick, which is legally used in stone quarries for blasting rocks. Despite these explosives being distributed only to licensed contractors, the Naxalites and militants manage to procure these either through extortion, force or terror. The gelatine sticks, however, are not as lethal as RDX. Even when used in small quantities, RDX gives a yield with high destructive capability. Though the militants in the North East use RDX, the RDX-IED combination has been used more often in Kashmir, because of the easy availability of the RDX to militant groups operating there.

RDX has a high explosive potential, is light, and is also malleable which allows its transport without suspicion. Though RDX is a military explosive and cannot be procured commercially, the external support available to various militant groups in Kashmir makes it easy for them to obtain it. Almost all the militant-related IED incidents in Kashmir have used RDX. The combination of RDX-IED in Kashmir increased during the second half of the 1990s. Reliance on RDX will continue and is certain to become a major strategy for the militants. In fact, militant groups in the North East seem to be shifting to RDX, instead of other explosives.

Given the easy availability of explosives and, appreciating the external involvement in providing RDX to militant and criminal groups, and the simple process involved in making an IED, the RDX-IED combination will be the real problem in the coming years; more so than the AK-47s in the hands of the militants.

20 October 2000

VII: Profile of Militant Groups in South Asia

National Democratic Front of Bodoland (NDFB)

BIBHU PRASAD ROUTRAY

History

THE BODOS, A MAJOR tribe in the State of Assam, have initiated their own form of insurgency to fight against the possession of their tribal land by Bengali settlers and the native Assamese, neglect of the Bodo language, and to express a sense of being exploited. The Bodos, being the earliest settlers in Assam, have cited economic and social neglect by the State government. The first Bodo organization, the All Bodo Students' Union (ABSU) was founded in 1967, and the Bodos started demanding a separate state within India towards the later half of the 1980s. In 1988, the National Democratic Front of Bodoland (NDFB) was founded, and it initiated guerrilla war. NDFB was originally established as the Bodo Security Force (BSF) in 1988 under the leadership of Ranjan Daimary. It was later renamed NDFB.

Objectives

The purported objective of this outfit is to secure a "sovereign Bodoland" in the areas north of the river Brahmaputra. While the other Bodo groups, such as the Bodo Liberation Tigers (BLT), demanded a separate state within Indian territory for the Bodo people, the NDFB wants a separate country for itself.

The other demand of the NDFB is regarding the script of the Bodo language. Currently the Bodo language is written in *Devanagri* script; NDFB, whose members are mostly Christians, prefer to use the Roman script.

Strategy

The NDFB was originally founded to protect the interests of the Bodos; but, over the years, this objective has been diluted, and it has joined hands with the ULFA (United Liberation front of Asom), which fights against the non-Assamese domination in the State. Presently, NDFB works in tandem with the ULFA. Sometime in 1999, the ULFA and NDFB formed a "coordination committee" for launching a "united struggle". NDFB has also established a "working arrangement" with the National Socialist Council of Nagaland-Isak-Muivah (NSCN-IM), an insurgent outfit in neighbouring Nagaland.

Their different objectives have put the NDFB at logger-heads with other Bodo outfits such as the Bodo Liberation Tigers (BLT), All Bodo Student's Union (ABSU) and the Bodo Sahitya Sabha (BSS). As the result of a decision taken on 10 January 2001 in Bhutan, the NDFB decided to target members of the BLT, BSS, ABSU, Bodo People Action Committee (BPAC), and the All Bodo Women's Welfare Federation (ABWWF), for selective killing.

The NDFB regularly indulges in acts of insurgency, targeting the symbols of governance and civilians. On 15 September 1998, NDFB insurgents killed fourteen Santhal *adivasis* (tribals) in Gossaigaon subdivision of Kokrajhar district. At least twelve security forces personnel were killed and ten others injured on 31 July 2000 when suspected NDFB militants triggered a powerful landmine explosion in a train near the Sonmohuri village in Kamrup district. On the next day, on 1 August 2000, NDFB terrorists exploded a bomb on a passenger train killing twelve and injuring several others near Tezpur. On 8 November 2000, eight civilians, including seven from the non-Assamese community were killed by suspected NDFB terrorists. On 25 November 2000, eight woodcutters were killed by NDFB terrorists in the Lung Sung forest reserve. On 21 December 2000 NDFB terrorists targeted Bhutan government vehicles, including a bus, killed two and injured sixteen others in Kokrajhar district. In Bongaigaon district, they set ablaze a Bhutanese police truck carrying rations to that country at Amlaiguri. In another incident, the ultras set fire to a vehicle going to Bhutan.

In the year 2000, NDFB terrorists were responsible for the deaths of twenty-nine security force personnel and 176 civilians. In the same period, ninety-five NDFB cadres were killed, eighty-three were arrested and hundred surrendered to the authorities.

It called for a boycott of the Republic Day celebration on 26 January 2001 to "draw the international eye to the colonial nature of Indian rule".

Dialogue with the Government

Except for occasional indications to initiate peace talks with the government, probably as a gesture to buy time to replenish its declining resources, the NDFB, unlike the Bodo Liberation Tigers Force (BLT), has still shown no real inclination for peace.

On 3 April 2000, the Union Minister for Home Affairs, L.K. Advani, expressed the government's readiness to enter into a dialogue process with the NDFB and ULFA, if they give up violence and agreed to negotiations within the framework of the Indian Constitution. Subsequently, some NDFB leaders met the Army's Tezpur based 4-Corps Commander and expressed their desire to hold peace talks. The Army authorities also decided to provide safe passage to the NDFB leaders to attend the proposed meeting. In May 2000, the head of the counter-insurgency operations in Assam, Lt Gen. D.B. Shekatkar, said that the NDFB had established direct contact with the army commanders for holding peace talks. In March 2001, the PDF demanded that the State government hold unconditional talks with the NDFB. However, this process has not moved beyond such expressions.

Command Structure

NDFB has an estimated strength of 1500 cadres, most of whom are holed up in camps inside Bhutan and Myanmar. Nothing is known regarding the command structure of the outfit whose activity revolves around the dictates of its Chairman. It announces its programmes through its publicity secretary. The Peoples' Democratic Party (PDP) is believed to be the political front of the NDFB in the State.

External Linkages

The NDFB has set up a number of camps in neighbouring Bhutan. According to some estimates, both ULFA and NDFB have more than twenty-one camps in the jungles of southern Bhutan. In July 2000, the Assam Chief Minister Prafulla Kumar Mahanta stated that he had "documentary evidence" of the alleged nexus between terrorist groups, including the NDFB, and the Bhutan government. Several Bhutanese government officials have visited the insurgent camps located inside Bhutan and have been openly aiding the Assam militants.

On 21 January 2001, Bhutan indicated that it would take army action against the NDFB and ULFA if these outfits do not stop operating from its territory. However, no such action has been taken though deliberations at various levels are going on. In one such meeting in Punakha on 16 March 2001, the leaders resolved to safeguard the country's sovereignty.

Popular Support

The NDFB is active in the districts of Bongaigaon, Kokrajhar, Darrang, Barpeta, Dhubri and Sonitpur. It also uses the Manas National Park, an important bio-diversity hotspot in South Asia, as a sanctuary. Taking advantage of the fact that the forests in the Park extend across the border into Bhutan, the insurgents use it as a corridor to slip in and out of Bhutan.

To garner support, NDFB occasionally promotes high visibility social issues. In February 2001, there were media reports suggesting that the NDFB have set up signboards and banners in and around the Manas reserve forest areas in Assam to save valuable trees from being smuggled out of the region.

Funds

Extortion and loot form the basic source of funding which is then used to purchase arms and ammunition for the outfit. Tea companies in the area, especially in the districts of Darrang and Sonitpur, have been regularly subjected to extortion by terrorist outfits, including the NDFB. In 1991, the Goodricke group allegedly paid about Rs 15 lakh (US $31,250) for the release of its Manager of the Nonoipara tea estate. In 1992, an executive of the Williamson Magor company, which has nearly forty-five tea gardens in the area, was abducted by the NDFB militants and the company had to airdrop Rs 1.3 crore (US $270,833) at a specified NDFB hideout for his release.

In 1996, the army claimed to have seized a NDFB document, which showed that the Williamson Magor group paid Rs 24 lakh (US $50,000) between September and October 1994. Another tea company, the Assam Frontier Company, with fifteen gardens, paid Rs 9 lakh (US $18,750). In addition, smaller companies paid regular installments. On 20 September 1997, the Tata Tea Company published a report in the newspapers explaining how it was being forced to pay extortion amounts to the terrorists of NDFB.

Another report revealed that (in the year 1995-6) government departments like Sales Tax, Forest and Inspectorate of Motor Vehicles, accounted for close to 50 per cent of the NDFB's collection of about Rs 1.3 crore (US $270,833). In 1997, the police arrested six officers of the transport department in the State on charges of providing funds to NDFB militants. Dutch NGOs such as Landlijke India Werk (LIW) and the Netherland Council of Indigenous Vodlesgeist (NCIV) are alleged to have provided funds for the outfit.

The outfit's extortion drive is directed against the non-Bodo families in various parts of Bongaigaon and Kokrajhar districts. Civilians and business establishments are served with regular notices for payment of "tax" and "donations". The NDFB also indulges in collecting "Bodoland tax" from the people in various districts of Lower Assam ranging from Rs 4,000 (US $83) to Rs 20,000 (US $417) depending on their financial position.

The Army, operating in the lower Assam districts of Kokrajhar and Bongaigaon, claimed that the NDFB is involved in illegal felling of trees. They also collect "taxes" from other illegal timber contractors at the rate of Rs 20,000 (US $417) per truck. Small time timber merchants also pay at the rate of Rs 50 (US $1.04) to Rs 100 (US $2.08) per hand-cart of timber. Those who fail to pay are attacked.

In July 2000, the Chief Minister of Assam alleged that the NDFB, along with the ULFA, were channeling funds through the "Bhutanese diplomatic pouch" to their leaders based in South East Asian capitals.

Leadership

Ranjan Daimary is the Chairman of the outfit. Lieutenant B. Irakdao is the outfit's self styled publicity secretary.

National Socialist Council of Nagaland (NSCN-IM)

BIBHU PRASAD ROUTRAY

History

NSCN WAS FORMED on 31 January 1980 by Isak Chisi Swu, Thuingaleng Muivah and S.S. Khaplang opposing the *Shillong Accord* signed by the then NNC (Naga National Council) with the Indian government. Since then it has been carrying on an armed struggle to end Indian sovereignty over the Naga people and establish a People's Republic of Nagaland. The Indian government's persistent efforts to start a dialogue process created differences among the leadership of NSCN and this disagreement took its toll on the organization. On 30 April 1988, after an attempt to assassinate Muivah failed, in which several of the cadres were killed, the NSCN split into two factions—namely the NSCN (K) led by S.S. Khaplang, NSCN (IM) the NSCN led by Isak and Muivah. The former suspected Isak and Muivah of secretly initiating talks with the Indian government.

NSCN (IM), as the dominant insurgent group in Nagaland, has been active in violent activities to further its cause. In May 1994, it was believed to be responsible for the massacre of sixteen people in a church in Nagaland. In December 1996, NSCN guerrillas boarded a bus in Guwahati (Nagaland), killed thirty people and injured a further twenty-four, all of whom were Kuki tribesman. A ceasefire was agreed upon between the group and the government in 1997 and came into operation on 1 August 1997. But it ran into rough weather when the Indian government, in April 1998, alleged that the NSCN had killed eight soldiers. On 29 November 1999, an attempt was made on the life of the Chief Minister of Nagaland, S.C. Jamir who is sympathetic towards the NSCN (K) faction. The organization suffered a major setback in January 2000 when its General Secretary Muivah was arrested in Thailand while travelling on a false South Korean passport. He was released on bail, but he was arrested again when he tried to leave the country and was sentenced to one year in prison. (To date he continues to languish in prison. In addition, the trial process for the passport forgery case has begun. The ceasefire came to an end on 31 July 2000. In the meanwhile, the Indian government and the NSCN (IM) have agreed to extend the ceasefire for one more year after a meeting in Bangkok.)

Objectives

The entire activity of the organization is aimed at achieving three alternate objectives. The first alternative is about establishing an independent Nagaland comprising the present territory of Nagaland and the Naga inhabited areas of Manipur and Myanmar. The second alternative aims at integrating the Naga inhabited districts of Manipur into a new state under the Indian constitution. The last alternative seeks to form a "Southern Nagaland" comprising the districts of Senapati, Ukhrul, Chandel and Tamenglong within the Indian Union.

NSCN (IM) aims to establish a People's Republic of Nagaland based on Mao's ideology. Its manifesto is based on the principle of socialism for economic development and a spiritual outlook—"Nagaland for Christ".

Strategy

NSCN (IM) tries to use the growing discontent among the different ethnic groups of the north-east region against the Indian state. This, it believes, will accelerate the disintegration of the latter and help the cause of Naga independence. With this objective in mind, it provides logistic support to other ethnic insurgent groups in the region like ULFA, NDFB, NLFT and PLA. It supports the militancy in Punjab and Jammu & Kashmir.

In addition to providing logistic support, NSCN (IM) has been instrumental in propping up new insurgent organizations among different ethnic groups in the region. For example, the formation of the Garo insurgent organisation ALMA (*A'Chik Liberation Matgrik Army*) was a handiwork of the NSCN (IM). The same is the case with HNLC (*Hynniewtrep National Liberation Council*) and ANVC (*A'Chik National Volunteers Council*) in Meghalaya, NLFT (*National Liberation Front of Tripura*) in Tripura and HPCD (*Hmar People's Convention [Democrat]*) in Mizoram. NSCN (IM) coordinates the activities of these organizations. Its aim is, thus, to turn its war against the Indian state into a war of the nationalities of the region. Keeping this aim in mind NSCN (IM) formed the ULFSS (*United Liberation Front of Seven Sisters*) in 1993 and SDUFSEHR (*Self-Defence United Front of the South-East Himalayan Region*) in November 1994.

The group has divided the entire region into several areas of operation with each of these militant outfits in charge of one. The NSCN (IM) plays the role of the coordinator and has tried to convert the whole north-eastern region into an anti-India battle zone. Additionally the smaller ethnic insurgent groups have served to open up different sectors of confrontation as well as centres for resource mobilisation in areas beyond the NSCN (IM)'s sphere of influence.

Dialogue with the Government

A serious process of dialogue with the Indian government started in the mid-nineties. On 15 June 1995, Prime Minister P.V. Narasimha Rao met both Isak and Muivah in Paris. It was decided to continue the process of dialogue to solve the problem. In 1996, Prime Minister Deve Gowda sent former Union Minister Rajesh Pilot on a secret mission to Bangkok to have a dialogue with the NSCN (IM) leadership. Later Deve Gowda met them on 3 February 1997 in Zurich. Following these meetings, a ceasefire came into force. While the army and other security forces complained that the group was using the ceasefire period to augment its stockpile of arms and is violating the truce conditions, the government stuck to its stand of holding negotiations. Several rounds of negotiations took place with Swaraj Kaushal as the chief interlocutor.

After the BJP government came to power installation in New Delhi, Prime Minister Vajpayee met the NSCN (IM) leadership in Paris in September 1998. Afterwards, the former Home Secretary, K. Padmanabhaiah acted as the centre's primary negotiator and met both Isak and Muivah in Bangkok for the first round of talks. The rebel leaders expressed unhappiness over the tardy progress in the negotiations. They stuck to the demand for a sovereign Nagaland, comprising many Naga-inhabited areas of neighbouring Assam and Manipur, besides the Nagaland State. Nothing concrete has emerged out of these meetings.

The peace process suffered a major setback with the arrest of Muivah in Bangkok on 19 January 2000. Padmanabhaiah was scheduled to meet Muivah in Bonn on 31 January and 1 February 2001 for another round of talks. With Muivah behind bars for one year, the dialogue process has come to a halt. While the NSCN (IM) demands that the Indian government should pressurize the Thai authorities for Muivah's early release, the government has refused to interfere in the legal processes of another country.

In the ongoing trial in the passport forgery case, the NSCN (IM) has appealed to both the Thai and Indian governments to recognise Muivah as an essential participant in the peace process and effect his immediate release. In the meantime the talks between the central government and the representatives of the NSCN(I-M) has resulted in the extension of the ceasefire till 31 July 2001. The ceasefire had been monitored by a Ceasefire Monitoring Group based at Kohima. Headed by the Additional Secretary, Home Ministry, Dr. P.D. Shenoy, this group comprises of representatives of the NSCN (IM), NGOs and the government. It meets at regular intervals and so far it has held twenty meetings.

Command Structure

The command structure of the NSCN (IM) is not known. But according to available sources, the top leadership comprises of Chairman Isak Chusi Swu and General Secretary Muivah. Below them are several *kilonsers* (ministers). Below them are senior members in charge of different regions. The organization also maintains an army wing. It boasts an army of nearly 2,000 dedicated guerrillas and enjoys a much wider support base.

External Linkages

NSCN (IM) has alliances with the Naga groups operating in Myanmar. It also has links with the Bodo Security Force. In addition, it promotes many insurgent organizations in almost all the north-eastern states. It has links with *Hynnilwtrep National Liberation Council* (HNLC) and *A'chik National Volunteers Council* (ANVC) of Meghalaya, *National Democratic Front of Bodoland* in Assam, *National Liberation Front of Tripura* (NLFT), *A'Chik Liberation Matgrik Army* (ALMA) in the Garo hills, and *Hmar People's Convention* (HPC) of Mizoram. It provides logistic support to insurgent groups such as the ULFA (*United Liberation Front of Assam*), the NDFB (*National Democratic Front for Bodoland*), NLFT (*National Liberation Front of Tripura*), and PLA (*People's Liberation Army*).

Internationally, it has opened up contacts with organizations like the UN Human Rights Organization in Geneva, Unrepresented Nations People's Organization (UNPO) at the Hague and the UN Working Group on Indigenous People (UNWGIP).

Popular Support

NSCN (IM) mostly consists of Tangkhul Nagas who are in a majority in the hills of Manipur. Its influence inside Manipur is restricted to the four districts of Senapati, Ukhrul, Chandel and Tamenglong.

Funds

Drug trafficking from Myanmar is a major source of income for the NSCN (IM). Apart from that, it indulges in extortion, bank robberies and other criminal pursuits to obtain finances. The smaller ethnic insurgent groups floated by NSCN (IM) carry out their operations in coordination with the parent organization. Seventy per cent of the total income goes to the NSCN (IM) and the remaining 30 per cent is left with the local groups.

In addition, the NSCN (IM) generates finances by international mobilization. Till 1971, the USA was a major provider of arms, finance and intelligence information. Till the late 1980s, China also provided support to the organization. Presently, Pakistan's ISI provides finance and arms to the NSCN (IM). Muivah was in Karachi before being arrested in Bangkok. This provides an indication of the ISI's support network in the region.

Towards the end of World War II, the retreating Japanese army left behind dumps of arms and ammunition in Nagaland, which at a later period was used by the insurgents against the security forces. The erstwhile East Pakistan had also trained a large number of Naga insurgents and had provided them money and arms. Weapons are widely available in the region in the black markets. Some of them have been stolen from the Indian security forces.

Leaders

The top leaders of the NSCN (IM) are Isak Chisi Swu and Thuingaleng Muivah. Apart from that, I. Shimre is another top leader who was arrested along with Muivah. Ng Hungshi is the press and publicity secretary of the organization. The army wing of the NSCN (IM) is headed by Ramting Thangkul and Peter Jajo.

Publications

NSCN (IM) does not have any regular publication, apart from the occasional papers it brings out. However, organizations such as "Other Media" in New Delhi publish materials sympathetic to their cause.

Kamatapur Liberation Organisation (KLO)

BIBHU PRASAD ROUTRAY

History

KLO IS ONE OF THE recently formed insurgent outfits in the Indian north-east. It was formed on 28 December 1995 by the Koch-Rajbongsi tribes who strove to carve out a separate Kamatapur State. Koch-Rajbongsis live in four lower Assam districts of Kokrajhar, Bongaigaon, Dhubri and Goalpara, West Garo Hills of Meghalaya and in the six districts of north Bengal. Intelligence sources reveal that the outfit was propped up by the United Liberation Front of Asom (ULFA) to use the area of north Bengal as a transit point to cross over from Bhutan to Bangladesh. The decision to prop-up a Rajbongsi insurgent outfit was taken by the ULFA in December 1995 at the initiative of Raju Baruah, the deputy leader of the outfit's military wing. The ULFA entrusted the then Chairman of its Darrang district Unit, Ajit Kachari with the task of setting up a Koch-Rajbongsi Organisation (KRLO) in lower Assam. Subsequently, the KLO was formed in north Bengal following a meeting at Kumaragram. KRLO became defunct after a brief spell of activity and most of its cadres joined the ULFA.

Objectives

The proposed State of Kamatapur comprises of six districts of north Bengal (South Dinajpur, North Dinajpur, Cooch Behar, Jalpaiguri, Malda and Darjeeling) and four districts of lower Assam (Kokrajhar,

Bongaigaon, Dhubri and Goalpara). Even though KLO was formed as an overground organization to seek its objective on the grounds of large-scale unemployment, land alienation and perceived ignorance of its language and a host of other grievances including economic deprivation, soon its strategy transformed into an armed struggle.

Strategy

The role of ULFA in transforming the character of KLO is considered to be significant. The ULFA, facing an uphill task in terms of maintaining its cadre strength and influence in face of repeated army operations, sought to use the relatively unmanned area of north Bengal for variety of purposes. Firstly, this area provides ULFA a transit point to commute from Bhutan to Bangladesh and vice versa, while some insurgents crossed over to Nepal through this area. Secondly, the area is being used by ULFA to trans-ship weapons to their camps in Bhutan. Thirdly, KLO maintains some hideouts for ULFA in this area. Fourthly, this area provides a safe haven for injured and battle-weary ULFA cadre.

KLO, till date, is not a very strong and capable outfit. Whenever it indulges in any act of insurgency, it invariably takes help from ULFA cadres. Even though ULFA oversaw the training of the KLO insurgents in the initial period, it is believed that the latter was given only a lower level training as compared to the ULFA cadres. Though the KLO insurgents also used sophisticated weapons like the AK series rifles, Chinese grenades, sources point out that those were joint operations by the KLO and ULFA, with the latter dominating and flexing its sophisticated arsenal.

The first reported KLO-ULFA armed operation was the abduction of a tea garden owner Roshanlal Garg from Latabari tea estate in central Dooars in July 1999. Garg was released after KLO was paid a huge ransom in February 2000. In November 1999, KLO and ULFA insurgents looted a railway cash counter near Siliguri.

In 2000, a KLO and ULFA joint operation resulted in the deaths of two prominent Communist Party of India-Marxist (CPI-M) activists. On 4 May 2000, Paresh Pal, a CPM leader was killed at Ghogsapara near the Assam-West Bengal border. On 7 August 2000, a CPM activist Nitai Das was killed at Jalpaiguri. In October

2000, a tea garden owner Om Prakash Agarwal was abducted by a joint team of KLO and ULFA insurgents.

In January 2001, KLO, along with ULFA, called for a boycott of the Republic Day celebrations on 26 January from 1 a.m. till 6 p.m. with the proclaimed objective of "overthrowing the Indian colonial rule".

Conflict Management Initiatives

Government initiative in terms of tackling this relatively nascent brand of insurgency ranged from outright refusal to acknowledge the presence of KLO and its threat to the region, to expression of helplessness due to the lack of a counter-insurgency force. Police in West Bengal were not geared up to deal with the KLO cadres and the purview of the Unified Command Structure, in charge of the counter-insurgency operations in Assam, excludes the region. Representatives of the government's of Assam and West Bengal met on 23 May 2000 and decided to jointly tackle the problem of cross-border insurgency. In the second half of the year 2000, Central Reserve Police Force (CRPF) was deployed to deal with the situation.

Command and Structure

KLO, until date, is not a very strong and capable insurgent outfit. According to some sources, it has an estimated cadre strength of one hundred, many of whom have been trained in ULFA-run camps in Bhutan. Nothing much is known regarding the command structure of the outfit whose activity revolves around the dictates of its chairman.

External Linkages

KLO operates in tandem with the ULFA. According to available information, initially thirty-five KLO insurgents were trained at the Kalikhola camp in Bhutan. In July 2000, about twenty KLO cadres were receiving training at that particular camp. Media reports in October 2000 quoted arrested KLO insurgents as having said that fifteen KLO cadres were being trained in the ULFA camps in Bhutan. Weapons such as AK-series rifles, United Machine Guns, Self-loading rifles, carbines, and pistols are available in the camp and the trainees have access to them.

The *Tiwa National Revolutionary Front* (TNRF), an insurgent outfit based in the Nagaon district of Assam also has working relationship with the KLO. In addition, the *National Socialist Council of Nagaland-Isak-Muivah* (NSCN-IM) understandably maintains links with the KLO.

Popular Support

The KLO tries to garner support from the Koch-Rajbongshis of lower Assam (Kokrajhar, Bongaigaon, Dhubri and Goalpara districts), West Garo Hills of Meghalaya and six districts of North Bengal. However, its support base is not that strong due to the presence of other Kamatapuri political organizations such as the *Kamatapuri People's Party* (KPP), *All Kamatapur Students' Union* (KSU), the *Kamatapur Women's Right Front* (KWRF) in West Bengal fighting for a similar cause.

Funds

KLO exhibits the typical characteristics of an insurgent outfit, which requires a regular flow of finances to buy arms, support its cadre and to maintain its effectiveness. Extortion forms the major source of its income. Like the ULFA, for its purpose, it has targeted the tea gardens in north Bengal, especially in the Dooars region. In the initial stages, the KLO insurgents used to come directly to the tea garden managers and demand money instead of sending demand notes and very often, the garden managers, in a bid to buy peace, came to a settlement rather than informing the police. However, this brand of extortion soon paved way for a more serious and organized mode of operation.

Loot of garden remittance in various attacks on the National Highway 31 passing through the heart of the tea belt, abductions, demand of huge ransom, theft of gardens' properties like green tea leaves, costly irrigation implements and even fence wiring became the common modes of acquiring finance.

The situation has reached such a level that the tea industry in the region, spread over nearly 300 tea gardens, has started contemplating in terms of raising a private protection force on the line of the one in Assam. In addition, ULFA also provides financial assistance to the KLO.

Leadership

Tushar Das alias Jibon Singha was the chairman of KLO, until he was arrested in October 1999. Nothing much is known regarding the succeeding leadership of the KLO after that. However, some of the prominent KLO insurgents who could be in positions of decision-making are Hiten Rai, Ravi Rajbongshi, Rahul Rai and Kajal Rai.

Hizbul Mujahideen (HM)

Suba Chandran

Master Ahsan Dar formed the *Hizbul Mujahideen* in 1990, along with Mohammad Abdullah Bangroo, with the support of Pakistan. Pakistan was looking for an alternative to the *Jammu and Kashmir Liberation Front* (JKLF). Pakistan preferred the *Hizbul Mujahideen* to the JKLF for two reasons. First, JKLF was no longer a pro-Pakistan outfit, but a pro-independence outfit, which Pakistan did not like. Secondly, the JKLF was secular, and Pakistan preferred an Islamic group.

Objectives

The *Hizbul Mujahideen* is very close to both the *Jamaat-e-Islami* (JI) in Kashmir and Pakistan. Most of the cadres of the *Hizbul* are drawn from the *Jamaat-e-Islami* of Kashmir. The *Hizbul* advocates Kashmir's merger with Pakistan and also campaigns for Islamisation of Kashmir.

Command and Structure

In 1991, the *Hizbul Mujahideen* set up a Supreme Advisory Council, which is the final decision making body. This Supreme Advisory Council replaced Master Ahsan Dar with Salahuddin, who, after becoming the Supreme Commander, re-organized the HM. He divided the organization into administrative and military wings. The leaders of the JI were in charge of the administrative wings of the HM and always had control over the commanders of the military wings. The Hizbul has a women wing—Binatul Islam, whose strength is not known.

Factions

When Ahsan Dar was replaced, he left the *Hizbul Mujahideen* and launched his own outfit—the Muslim *Mujahideen*. However, the Muslim *Mujahideen* could not retain its identity, as Ahsan Dar was kidnapped by the HM in 1992 wherafter, both he and his outfit lost their influence. There was another faction led by Nasir-ul-Islam known as *Jamait-ul-Mujahideen*. This faction also lost its relevance after Nasir-ul-Islam was killed.

Strength

The *Hizbul Mujahideen*, in the early 1990s had a strength of 12,000 cadres, especially after Abdul Majid Dar merged his *Tehreek-e-Jihad-e-Islami* in 1991. However it has only 1500 cadres now, half of whom are in Pakistan occupied Kashmir (PoK). There are around 700-800 members of the *Hizbul Mujahideen* fighting in the Kashmir Valley. The decline in its strength was due to several factors. Firstly, it lost most of its members in its fight against the Indian security forces. Secondly, the counter insurgents, known as *Ikhwans* were also responsible for killing many of its members. It is estimated that nearly 2000 *Hizbul* cadres were killed by the *Ikhwans*.

Areas of Influence

The *Hizbul*, being comprised of the local militants, have influence all over the Valley. Besides, it also has influence in Poonch, Rajouri and Doda districts of the Jammu region.

Training Camps

The *Hizbul Mujahideen* has training camps in Pakistan and in PoK. Ever since the Taliban came on the scene in Afghanistan, the training camps for the *Hizbul* were closed, as the *Hizbul* is viewed as the militant wing of the *Jamaat-e-Islami*. The Taliban does not have cordial relations with the *Jamaat-e-Islami* of Pakistan as the latter has been supporting the former's opponents in Afghanistan.

External Linkages

Though the *Hizbul* was founded with active help from Pakistan, in the second half of the nineties, the *Hizbul* found itself getting distanced from Pakistan. *Hizbul*'s closeness to the *Jamaat-e-Islami* (JI) of Pakistan and the changed equations between the Pakisan government and JI in Pakistan was the main reason for *Hizbul* losing its significance. In the late 1980s and the early 1990s, the ISI and Nawaz Sharif were very close to the JI and its chief, Qazi Hussain Ahmed. Later, when the equations between the ISI and Qazi changed, *Hizbul*'s closeness to Qazi became a factor in ISI-*Hizbul* relations.

Secondly, the Pakistani distrust towards Kashmiri militants resulted in its propping up foreign militants at the cost of the local Kashmiri militants. The *Hizbul* did not like to be porters, couriers and guides for the foreign militants. The differences in ideology between the *Hizbul* and other militant groups such as the *Lashkar-e-Toiba* and *Harkat-ul-Ansar* also resulted in *Hizbul* distancing itself from these groups, which further alienated the ISI from it.

Liberation Tigers of Tamil Eelam

N. MANOHARAN

History

CLAIMED TO BE "the most powerful extra-parliamentary liberation movement in the Tamil nation", the *Liberation Tigers of the Tamil Eelam* (LTTE) was founded by Vellupillai Prabhakaran on 5 March 1976, the day he conducted a successful bank robbery in Puttur. However, its origin can be traced to many youth organiZations like *Pulip Padai* (the Army of Tigers), the *Tamil Liberation Organization*, the *Tamil Students League*, the *Tamil Youth League* and, finally, the *Tamil New Tigers*, which emerged as a result of transformation from national consciousness to defensive nationalism. After a few years of militancy, the LTTE faced a split with the formation of the *People's Liberation Organization of Tamil Eelam* (PLOTE) by Uma Maheswaran; thereafter many splinter groups emerged. At one time, thirty-seven groups were existing; five were prominent—LTTE, TELO, EPRLF, PLOT and EROS. In due course, LTTE emerged as the most powerful militant organization.

Objectives

An egalitarian ideology governs the combatants. Their aim is to establish a casteless Tamil society by armed struggle. Lenin's conception of "self-determination" and the "revolutionary vanguard" forms the organization's basic ideology. Earlier, the LTTE's struggle was defined in Marxist terms, but as Prabhakaran rose to prominence, Marx "withered away". The "class war" got transformed into a "race war". The Tiger symbol, an allusion to the military character of the South Indian Chola Empire, used by the LTTE, highlights its links of "Tamilness". The ideology of violence in Tigers is drawn from the Dravidian National Movement in Tamil Nadu in the 1950s and 1960—sit marked a revival of martial culture of the long suppressed military castes of South India, like *Maravar*. The cult of martyrdom and the ideology of vengeance are based on such appeals to a heroic past. On the other hand, unlike other guerrilla organizations, its leader Prabhakaran has a deep impact on the LTTE's ideology—the character of deep suspicion, fanatic braveness, relentless pursuit of vengeance and disregard for human life.

Strategy

At the macro level, the Tigers' strategy has four key components:

(i) the use of times of peace to prepare for war, in line with the Maoist doctrine of "retreat and recuperate".

(ii) an attempt to attain total control over the Tamil struggle to gain legitimacy as the sole representative of Sri Lankan Tamils. It is with this motive that the LTTE has eliminated almost all opposition to it;

(iii) a subordination of the political struggle to the military one; hence it is not interested in a political solution through dialogue; and,

(iv) a mixture of guerrilla and conventional warfare tactics in battle.

In addition, the Tigers make use of suicide bombers as a tactic. Though many militant groups follow this technique, the LTTE is one of the few organizations to adopt it as an article of faith. A separate unit known as the "Black Tigers" exists to organize attacks on civilian and military targets and eliminate key leaders by these means.

Dialogue with Government

The underlying point to emphasize is that the LTTE has never been sincere about a dialogue. If it was willing at times, it was a tactical ploy, either to buy time to regroup or to coalesce against a common enemy or gain legitimacy from the international community. Looked at in this perspective, starting with the 1984 Thimpu talks and coming to the last dialogue in 1995, have been failures due to the LTTE's intransigence by placing unreasonable demands on the Sri Lankan state. Efforts by third parties like India, Norway, Britain and the United States have been fruitless. However, in the initial stages (early 1980s) the Sri Lankan Government missed the opportunity for a constructive dialogue with the militant groups due to their deep mistrust of the Tamils. But, with the assumption of UNP government in December 2001 under Ranil Wickremasinge, serious process of peace was initiated with the LTTE. A MoU was signed in February 2002 and direct talks with Norwegian facilitation began in September 2002. Intense international pressure is believed to be the main reason behind the ongoing talks.

Structure

The LTTE differs from other classical guerilla organizations, which do not promote the cult of leader. For the Tigers, Prabhakaran is supreme. At the helm is the military wing. It reflects classical Maoist doctrine by emphasising discipline and the absence of a formal ranking system. The Central Committee is the highest decision-making body with Prabhakaran as its Chairman. The structure has both political and military wings. Area commanders are responsible for tactical decision-making. They are men with many years of fighting experience.

External Linkages

The paws of the Tigers extend from Canada and the United States in the West to Australia in the east. The linkages are due to the presence of Tamil refugees in those countries who fled from the ethnic conflict in Sri Lanka. Of late, due to crackdowns on the Tigers by the United States, Canada, India and South Africa, the support base of the LTTE has dwindled. Their links are more confined to some West European countries like Britain and Germany, Nordic countries, besides Australia, Thailand, Myanmar, Cambodia, and South Africa, but not at the governmental level. India, which was once highly sympathetic towards the LTTE outlawed the organization soon after the assassination of Rajiv Gandhi by the Tigers. As of now only a tenuous linkage continues in Tamil Nadu for political purposes.

Popular Support

The popular support to the LTTE comes from three: intra-Sri Lankan Tamil constituency, Sri Lankan Tamil diaspora, and other Tamils including those in India. However, the Tigers are slowly losing their support among the masses at all levels. Within Sri Lanka people are slowly shifting their loyalties, due to the Tigers' extortion, conscription and displacement. In addition, the re-construction programmes and confidence building efforts by the Government through its peace packages acts against the LTTE. The Sri Lankan Tamil refugees abroad have become, of late, tired of the extortion racket by the LTTE. Moreover, the crackdowns on them by United States, Canada and India is preventing Tamil refugees from actively supporting the rebels. The combination of all these factors have reduced the support base of the Tigers. However, the LTTE still enjoys considerable mass support either due to fear or the absence of a credible alternative.

Funds

The funds for the LTTE come from three major sources:

1. Diaspora contribution: The major source of funding is by the Sri Lankan Tamil expatriates living in developed countries.
2. Extortion: The LTTE also collects money from the people living in areas controlled by it in Sri Lanka as taxation.
3. Narcotics: The Tigers are also earning huge amounts of money through the drugs trade, as Sri Lanka is strategically located between the "Golden Crescent" and the "Golden Triangle".

It is this large funding which has enabled the LTTE to increase its firepower by acquiring sophisticated weapons and weapon systems including surface-to-air missiles. The Tigers are also using weapons captured from the Lankan Army.

Leaders

The entire organization revolves around Prabhakaran. Though most of the second rung leaders are no more, some of the notable remaining personalities are Anton Balasingham, the LTTE ideologue; Lawrance Thilagar, Secretary of the International Secretariat of the LTTE; Tamil Selvam, leader of the political wing; Pottu Amman, intelligence; Pararajasingham, judicial matters; Javan, Voice of Tigers; Soosai, Sea Tigers; Ranjith Appa, finance; Shankar, Air Tigers; and Radi, Women's wing.

Appendices

Regional Conventions

A. INTER AMERICAN COMMITTEE AGAINST TERRORISM

The Second Specialized Conference on Terrorism held in Mar del Plata, Argentina on November 23-24, 1998 concluded with the adoption of the Commitment of Mar del Plata. That commitment called for establishing within the Organization of American States an "Inter-American Committee Against Terrorism" composed of "competent national authorities" of the member states. This effort was further endorsed by the heads of state of the hemisphere in the Plan of Action of the Second Summit of the Americas in Santiago, Chile. The subsequent meeting of the General Assembly endorsed the recommendations and decisions contained in the Commitment of Mar Del Plata and established CICTE by resolution AG/RES. 1650 (XXIX-O/99). The basic objectives of CICTE, as set forth in the Commitment of Mar del Plata, are to:

- Enhance the exchange of information via the competent national authorities, including the establishment of an Inter-American database on terrorism issues
- Formulate proposal to assist member states in drafting appropriate counter-terrorism legislation in all states
- Compile the bilateral, sub-regional, regional and multilateral treaties and agreements signed by member states and promote universal adherence to international counter-terrorism conventions
- Enhance border cooperation and travel documentation security measures
- Develop activities for training and crisis management.

The first regular session of CICTE was held in Miami, Florida in October 1999 which developed a plan of work. A second regular session planned for Bolivia in 2000 had to be cancelled at the last moment. No session was scheduled in 2001.

The events of September 11, 2001 brought renewed focus to the Inter-American efforts to confront terrorism. The attacks were immediately condemned by the General Assembly, which coincidentally was meeting in

Special Session in Lima, Peru to approve the Inter-American Democratic Charter. This was followed by the Resolution Strengthening Cooperation to Prevent, Combat, and Eliminate Terrorism (RC.23/RES.1/01) adopted by the 23rd Meeting of Consultation of Ministers of Foreign Affairs September 21, 2001 in Washington, DC.

This resolution included among other items the following issues pertinent to CICTE:

- To call upon all member states to strengthen cooperation, at the regional and international levels, to pursue, capture, prosecute, and punish and, as appropriate, to expedite the extradition of the perpetrators, organizers, and sponsors of these terrorist acts, strengthen mutual legal assistance, and exchange information in a timely manner.
- To instruct the Permanent Council to convoke, as soon as possible, a meeting of the Inter-American Committee Against Terrorism so that it may identify urgent actions aimed at strengthening Inter-American cooperation to prevent, combat, and eliminate terrorism in the Hemisphere.
- To entrust the Permanent Council with preparing a draft Inter-American Convention Against Terrorism with a view to presenting it to the next session of the OAS General Assembly. Also, to urge the states to study the international legal repercussions of the conduct of government authorities who provide financial support to, protect, or harbor terrorist individuals or groups.

In light of these and subsequent resolutions of the organs of the Inter-American system, CICTE held two special sessions October 15, 2001 and November 29, 2001. Between these sessions, three subcommittees (Financial Controls, Border Controls, and Work Plan) worked diligently to identify counter-terrorism actions for OAS Member States to implement at the multilateral, regional, sub-regional and national levels and to draft an ambitious although concrete agenda for CICTE to pursue in 2002-2003.

At the Second Regular Session of CICTE January 28-29, 2002 in Washington DC, the ministers of interior and public Security and the other heads of delegations reported on the action taken by their respective nations to implement Resolution RC. 23 of September 21. On January 30, policy experts from the member states participated in a Policy Development Role Playing Exercise hosted by the United States to examine possible courses of action in response to a terrorist scenario.

B. EUROPEAN CONVENTION ON THE SUPPRESSION OF TERRORISM, STRASBOURG, 27.1.1977

THE MEMBER STATES of the Council of Europe, signatory hereto,

CONSIDERING that the aim of the Council of Europe is to achieve a greater unity between its members;

AWARE of the growing concern caused by the increase in acts of terrorism;

WISHING to take effective measures to ensure that the perpetrators of such acts do not escape prosecution and punishment;

CONVINCED that extradition is a particularly effective measure for achieving this result,

HAVE agreed as follows:

Article 1

For the purposes of extradition between Contracting States, none of the following offences shall be regarded as a political offence or as an offence connected with a political offence or as an offence inspired by political motives:

a an offence within the scope of the Convention for the Suppression of Unlawful Seizure of Aircraft, signed at The Hague on 16 December 1970;

b an offence within the scope of the Convention for the Suppression of Unlawful Acts against the Safety of Civil Aviation, signed at Montreal on 23 September 1971;

c a serious offence involving an attack against the life, physical integrity or liberty of internationally protected persons, including diplomatic agents;

d an offence involving kidnapping, the taking of a hostage or serious unlawful detention;

e an offence involving the use of a bomb, grenade, rocket, automatic firearm or letter or parcel bomb if this use endangers persons;

f an attempt to commit any of the foregoing offences or participation as an accomplice of a person who commits or attempts to commit such an offence.

Article 2

1. For the purpose of extradition between Contracting States, a Contracting State may decide not to regard as a political offence or as an offence connected with a political offence or as an offence inspired by political motives a serious offence involving an act of violence, other than one covered by Article 1, against the life, physical integrity or liberty of a person.

2. The same shall apply to a serious offence involving an act against property, other than one covered by Article 1, if the act created a collective danger for persons.

3. The same shall apply to an attempt to commit any of the foregoing offences or participation as an accomplice of a person who commits or attempts to commit such an offence.

Article 3

The provisions of all extradition treaties and arrangements applicable between Contracting States, including the European Convention on Extradition, are modified as between Contracting States to the extent that they are incompatible with this Convention.

Article 4

For the purpose of this Convention and to the extent that any offence mentioned in Article 1 or 2 is not listed as an extraditable offence in any extradition convention or treaty existing between Contracting States, it shall be deemed to be included as such therein.

Article 5

Nothing in this Convention shall be interpreted as imposing an obligation to extradite if the requested State has substantial grounds for believing that the request for extradition for an offence mentioned in Article 1 or 2 has been made for the purpose of prosecuting or punishing a person on account of his race, religion, nationality or political opinion, or that that person's position may be prejudiced for any of these reasons.

Article 6

1. Each Contracting State shall take such measures as may be necessary to establish its jurisdiction over an offence mentioned in Article 1 in the case where the suspected offender is present in its territory and it does not

extradite him after receiving a request for extradition from a Contracting State whose jurisdiction is based on a rule of jurisdiction existing equally in the law of the requested State.

2. This Convention does not exclude any criminal jurisdiction exercised in accordance with national law.

Article 7

A Contracting State in whose territory a person suspected to have committed an offence mentioned in Article 1 is found and which has received a request for extradition under the conditions mentioned in Article 6, paragraph 1, shall, if it does not extradite that person, submit the case, without exception whatsoever and without undue delay, to its competent authorities for the purpose of prosecution. Those authorities shall take their decision in the same manner as in the case of any offence of a serious nature under the law of that State.

Article 8

1. Contracting States shall afford one another the widest measure of mutual assistance in criminal matters in connection with proceedings brought in respect of the offences mentioned in Article 1 or 2. The law of the requested State concerning mutual assistance in criminal matters shall apply in all cases. Nevertheless this assistance may not be refused on the sole ground that it concerns a political offence or an offence connected with a political offence or an offence inspired by political motives.

2. Nothing in this Convention shall be interpreted as imposing an obligation to afford mutual assistance if the requested State has substantial grounds for believing that the request for mutual assistance in respect of an offence mentioned in Article 1 or 2 has been made for the purpose of prosecuting or punishing a person on account of his race, religion, nationality or political opinion or that that person's position may be prejudiced for any of these reasons.

3. The provisions of all treaties and arrangements concerning mutual assistance in criminal matters applicable between Contracting States, including the European Convention on Mutual Assistance in Criminal Matters, are modified as between Contracting States to the extent that they are incompatible with this Convention.

Article 9

1. The European Committee on Crime Problems of the Council of Europe shall be kept informed regarding the application of this Convention.

2. It shall do whatever is needful to facilitate a friendly settlement of any difficulty which may arise out of its execution.

Article 10

1. Any dispute between Contracting States concerning the interpretation or application of this Convention, which has not been settled in the framework of Article 9, paragraph 2, shall, at the request of any Party to the dispute, be referred to arbitration. Each Party shall nominate an arbitrator and the two arbitrators shall nominate a referee. If any Party has not nominated its arbitrator within the three months following the request for arbitration, he shall be nominated at the request of the other Party by the President of the European Court of Human Rights. If the latter should be a national of one of the Parties to the dispute, this duty shall be carried out by the Vice-President of the Court or if the Vice-President is a national of one of the Parties to the dispute, by the most senior judge of the Court not being a national of one of the Parties to the dispute. The same procedure shall be observed if the arbitrators cannot agree on the choice of referee.

2. The arbitration tribunal shall lay down its own procedure. Its decisions shall be taken by majority vote. Its award shall be final.

Article 11

1. This Convention shall be open to signature by the member States of the Council of Europe. It shall be subject to ratification, acceptance or approval. Instruments of ratification, acceptance or approval shall be deposited with the Secretary General of the Council of Europe.

2. The Convention shall enter into force three months after the date of the deposit of the third instrument of ratification, acceptance or approval.

3. In respect of a signatory State ratifying, accepting or approving subsequently, the Convention shall come into force three months after the date of the deposit of its instrument of ratification, acceptance or approval.

Article 12

1. Any State may, at the time of signature or when depositing its instrument of ratification, acceptance or approval, specify the territory or territories to which this Convention shall apply.

2. Any State may, when depositing its instrument of ratification, acceptance or approval or at any later date, by declaration addressed to the

Secretary General of the Council of Europe, extend this Convention to any other territory or territories specified in the declaration and for whose international relations it is responsible or on whose behalf it is authorised to give undertakings.

3. Any declaration made in pursuance of the preceding paragraph may, in respect of any territory mentioned in such declaration, be withdrawn by means of a notification addressed to the Secretary General of the Council of Europe. Such withdrawal shall take effect immediately or at such later date as may be specified in the notification.

Article 13

1. Any State may, at the time of signature or when depositing its instrument of ratification, acceptance or approval, declare that it reserves the right to refuse extradition in respect of any offence mentioned in Article 1 which it considers to be a political offence, an offence connected with a political offence or an offence inspired by political motives, provided that it undertakes to take into due consideration, when evaluating the character of the offence, any particularly serious aspects of the offence, including:

a that it created a collective danger to the life, physical integrity or liberty of persons; or

b that it affected persons foreign to the motives behind it; or

c that cruel or vicious means have been used in the commission of the offence.

2. Any State may wholly or partly withdraw a reservation it has made in accordance with the foregoing paragraph by means of a declaration addressed to the Secretary General of the Council of Europe which shall become effective as from the date of its receipt.

3. A State which has made a reservation in accordance with paragraph 1 of this article may not claim the application of Article 1 by any other State; it may, however, if its reservation is partial or conditional, claim the application of that article in so far as it has itself accepted it.

Article 14

Any Contracting State may denounce this Convention by means of a written notification addressed to the Secretary General of the Council of Europe. Any such denunciation shall take effect immediately or at such later date as may be specified in the notification.

Article 15

This Convention ceases to have effect in respect of any Contracting State which withdraws from or ceases to be a member of the Council of Europe.

Article 16

The Secretary General of the Council of Europe shall notify the member States of the Council of:

a any signature;
b any deposit of an instrument of ratification, acceptance or approval;
c any date of entry into force of this Convention in accordance with Article 11 thereof;
d any declaration or notification received in pursuance of the provisions of Article 12;
e any reservation made in pursuance of the provisions of Article 13, paragraph 1;
f the withdrawal of any reservation effected in pursuance of the provisions of Article 13, paragraph 2;
g any notification received in pursuance of Article 14 and the date on which denunciation takes effect;
h any cessation of the effects of the Convention pursuant to Article 15.

IN WITNESS WHEREOF, the undersigned, being duly authorised thereto, have signed this Convention.

DONE at Strasbourg, this 27th day of January 1977, in English and in French, both texts being equally authoritative, in a single copy which shall remain deposited in the archives of the Council of Europe. The Secretary General of the Council of Europe shall transmit certified copies to each of the signatory States.

C. THE ARAB CONVENTION FOR THE SUPPRESSION OF TERRORISM

Adopted by the Council of Arab Ministers of the Interior and the Council of Arab Ministers of Justice, Cairo, April 1998.

Unofficial translation from Arabic by the United Nations English translation service.

Preamble

THE ARAB STATES signatory hereto,

DESIRING to promote mutual cooperation in the suppression of terrorist offences, which pose a threat to the security and stability of the Arab Nation and endanger its vital interests,

BEING committed to the highest moral and religious principles and, in particular, to the tenets of the Islamic Sharia, as well as to the humanitarian heritage of an Arab Nation that rejects all forms of violence and terrorism and advocates the protection of human rights, with which precepts the principles of international law conform, based as they are on cooperation among peoples in the promotion of peace,

BEING FURTHER committed to the Pact of the League of Arab States, the Charter of the United Nations and all the other international convents and instruments to which the Contracting States to this Convention are parties,

AFFIRMING the right of peoples to combat foreign occupation and aggression by whatever means, including armed struggle, in order to liberate their territories and secure their right to self-determination, and independence and to do so in such a manner as to preserve the territorial integrity of each Arab country, of the foregoing being in accordance with the purposes and principles of the Charter of the United Nations and with the Organization's resolutions,

HAVE agreed to conclude this convention and to invite any Arab State that did not participate in its conclusion to accede hereto.

PART ONE

DEFINITIONS AND GENERAL PROVISIONS

Article 1

Each of the following terms shall be understood in the light of the definition give;

1. CONTRACTING STATE

Any member State of the League of Arab States that has ratified this Convention and that has deposited its instruments of ratification with the General Secretariat of the League.

2. TERRORISM

Any act or threat of violence, whatever its motives or purposes, that occurs in the advancement of an individual or collective criminal agenda and seeking to sow panic among people, causing fear by harming them, or placing their lives, liberty or security in danger, or seeking to cause damage to the environment or to public or private installations or property or to occupying or seizing them, or seeking to jeopardize a national resources.

3. TERRORIST OFFENCE

Any offence or attempted offence committed in furtherance of a terrorist objective in any of the Contracting States, or against their nationals, property or interests, that is punishable by their domestic law. The offences stipulated in the following conventions, except where conventions have not been ratified by Contracting States or where offences have been excluded by their legislation, shall also be regarded as terrorist offences:

(a) The Tokyo Convention on offences and Certain Other Acts Committed on Board Aircraft, of 14 September 1963;
(b) The Hague Convention for the Suppression of Unlawful Seizure of Aircraft, of 16 December 1970;
(c) The Montreal Convention for the Suppression of Unlawful Acts against the Safety of Civil Aviation, of 23 September 1971, and the Protocol thereto of 10 May 1984;
(d) The Convention on the Prevention and Punishment of Crimes

against Internationally Protected Persons, including Diplomatic Agents, of 14 December 1973;

(e) The International Convention against the Taking of Hostages, of 17 December 1979;

(f) The provisions of the United Nations Convention on the Law of the Sea, of 1982, relating to piracy on the high seas.

Article 2

(a) All cases of struggle by whatever means, including armed struggle, against foreign occupation and aggression for liberation and self-determination, in accordance with the principles of international law, shall not be regarded as an offence. This provision shall not apply to any act prejudicing the territorial integrity of any Arab State.

(b) None of the terrorist offences indicated in the preceding article shall be regarded as a political offence. In the application of this Convention, none of the following offences shall be regarded as a political offence, even if committed for political motives:

(i) Attacks on the kings, Heads of State or rulers of the contracting States or on their spouses and families;

(ii) Attacks on crown princes, vice-presidents, prime ministers or ministers in any of the Contracting States;

(iii) Attacks on persons enjoying diplomatic immunity, including ambassadors and diplomats serving in or accredited to the Contracting States;

(iv) Premeditated murder or theft accompanied by the use of force directed against individuals, the authorities or means of transport and communications;

(v) Acts of sabotage and destruction of public property and property assigned to a public service, even if owned by another Contracting State;

(vi) The manufacture, illicit trade in or possession of weapons, munitions or explosives, or other items that may be used to commit terrorist offences.

PART TWO

PRINCIPLES OF ARAB COOPERATION FOR THE SUPPRESSION OF TERRORISM

CHAPTER I

THE SECURITY FIELD

SECTION I

Measures for the Prevention and Suppression of Terrorist Offences

Article 3

Contracting States undertake not to organize, finance or commit terrorist acts or to be accessories thereto in any manner whatsoever. In their commitment to the prevention and suppression of terrorist offence in accordance with their domestic laws and procedures, they shall endeavour:

I. PREVENTIVE MEASURE

1. To prevent the use of their territories as a base for planning, organizing, executing, attempting or taking part in terrorist crime in any manner whatsoever. This includes the prevention of terrorists; infiltration into, or residence in their territories either as individuals or groups, receiving or giving refuge to them, training, arming, financing, or providing any facilitation to them;

2. To cooperate and coordinate action among Contracting States, particularly neighbouring countries suffering from similar or common terrorist offences;

3. To develop and strengthen systems for the detection of the movement, importation, exportation, stockpilling and use of weapons, munitions and explosives and of other means of aggression, murder and destruction as well as procedures for monitoring their passage through customs and across borders in order to prevent their transfer from one Contracting State to another or to third-party States other than for lawful purposes;

4. To develop and strengthen systems concerned with surveillance procedures and the securing of borders and points of entry overland and by air in order to prevent illicit entry thereby;

5. To strengthen mechanisms for the security and protection of eminent persons, vital installations and means of public transportation,

6. To enhance the protection, security and safety of diplomatic and consular persons and missions and international and regional organizations accredited to Contracting Stages, in accordance with the relevant international agreements, which govern this subject;

7. To reinforce security-related information activities and to coordinate them with those of each State in accordance with its information policy, with a view to exposing the objectives of terrorist groups and organizations, thwarting their schemes and demonstrating the danger they pose to security and stability;

8. To establish, in each Contracting State, a database for the accumulation and analysis of information relating to terrorist elements, groups, movements and organizations and for the monitoring of developments with respect to the terrorist phenomenon and of successful experiences in counter-terrorism, and to keep such information up to date and make it available to the competent authorities of Contracting States, within the limits established by the domestic laws and procedures of each State;

II. MEASURES OF SUPPRESSION

1. To arrest the perpetrators of terrorist offences and to prosecute them in accordance with national law or extradite them in accordance with the provision's of this Convention or of any bilateral treaty between the requesting State and the requested State;

2. To provide effective protection for those working in the criminal justice field;

3. To provide effective protection for sources of information concerning terrorist offences and for witnesses thereof;

4. To extend necessary assistance to victims of terrorism;

5. To establish effective cooperation between the relevant agencies and the public in countering terrorism by, inter alia, establishing appropriate guarantees and incentives to encourage the reporting of terrorist acts, the provision of information to assist in their investigation, and cooperation in the arrest of perpetrators.

SECTION II

ARAB COOPERATION FOR THE PREVENTION AND SUPPRESSION OF TERRORIST OFFENCES

Article 4

Contracting States shall cooperate for the prevention and suppression of terrorist offences, in accordance with the domestic laws and regulations of each State, as set forth hereunder:

I. EXCHANGING OF INFORMATION

1. Contracting States shall undertake to promote the exchange of information between and among them concerning:

(a) The activities and crimes of terrorist groups and of their leaders and members; their headquarters and training; the means and sources by which they are funded and armed; the types of weapons, munitions and explosives used by them; and other means of aggression, murder and destruction;
(b) The means of communication and propaganda used by terrorist groups, their modus operandi; the movements of their leaders and members; and the travel documents that they use.

2. Each contracting State shall undertake to notify any other Contracting State in an expeditious manner of the information it has concerning any terrorist offence that takes place in its territory and is intended to harm the interests of that State or of its nationals and to include in such notification statements concerning the circumstances surrounding the offence, those who committed it, its victims, the losses occasioned by it and the devices and methods used in its perpetration, to the extent compatible with the requirements of the investigation and inquiry.

3. Contracting States shall undertake to cooperate with each other in the exchange of information for the suppression of terrorist offences and promptly to notify other Contracting States of all the information or data in their possession that may prevent the occurrence of terrorist offences in their territory, against their nationals or residents or against their interests.

4. Each Contracting State shall undertake to furnish any other Contracting State with any information or data in its possession that may:

(a) Assist in the arrest of a person or persons accused of committing a terrorist offence against the interests of that State or of being implicated in such an offence whether by aiding and abetting, collusion or incitement;

(b) Lead to the seizure of any weapons, munitions or explosives or any devices or funds used or intended for use to commit a terrorist offence.

5. Contracting States shall undertake to maintain the confidentiality of the information that they exchange among themselves and not to furnish it to any State that is not a Contracting State or any other party without the prior consent of the State that was the source of the information.

II. INVESTIGATIONS

Contracting States shall undertake to promote cooperation among themselves and to provide assistance with respect to measures for the investigation and arrest of fugitives suspected or convicted of terrorist offences in accordance with the laws and regulations of each state.

III. EXCHANGE OF EXPERTISE

1. Contracting States shall cooperate in the conduct and exchange of research studies for the suppression of terrorist offences and shall exchange expertise in the counter-terrorism field.

2. Contracting States shall cooperate, within the limits of their resources, in providing all possible technical assistance for the formulation of programmes or the holding of joint training courses or training courses intended for one state or for a group of Contracting States, as required for the benefit of those working in counter-terrorism with the aim of developing their scientific and practical abilities and enhancing their performance.

CHAPTER II

THE JUDICIAL FIELD

SECTION I

Extradition of Offenders

Article 5

Contracting States shall undertake to extradite those indicated for or convicted of terrorist offences whose extradition is requested by any of these states in accordance with the rules and conditions stipulated in this convention.

Article 6

Extradition shall not be permissible in any of the following circumstances:

(a) If the offence for which extradition is requested is regarded under the laws in force in the requested State as an offence of a political nature;
(b) If the offence for which extradition is requested relates solely to a dereliction of military duties;
(c) If the offence for which extradition is requested was committed in the territory of the requested contracting State, except where the offence has harmed the interests of the requesting State and its laws provide for the prosecution and punishment for such offences and where the requested State has not initiated any investigation or prosecution;
(d) If a final judgement having the force of res judicata has been rendered in respect of the offence in the requested Contracting State or in a third Contracting State;
(e) If, on delivery of the request for extradition, proceedings have been terminated or punishment has, under the law of the requesting State, lapsed because of the passage of time;
(f) If the offence was committed outside the territory of the requesting State by a person who is not a national of that State and the law of the requested State does not allow prosecution for the same category of offence when committed outside its territory by such a person;
(g) If the requesting State has granted amnesty to perpetrators of offences that include the offence in question;
(h) If the legal system of the requested State does not allow it to extradite its nationals. In this case, the requested State shall prosecute any such persons who commit in any of the other Contracting States a terrorist offence that is punishable in both States by deprivation of liberty for a period of at least one year or more. The nationality of the person whose extradition is sought shall be determined as at the date on which the offence in question was committed, and use shall be made in this regard of the investigation conducted by the requesting State.

Article 7

Should the person whose extradition is sought be under investigation, on trial or already convicted for another offence in the requested State, his concluded, the trial is completed or the sentence is imposed. The requested State may nevertheless extradite him on an interim basis for questioning or trial provided that he is returned to that State before serving the sentence imposed on him in the requesting State.

Article 8

For purposes of the extradition of offenders under this Convention, no account shall be taken of any difference there may be in the domestic legislation of Contracting States in the legal designation of the offence as a felony or a misdemeanour or in the penalty assigned to it, provided that it is punishable under the laws of both States by deprivation of liberty for a period of at least one year or more.

SECTION II

JUDICIAL DELEGATION

Article 9

Each Contracting State may request any other Contracting State to undertake in its territory and on its behalf any judicial procedure relating to an action arising out of a terrorist offence and, in particular:

(a) To hear the testimony of witnesses and take depositions as evidence;
(b) To effect service of judicial documents;
(c) To execute searches and seizures;
(d) To examine and inspect evidence;
(e) To obtain relevant documents and records or certified copies thereof.

Article 10

Each of the Contracting States shall undertake to implement judicial delegations relating to terrorist offences, but such assistance may be refused in either of the two following cases:

(a) Where the request relates to an offence that is subject to investigation or prosecution in the requested State;

(b) Where granting the request might be prejudicial to the sovereignty, security or public order of the requested State.

Article 11

The request for judicial delegation shall be granted promptly in accordance with the provisions of the domestic law of the requested State. The latter may postpone the execution of the request until such time as any ongoing investigation or prosecution involving the same matter are completed or any compelling reasons for postponement cease to exist, provided that the requesting State is notified of such postponement.

Article 12

(a) A measure that is undertaken by means of a judicial delegation, in accordance with the provisions of this Conventions, shall have the same legal effect as if it had been taken by the competent authority of the requesting State;
(b) The result of implementing the judicial delegation may be used only for the purpose for which the delegation is issued.

SECTION III

JUDICIAL COOPERATION

Article 13

Each contracting State shall provide the other States with all possible and necessary assistance for investigations or prosecutions relating to terrorist offences.

Article 14

(a) Where one of the Contracting States has jurisdiction to prosecute a person suspected of a terrorist offence, it may request the State in which the suspect is present to take proceedings against him for that offence, subject to the agreement of that State and provided that the offence is punishable in the prosecuting State by deprivation of liberty for a period of at least one your or more. The requesting state shall, in this event, provide the requested state with all the investigation documents and evidence relating to the offence.

(b) The investigation or prosecution shall be conducted on the basis of the charge or charges made by the requesting state against the suspect, in accordance with the provisions and procedures of the law of the prosecuting state.

Article 15

The submission by the requesting state of a request for prosecution in accordance with paragraph (a) of the preceding article shall entail the suspension of the measures taken by it to pursue, investigate and prosecute the suspect whose prosecution is being requested, with the exception of those required for the purposes of the judicial cooperation and assistance, or the judicial delegation, sought by the State requested to conduct the prosecution.

Article 16

(a) The measures taken in either the requesting State or that in which the prosecution takes place shall be subject to the law of the State in which they are taken and they shall have the force accorded to them by that law.

(b) The requesting State may try or retry a person whose prosecution it has requested only if the requested State declines to prosecute him.

(c) The State requested to take proceedings shall in all cases undertake to notify the requesting State of what action it has taken with regard to the request and of the outcome of the investigation or prosecution.

Article 17

The State requested to take proceedings may take all the measures and steps established by its law with respect to the accused both before the request to take proceedings reaches it and subsequently.

Article 18

The transfer of competence for prosecution shall not prejudice the rights of the victim of the offence, who reserves the right to approach the courts of the requesting State or the prosecuting State with a view to claiming his civil-law rights as a result of the offence.

SECTION IV

SEIZURE OF ASSETS AND PROCEEDS DERIVED FROM THE OFFENCE

Article 19

(a) If it is decided to extradite the requested person, any Contracting State shall undertake to seize and hand over to the requesting State the property used and proceeds derived from or relating to the terrorist offence, whether in the possession of the person whose extradition is sought or that of a third party.
(b) Once it has been established that they relate to the terrorist offence, the items indicated in the preceding paragraph shall be surrendered even if the person to be extradited is not handed over because he has absconded or died or for any other reason.
(c) The provisions of the two preceding paragraphs shall be without prejudice to the rights of any Contracting State or of bona fide third parties in the property or proceeds in question.

Article 20

The State requested to hand over property and proceeds may take all the precautionary measures necessary to discharge its obligation to hand them over. It may also retain such property or proceeds on a temporary basis if they are required for pending criminal proceedings or may, for the same reason, hand them over to the requesting State on condition that they are returned.

SECTION V

EXCHANGE OF EVIDENCE

Article 21

Contracting States shall undertake to have the evidence of any terrorist offence committed in their territory against another Contracting State examined by their competent agencies, and they may seek the assistance of any other Contracting State in doing so. They shall take the necessary measures to preserve such evidence and ensure its legal validity. They alone shall examination to the State against whose interests the offence was committed, and the Contracting State or States whose assistance is sought shall not pass this information to any third party.

PART THREE

MECHANISMS FOR IMPLEMENTING COOPERATION

CHAPTER I

EXTRADITION PROCEDURES

Article 22

Requests for extradition shall be made between the competent authorities in the Contracting States directly, through their ministries of justice or the equivalent or through the diplomatic channel.

Article 23

The request for extradition shall be made in writing and shall be accompanied by the following:

(a) The original or an authenticated copy of the indictment or detention order or any other documents having the same effect and issued in accordance with the procedure laid down in the law of the requesting State;
(b) A statement of the offences for which extradition is requested, showing the time and place of their commission, their legal designation and a reference to the legal provisions applicable thereto, together with a copy of the relevant provisions;
(c) As accurate a description as possible of the person whose extradition is sought, together with any other information that may serve to establish his identity and nationality.

Article 24

1. The judicial authorities in the requesting State may apply to the requested State by any of the means of written communication for the provisional detention of the person being sought pending the presentation of the request for extradition.

2. In this case, the State from which extradition is requested may detain

the person being sought on a provisional basis. If the request for extradition is not presented together with the necessary documents specified in the preceding article, the person whose extradition is being sought may not be detained for more than 30 days from the date of his arrest.

Article 25

The requesting State shall submit a request accompanied by the documents specified in article 23 of this Convention. If the requested State determines that the request is in order, its competent authorities shall grant the request in accordance with its own law and its decision shall be promptly communicated to the requesting State.

Article 26

1. In all of the cases stipulated in the two preceding articles, the period of provisional detention shall not exceed 60 days from the date of arrest.

2. During the period specified in the preceding paragraph, the possibility of provisional release is not excluded provided that the State from which extradition is requested takes any measures it considers necessary to prevent the escape of the person sought.

3. Such release shall not prevent the rearrest of the person concerned or his extradition if a request for extradition is received subsequently.

Article 27

Should the requested State consider that it requires supplementary information in order to ascertain whether the conditions stipulated in this Chapter has been met, it shall notify the requesting State accordingly and a date for the provision of such information shall be established.

Article 28

Should the requested State receive several requests for extradition from different States, either for the same offence or for different offences, it shall make its decision having regard to all the circumstances and, in particular, the possibility of subsequent extradition, the respective dates or when the requests were received, the relative seriousness of the offences and the place where the offences were committed.

CHAPTER II

PROCEDURES FOR JUDICIAL DELEGATION

Article 29

Request relating to judicial delegations shall contain the following information:

(a) The authority presenting the request;
(b) The subject of and reason for the request;
(c) An exact statement, to the extent possible, of the identity and nationality of the person concerned;
(d) A description of the offence in connection with which the request for a judicial delegation is being made, its legal designation, the penalty established for its commission, and as much information as possible on the circumstances so as to facilitate the proper functioning of the judicial delegation.

Article 30

1. The request for a judicial delegation shall be addressed by the Ministry of Justice of the requesting State to the Ministry of Justice of the requested State and shall be returned through the same channel.

2. In case of urgency, the request for a judicial delegation shall be addressed by the judicial authorities of the requesting State directly to the judicial authorities of the requested State, and a copy of the request shall be sent at the same time to the Ministry of Justice of the requested State. The request, accompanied by the documents relating to its implementation, shall be returned through the channel stipulated in the preceding paragraph.

3. The request for a judicial delegation may be sent by the judicial authorities directly to the competent authority in the requested State, and replies may be forwarded directly through this authority.

Article 31

Requests for judicial delegation and their accompanying documents must be signed and must bear the seal of the competent authority or be authenticated by it. Such documents shall be exempt from all formalities that may be required by the legislation of the requested State.

Article 32

Should an authority that receives a request for a judicial delegation not have the competence to deal with it, it shall automatically refer it to the competent authority in its State. In the event the request has been sent directly, it shall notify the requesting State in the same manner.

Article 33

Every refusal of a request for a judicial delegation must be accompanied by a statement of the grounds for such refusal.

CHAPTER III

MEASURES FOR THE PROTECTION OF WITNESSES AND EXPERTS

Article 34

If, in the estimation of a requesting State, the appearance of a witness or expert before its judicial authority is of particular importance, it shall indicate this fact in its request. The request or summons to appear shall indicate the approximate amount of the allowances and the travel and subsistence expenses and shall include an undertaking to pay them. The requested State shall invite the witness or expert to appear and shall inform the requesting State of the response.

Article 35

1. A witness or an expert who does not comply with a summons to appear shall not be subject to any penalty or coercive measure, not withstanding any contrary statement in the summons.

2. Where a witness or an expert travels to the territory of the requesting State of his own accord, he should be summoned to appear in accordance with the provisions of the domestic legislation of that State.

Article 36

1. A witness or an expert shall not be prosecuted, detained or subjected to any restrictions on his personal liberty in the territory of the requesting State in respect of any acts or convictions that preceded the person's departure from the requested State, regardless of his nationality, as long as

his appearance before the judicial authorities of that State is in response to a summons.

2. No witness or expert, regardless of his nationality, who appears before the judicial authorities of a requesting State in response to a summons may be prosecuted, detained or subjected to any restriction on his personal liberty in the territory of that State in respect of any acts or convictions not specified in the summons and that preceded the person's departure from the territory of the requested State.

3. The immunity stipulated in this article shall lapse if the witness or expert sought, being free to leave, remains in the territory of the requesting State for a period of 30 consecutive days after his presence is no longer required by the judicial authorities or, having left the territory of the requesting State, has voluntarily returned.

Article 37

1. The requesting State shall take all necessary measures to protect witnesses and experts from any publicity that might endanger them, their families or their property as a result of their provision of testimony or expertise and shall, in particular, guarantee confidentiality with respect to:

(a) The date, place and means of their arrival in the requesting state;
(b) Their place of residence, their movements and the places they frequent;
(c) Their testimony and the information they provide before the competent judicial authorities.

2. The requesting State shall undertake to provide the necessary protection for the security of witnesses and experts and of members of their families that is required by their situation, the circumstances of the case in connection with which they are sought and the types of risks that can be anticipated.

Article 38

1. Where a witness or expert whose appearance, is sought by a requesting State is in custody in the requested State, he may be temporarily transferred to the location of the hearing where he is requested to provide his testimony under conditions and at times to be determined by the requested State. Such transfer may be refused if:

(a) The witness or expert in custody objects;
(b) His presence is required for criminal proceedings in the territory of the requested State;
(c) His transfer would prolong the term of his detention;
(d) There are considerations militating against his transfer.

2. The witness or expert thus transferred shall continue to be held in custody in the territory of the requesting State until such time as he is returned to the requested State unless the latter State requests that he be released.

PART FOUR

FINAL PROVISIONS

Article 39

This Convention is subject to ratification, acceptance or approval by the signatory States, and instruments of ratification, acceptance or approval shall be deposited with the General Secretariat of the League of Arab States within 30 days of the date of such ratification, acceptance or approval. The General Secretariat shall notify member States of the deposit of each such instrument and of its date.

Article 40

1. This convention shall enter into force on the thirtieth day after the date as of which instruments of ratification, acceptance or approval have been deposited by seven Arab States.

2. This Convention shall enter into force for any other Arab State only after the instrument of ratification, acceptance or approval has been deposited and 30 days have elapsed from the date of that deposit.

Article 41

No Contracting State may make any reservation that explicitly or implicitly violates the provisions of this Convention or is incompatible with its objectives.

Article 42

A contracting State may denounce this Convention only by written request addressed to the Secretary-General of the League of Arab States.

Denunciation shall take effect six months from the date the request is addressed to the Secretary-General of the League of Arab States.

The provisions of this Convention shall remain in force in respect of requests submitted before this period expires.

DONE at Cairo, this twenty-second day of April 1998, in a single copy, which shall be deposited with the General Secretariat of the League of Arab States. A certified copy shall be kept at the General Secretariat of the

Council of Arab Ministers of the Interior, and certified copies shall be transmitted to each of the parties that are signatories to this Convention or that accede hereto.

IN WITNESS WHEREOF, the Arab Ministers of the Interior and Ministers of Justice have signed this Convention on behalf of their respective states.

D. SAARC REGIONAL CONVENTION ON THE SUPPRESSION OF TERRORISM

The South Asian Association For Regional Cooperation (SAARC)
South Asia Terrorism Porta, November 4, 1987

SAARC Regional Convention on the Suppression of Terrorism

The Member States of the South Asian Association For Regional Cooperation (SAARC)

MINDFUL of the principles of cooperation enshrined in the SAARC Charter;

RECALLING that at the Dhaka Summit on December 7-8, 1985, the Heads of State or Government of the member States of the SAARC recognized the seriousness of the problem of terrorism as it affects the security and stability of the region;

ALSO RECALLING the Bangalore Summit Declaration of 17 November 1986, in which the Heads of State or Government of SAARC agreed that cooperation among SAARC States was vital if terrorism was to be prevented and eliminated from the region; unequivocally condemned all acts, methods and practices of terrorism as criminal and deplored their impact on life and property, socio-economic development, political stability, regional and international peace and cooperation; and recognized the importance of the principles laid down in UN Resolution 2625 (XXV) which among others required that each state should refrain from organizing instigating, assisting or participating in acts of civil strife or terrorist acts in another state or acquiescing in organized activities within its territory directed towards the commission of such acts;

AWARE of the danger posed by the spread of terrorism and its harmful effect on peace, cooperation, friendship and good neighbourly relations and which could also jeopardize the sovereignty and territorial integrity of states;

HAVE resolved to take effective measures to ensure that perpetrators of terroristic acts do not escape prosecution and punishment by providing for their extradition or prosecution, and to this end,

HAVE agreed as follows:

Article 1

Subject to the overall requirements of the law of extradition, conduct constituting any of the following offencezs, according to the law of the Contracting State, shall be regarded as terroristic and for the purpose of extradition shall not be regarded as a political offence or as an offence connected with a political offence or as an offence inspired by political motives:

a. An offence within the scope of the Convention for the Suppression of Unlawful Seizure of Aircraft, signed at the Hague on December 16, 1970;
b. An offence within the scope of the Convention for the Suppression of Unlawful Acts against the Safety of Civil Aviation, signed at Montreal on September 23, 1971;
c. An offence within the scope of the Convention on the Prevention and Punishment of Crimes against Internationally Protected Persons, including Diplomatic Agents, signed at New York on December 14, 1973;
d. An offence within the scope of any Convention to which the SAARC member States concerned are parties and which obliges the parties to prosecute or grant extradition.
e. Murder, manslaughter, assault causing bodily harm, kidnapping, hostage-taking and offences relating to firearms, weapons, explosives and dangerous substances when used as a means to perpetrate indiscriminate violence involving death or serious bodily injury to persons or serious damage to property;
f. An attempt or conspiracy to commit an offence described in sub-paragraphs (a) to (e), aiding, abetting or counselling the commission of such an offence or participating as an accomplice in the offences so described.

Article 2

For the purpose of extradition between SAARC member States, any two or more Contracting States may, by agreement, decide to include any other serious offence involving violence, which shall not be regarded as a political offence or an offence connected with a political offence or an offence inspired by political motives.

Article 3

1. The provisions of all extradition treaties and arrangements applicable between Contracting States are hereby amended as between Contracting States to the extent that they are incompatible with the Convention.

2. For the purpose of this Convention and to the extent that any offence referred to in Article 1 or agreed to in terms of Article 2 is not listed as an extraditable offence in any extradition treaty existing between Contracting States, it shall be deemed to be included as such therein.

3. Contracting States undertake to include these offences as extraditable offences in any future extradition treaty to be concluded between them.

4. If a Contracting State which makes extradition conditional on the existence of a treaty receives a request for extradition from another Contracting State with which it has no extradition treaty, the requested State may, at its option, consider this Convention as the basis for extradition in respect of the offences set forth in Article 1 or agreed to in terms of Article 2. Extradition shall be subject to the law of the requested State.

5. Contracting States which do not make extradition conditional on the existence of a treaty, shall recognize the offences set forth in Article 1 or agreed to in terms of Article 2 as extraditable offences between themselves, subject to the law of the requested State.

Article 4

A Contracting State in whose territory a person suspected of having committed an offence referred to in Article 1 or agreed to in terms of Article 2 is found and which has received a request for extradition from another Contracting State, shall, if it does not extradite that person, submit the case without exception and without delay, to its competent authorities, so that prosecution may be considered. These authorities shall take their decisions in the same manner as in the case of any offence of a serious under the law of that State.

Article 5

For the purpose of Article 4, each Contracting State may take such measures as it deems appropriate, consistent with its national laws, subject to reciprocity, to exercise its jurisdiction in the case of an offence under Article 1 or agreed to in terms of Article 2.

Article 6

A Contracting State in whose territory an alleged offender is found, shall upon receiving a request for extradition from another Contracting State, take appropriate measures, subject to its national laws, so as to ensure his presence for purposes of extradition or prosecution. Such measures shall immediately be notified to the requesting State.

Article 7

Contracting States shall not be obliged to extradite, if it appears to the requested State that by reason of the trivial nature of the case or by reason of the request for the surrender or return of a fugitive offender not being made in good faith or in the interests of justice or for any other reason it is unjust or inexpedient to surrender or return the fugitive offender.

Article 8

1. Contracting States shall, subject to their national laws, afford one another the greatest measure of mutual assistance in connection with proceedings brought in respect of the offences referred to in Article 1 or agreed to in terms of Article 2, including the supply of all evidence at their disposal necessary for the proceedings.

2. Contracting States shall cooperate among themselves, to the extent permitted by their national laws, through consultations between appropriate agencies, exchange of information, intelligence and expertise and such other cooperative measures as may be appropriate, with a view to preventing terroristic activities through precautionary measures.

Article 9

1. The Convention shall be open for signature by the member States of SAARC at the SAARC Secretariat in Kathmandu.

2. It shall be subject to ratification. Instruments of Ratification shall be deposited with the Secretary-General of SAARC.

Article 10

The Convention shall enter into force on the fifteenth day following the date of the deposit of the seventh Instrument of Ratification with the Secretary-General of SAARC.

Article 11

The Secretary-General of SAARC shall be depository of this Convention and shall notify member States of signatures to this Convention and all deposits of Instruments of Ratification. The Secretary-General shall transit certified copies of such Instruments to each member State. The Secretary-General shall also inform member States of the date on which this Convention will have entered into force in accordance with Article 10.

IN WITNESS WHEREOF the undersigned, being duly authorized thereto by their respective Governments, have signed this Convention.

DONE at Kathmandu on this Fourth Day of November One Thousand Nine Hundred and Eighty Seven, in eight originals, in the English Language, all texts being equally authentic.

HUMAYUN RASHEED CHOUDHURY
Minister of Foreign Affairs People's Republic of Bangladesh

K. NATWAR SINGH
Minister of State for External Affairs Republic of India

SHAILENDRA KUMAR
Minister for Foreign Affairs and Land Reforms
His Majesty's Government of Nepal

DAWA TSERING
Minister of Foreign Affairs
Kingdom of Bhutan

FATHULLA JAMEEL
Minister of Foreign Affairs
Republic of Maldives

UPADHYAYA ZAIN NOORANI
Minister of State for Foreign Affairs
Islamic Republic of Pakistan

A.C. SHAHUL HAMEED
Minister of Foreign Affairs
Democratic Socialist Republic of Sri Lanka

Source: http://www.ciaonet.org/cbr/cbr00/video/cbr_ctd/cbr_ctd_36.html

International Conventions

E. CONVENTION ON OFFENCES AND CERTAIN OTHER ACTS COMMITTED ON BOARD AIRCRAFT

Signed at Tokyo on 14 September 1963 (Tokyo Convention)

THE STATES PARTIES to this Convention, have agreed as follows:

CHAPTER I

SCOPE OF THE CONVENTION

Article 1

1. This Convention shall apply in respect of:

a. offences against penal law;
b. acts which, whether or not they are offences, may or do jeopardize the safety of the aircraft or of persons or property therein or which jeopardize good order and discipline on board.

2. Except as provided in Chapter III, this Convention shall apply in respect of offences committed or acts done by a person on board any aircraft registered in a Contracting State, while that aircraft is in flight or on the surface of the high seas or of any other area outside the territory of any State.

3. For the purposes of this Convention, an aircraft is considered to be in flight from the moment when power is applied for the purpose of take-off until the moment when the landing run ends.

4. This Convention shall not apply to aircraft used in military, customs or police services.

Article 2

Without prejudice to the provisions of Article 4 and except when the safety of the aircraft or of persons or property on board so requires, no provision of this Convention shall be interpreted as authorizing or requiring any action in respect of offences against penal laws of a political nature or those based on racial or religious discrimination.

CHAPTER II

JURISDICTION

Article 3

1. The State of registration of the aircraft is competent to exercise jurisdiction over offences and acts committed on board.

2. Each Contracting State shall take such measures as may be necessary to establish its jurisdiction as the State of registration over offences committed on board aircraft registered in such State.

3. This Convention does not exclude any criminal jurisdiction exercised in accordance with national law.

Article 4

A Contracting State which is not the State of registration may not interfere with an aircraft in flight in order to exercise its criminal jurisdiction over an offence committed on board except in the following cases:

a. the offence has effect on the territory of such State;
b. the offence has been committed by or against a national or permanent resident of such State;
c. the offence is against the security of such State;
d. the offence consists of a breach of any rules or regulations relating to the flight or manoeuvre of aircraft in force in such State;
e. the exercise of jurisdiction is necessary to ensure the observance of any obligation of such State under a multilateral international agreement.

CHAPTER III

POWERS OF THE AIRCRAFT COMMANDER

Article 5

1. The provisions of this Chapter shall not apply to offences and acts committed or about to be committed by a person on board an aircraft in

flight in the airspace of the State of registration or over the high seas or any other area outside the territory of any State unless the last point of take-off or the next point of intended landing is situated in a State other than that of registration, or the aircraft subsequently flies in the airspace of a State other than that of registration with such person still on board.

2. Notwithstanding the provisions of Article 1, paragraph 3, an aircraft shall for the purposes of this Chapter, be considered to be in flight at any time from the moment when all its external doors are closed following embarkation until the moment when any such door is opened for disembarkation. In the case of a forced landing, the provisions of this Chapter shall continue to apply with respect to offences and acts committed on board until competent authorities of a State take over the responsibility for the aircraft and for the persons and property on board.

Article 6

1. The aircraft commander may, when he has reasonable grounds to believe that a person has committed, or is about to commit, on board the aircraft, an offence or act contemplated in Article 1, paragraph 1, impose upon such person reasonable measures including restraint which are necessary:

a. to protect the safety of the aircraft, or of persons or property therein; or
b. to maintain good order and discipline on board; or
c. to enable him to deliver such person to competent authorities or to disembark him in accordance with the provisions of this Chapter.

2. The aircraft commander may require or authorize the assistance of other crew members and may request or authorize, but not require, the assistance of passengers to restrain any person whom he is entitled to restrain. Any crew member or passenger may also take reasonable preventive measures without such authorization when he has reasonable grounds to believe that such action is immediately necessary to protect the safety of the aircraft, or of persons or property therein.

Article 7

1. Measures of restraint imposed upon a person in accordance with Article 6 shall not be continued beyond any point at which the aircraft lands unless:

a. such point is in the territory of a non-Contracting State and its authorities refuse to permit disembarkation of that person or those measures have been imposed in accordance with Article 6, paragraph 1(c) in order to enable his delivery to competent authorities;

b. the aircraft makes a forced landing and the aircraft commander is unable to deliver that person to competent authorities; or

c. that person agrees to onward carriage under restraint.

2. The aircraft commander shall as soon as practicable, and if possible before landing in the territory of a State with a person on board who has been placed under restraint in accordance with the provisions of Article 6, notify the authorities of such State of the fact that a person on board is under restraint and of the reasons for such restraint.

Article 8

1. The aircraft commander may, in so far as it is necessary for the purpose of subparagraph (a) or (b) or paragraph 1 of Article 6, disembark in the territory of any State in which the aircraft lands any person who he has reasonable grounds to believe has committed, or is about to commit, on board the aircraft an act contemplated in Article 1, paragraph 1(b).

2. The aircraft commander shall report to the authorities of the State in which he disembarks any person pursuant to this Article, the fact of, and the reasons for, such disembarkation.

Article 9

1. The aircraft commander may deliver to the competent authorities of any Contracting State in the territory of which the aircraft lands any person who he has reasonable grounds to believe has committed on board the aircraft an act which, in his opinion, is a serious offence according to the penal law of the State of registration of the aircraft.

2. The aircraft commander shall as soon as practicable and if possible before landing in the territory of a Contracting State with a person on board whom the aircraft commander intends to deliver in accordance with the preceding paragraph, notify the authorities of such State of his intention to deliver such person and the reasons therefor.

3. The aircraft commander shall furnish the authorities to whom any suspected offender is delivered in accordance with the provisions of this Article with evidence and information which, under the law of the State of registration of the aircraft, are lawfully in his possession.

Article 10

For actions taken in accordance with this Convention, neither the aircraft commander, any other member of the crew, any passenger, the owner or operator of the aircraft, nor the person on whose behalf the flight was performed shall be held responsible in any proceeding on account of the treatment undergone by the person against whom the actions were taken.

CHAPTER IV

UNLAWFUL SEIZURE OF AIRCRAFT

Article 11

1. When a person on board has unlawfully committed by force or threat thereof an act of interference, seizure, or other wrongful exercise of control of an aircraft in flight or when such an act is about to be committed, Contracting States shall take all appropriate measures to restore control of the aircraft to its lawful commander or to preserve his control of the aircraft.

2. In the cases contemplated in the preceding paragraph, the Contracting State in which the aircraft lands shall permit its passengers and crew to continue their journey as soon as practicable, and shall return the aircraft and its cargo to the persons lawfully entitled to possession.

CHAPTER V

POWERS AND DUTIES OF STATES

Article 12

Any Contracting State shall allow the commander of an aircraft registered in another Contracting State to disembark any person pursuant to Article 8, paragraph 1.

Article 13

1. Any Contracting State shall take delivery of any person whom the aircraft commander delivers pursuant to Article 9, paragraph 1.

2. Upon being satisfied that the circumstances so warrant, any Contracting State shall take custody or other measures to ensure the presence of any person suspected of an act contemplated in Article 11, paragraph 1 and of

any person of whom it has taken delivery. The custody and other measures shall be as provided in the law of that State but may only be continued for such time as is reasonably necessary to enable any criminal or extradition proceedings to be instituted.

3. Any person in custody pursuant to the previous paragraph shall be assisted in communicating immediately with the nearest appropriate representative of the State of which he is a national.

4. Any Contracting State, to which a person is delivered pursuant to Article 9, paragraph 1, or in whose territory an aircraft lands following the commission of an act contemplated in Article 11, paragraph 1, shall immediately make a preliminary enquiry into the facts.

5. When a State, pursuant to this Article, has taken a person into custody, it shall immediately notify the State of registration of the aircraft and the State of nationality of the detained person and, if it considers it advisable, any other interested State of the fact that such person is in custody and of the circumstances which warrant his detention. The State which makes the preliminary enquiry contemplated in paragraph 4 of this Article shall promptly report its findings to the said States and shall indicate whether it intends to exercise jurisdiction.

Article 14

1. When any person has been disembarked in accordance with Article 8, paragraph 1, or delivered in accordance with Article 9, paragraph 1, or has disembarked after committing an act contemplated in Article 11, paragraph 1, and when such person cannot or does not desire to continue his journey and the State of landing refuses to admit him, that State may, if the person in question is not a national or permanent resident of that State, return him to the territory of the State of which he is a national or permanent resident or to the territory of the State in which he began his journey by air.

2. Neither disembarkation, nor delivery, not the taking of custody or other measures contemplated in Article 13, paragraph 2, nor return of the person concerned, shall be considered as admission to the territory of the Contracting State concerned for the purpose of its law relating to entry or admission of persons and nothing in this Convention shall affect the law of a Contracting State relating to the expulsion of persons from its territory.

Article 15

1. Without prejudice to Article 14, any person who has been disembarked in accordance with Article 8, paragraph 1, or delivered in accordance with

Article 9, paragraph 1, or has disembarked after committing an act contemplated in Article 11, paragraph 1, and who desires to continue his journey shall be at liberty as soon as practicable to proceed to any destination of his choice unless his presence is required by the law of the State of landing for the purpose of extradition or criminal proceedings.

2. Without prejudice to its law as to entry and admission to, and extradition and expulsion from its territory, a Contracting State in whose territory a person has been disembarked in accordance with Article 8, paragraph 1, or delivered in accordance with Article 9, paragraph 1 or has disembarked and is suspected of having committed an act contemplated in Article 11, paragraph 1, shall accord to such person treatment which is no less favourable for his protection and security than that accorded to nationals of such Contracting State in like circumstances.

CHAPTER VI

OTHER PROVISIONS

Article 16

1. Offences committed on aircraft registered in a Contracting State shall be treated, for the purpose of extradition, as if they had been committed not only in the place in which they have occurred but also in the territory of the State of registration of the aircraft.

2. Without prejudice to the provisions of the preceding paragraph, nothing in this Convention shall be deemed to create an obligation to grant extradition.

Article 17

In taking any measures for investigation or arrest or otherwise exercising jurisdiction in connection with any offence committed on board an aircraft the Contracting States shall pay due regard to the safety and other interests of air navigation and shall so act as to avoid unnecessary delay of the aircraft, passengers, crew or cargo.

Article 18

If Contracting States establish joint air transport operating organizations or international operating agencies, which operate aircraft not registered in any one State those States shall, according to the circumstances of the case, designate the State among them which, for the purposes of this Convention, shall be considered as the State of registration and shall give notice thereof to the International Civil Aviation Organization which shall communicate the notice to all States Parties to this Convention.

CHAPTER VII

FINAL CLAUSES

Article 19

Until the date on which this Convention comes into force in accordance with the provisions of Article 21, it shall remain open for signature on behalf of any State which at that date is a Member of the United Nations or of any of the Specialized Agencies.

Article 20

1. This Convention shall be subject to ratification by the signatory States in accordance with their constitutional procedures.

2. The instruments of ratification shall be deposited with the International Civil Aviation Organization.

Article 21

1. As soon as twelve of the signatory States have deposited their instruments of ratification of this Convention, it shall come into force between them on the ninetieth day after the date of the deposit of the twelfth instrument of ratification. It shall come into force for each State ratifying thereafter on the ninetieth day after the deposit of its instrument of ratification.

2. As soon as this Convention comes into force, it shall be registered with the Secretary-General of the United Nations by the International Civil Aviation Organization.

Article 22

1. This Convention shall, after it has come into force, be open for accession by any State Member of the United Nations or of any of the Specialized Agencies.

2. The accession of a State shall be effected by the deposit of an instrument of accession with the International Civil Aviation Organization and shall take effect on the ninetieth day after the date of such deposit.

Article 23

1. Any Contracting State may denounce this Convention by notification addressed to the International Civil Aviation Organization.

2. Denunciation shall take effect six months after the date of receipt by the International Civil Aviation Organization of the notification of denunciation.

Article 24

1. Any dispute between two or more Contracting States concerning the interpretation or application of this Convention, which cannot be settled through negotiation, shall, at the request of one of them, be submitted to arbitration. If within six months from the date of the request for arbitration the Parties are unable to agree on the organization of the arbitration, any one of those Parties may refer the dispute to the International Court of Justice by request in conformity with the Statute of the Court.

2. Each State may at the time of signature or ratification of this Convention or accession thereto, declare that it does not consider itself bound by the preceding paragraph. The other Contracting States shall not be bound by the preceding paragraph with respect to any Contracting State having made such a reservation.

3. Any Contracting State having made a reservation in accordance with the preceding paragraph may at any time withdraw this reservation by notification to the International Civil Aviation Organization.

Article 25

Except as provided in Article 24 no reservation may be made to this Convention.

Article 26

The International Civil Aviation Organization shall give notice to all States Members of the United Nations or of any of the Specialized Agencies:

a. of any signature of this Convention and the date thereof;
b. of the deposit of any instrument of ratification or accession and the date thereof;
c. of the date on which this Convention comes into force in accordance with Article 21, paragraph 1;

d. of the receipt of any notification of denunciation and the date thereof; and
e. of the receipt of any declaration or notification made under Article 24 and the date thereof.

IN WITNESS WHEREOF the undersigned Plenipotentiaries, having been duly authorized, have signed this Convention.

DONE at Tokyo on the fourteenth day of September One Thousand Nine Hundred and Sixty-three in three authentic texts drawn up in the English, French and Spanish languages.

This Convention shall be deposited with the International Civil Aviation Organization with which, in accordance with Article 19, it shall remain open for signature and the said Organization shall send certified copies thereof to all States Members of the United Nations or of any Specialized Agency.

Disclaimer

The present version of the Conventions and Protocols might differ slightly from the consolidated official English versions which were—by end of November 2000—not available to TPB in electronic form. Please contact the Codification Division of the UN Office of Legal Affairs (United Nations, Room S-3450 A, New York, N.Y. 10017, USA) for the official versions in English and other official UN languages.

F. CONVENTION FOR THE SUPPRESSION OF UNLAWFUL SEIZURE OF AIRCRAFT

16 December 1970 (The Hague Convention 1970)

THE STATES PARTIES to this Convention,

CONSIDERING that unlawful acts of seizure or exercise of control of aircraft in flight jeopardize the safety of persons and property, seriously affect the operation of air services, and undermine the confidence of the peoples of the world in the safety of civil aviation;

CONSIDERING that the occurrence of such acts is a matter of grave concern;

CONSIDERING that, for the purpose of deterring such acts, there is an urgent need to provide appropriate measures for punishment of offenders;

HAVE agreed as follows:

Article 1

Any person who on board an aircraft in flight:

a. unlawfully, by force or threat thereof, or by any other form of intimidation, seizes, or exercises control of, that aircraft, or attempts to perform any such act, or
b. is an accomplice of a person who performs or attempts to perform any such act commits an offence (hereinafter referred to as "the offence").

Article 2

Each Contracting State undertakes to make the offence punishable by severe penalties.

Article 3

1. For the purposes of this Convention, an aircraft is considered to be in flight at any time from the moment when all its external doors are closed following embarkation until the moment when any such door is opened for disembarkation. In the case of a forced landing, the flight shall be deemed

to continue until the competent authorities take over the responsibility for the aircraft and for persons and property on board.

2. This Convention shall not apply to aircraft used in military, customs or police services.

3. This Convention shall apply only if the place of take-off or the place of actual landing of the aircraft on board which the offence is committed is situated outside the territory of the State of registration of that aircraft; it shall be immaterial whether the aircraft is engaged in an international or domestic flight.

4. In the cases mentioned in Article 5, this Convention shall not apply if the place of take-off and the place of actual landing of the aircraft on board which the offence is committed are situated within the territory of the same State where that State is one of those referred to in that Article.

5. Notwithstanding paragraphs 3 and 4 of this Article, Articles 6, 7, 8, and 10 shall apply whatever the place of take-off or the place of actual landing of the aircraft, if the offender or the alleged offender is found in the territory of a State other than the State of registration of that aircraft.

Article 4

1. Each Contracting State shall take such measures as may be necessary to establish its jurisdiction over the offence and any other act of violence against passengers or crew committed by the alleged offender in connection with the offence, in the following cases:

a. when the offence is committed on board an aircraft registered in that State;
b. when the aircraft on board which the offence is committed lands in its territory with the alleged offender still on board;
c. when the offence is committed on board an aircraft leased without crew to a lessee who has his principal place of business or, if the lessee has no such place of business, his permanent residence, in that State.

2. Each Contracting State shall likewise take such measures as may be necessary to establish its jurisdiction over the offence in the case where the alleged offender is present in its territory and it does not extradite him pursuant to Article 8 to any of the States mentioned in paragraph 1 of this Article.

3. This Convention does not exclude any criminal jurisdiction exercised in accordance with national law.

Article 5

The Contracting States which establish joint air transport operating organizations or international operating agencies, which operate aircraft which are subject to joint or international registration shall, by appropriate means, designate for each aircraft the State among them which shall exercise the jurisdiction and have the attributes of the State of registration for the purpose of this Convention and shall give notice thereof to the International Civil Aviation Organization which shall communicate the notice to all States Parties to this Convention.

Article 6

1. Upon being satisfied that the circumstances so warrant, any Contracting State in the territory of which the offender or the alleged offender is present, shall take him into custody or take other measures to ensure his presence. The custody and other measures shall be as provided in the law of that State but may only be continued for such time as is necessary to enable any criminal or extradition proceedings to be instituted.

2. Such State shall immediately make a preliminary enquiry into the facts.

3. Any person in custody pursuant to paragraph 1 of this Article shall be assisted in communicating immediately with the nearest appropriate representative of the State of which he is a national.

4. When a State, pursuant to this Article, has taken a person into custody, it shall immediately notify the State of registration of the aircraft, the State mentioned in Article 4, paragraph 1(c), the State of nationality of the detained person and, if it considers it advisable, any other interested States of the fact that such person is in custody and of the circumstances which warrant his detention. The State which makes the preliminary enquiry contemplated in paragraph 2 of this Article shall promptly report its findings to the said States and shall indicate whether it intends to exercise jurisdiction.

Article 7

The Contracting State in the territory of which the alleged offender is found shall, if it does not extradite him, be obliged, without exception whatsoever and whether or not the offence was committed in its territory, to submit the case to its competent authorities for the purpose of prosecution. Those authorities shall take their decision in the same manner as in the case of any ordinary offence of a serious nature under the law of that State.

Article 8

1. The offence shall be deemed to be included as an extraditable offence in any extradition treaty existing between Contracting States. Contracting States undertake to include the offence as an extraditable offence in every extradition treaty to be concluded between them.

2. If a Contracting State which makes extradition conditional on the existence of a treaty receives a request for extradition from another Contracting State with which it has no extradition treaty, it may at its option consider this Convention as the legal basis for extradition in respect of the offence. Extradition shall be subject to the other conditions provided by the law of the requested State.

3. Contracting States which do not make extradition conditional on the existence of a treaty shall recognize the offence as an extraditable offence between themselves subject to the conditions provided by the law of the requested State.

4. The offence shall be treated, for the purpose of extradition between Contracting States, as if it had been committed not only in the place in which it occurred but also in the territories of the States required to establish their jurisdiction in accordance with Article 4, paragraph 1.

Article 9

1. When any of the acts mentioned in Article 1(a) has occurred or is about to occur, Contracting States shall take all appropriate measures to restore control of the aircraft to its lawful commander or to preserve his controi of the aircraft.

2. In the cases contemplated by the preceding paragraph, any Contracting State in which the aircraft or its passengers or crew are present shall facilitate the continuation of the journey of the passengers and crew as soon as practicable, and shall without delay return the aircraft and its cargo to the persons lawfully entitled to possession.

Article 10

1. Contracting States shall afford one another the greatest measure of assistance in connection with criminal proceedings brought in respect of the offence and other acts mentioned in Article 4. The law of the State requested shall apply in all cases.

2. The provisions of paragraph 1 of this Article shall not affect obligations under any other treaty, bilateral or multilateral, which governs or will govern, in whole or in part, mutual assistance in criminal matters.

Article 11

Each Contracting State shall in accordance with its national law report to the Council of the International Civil Aviation Organization as promptly as possible any relevant information in its possession concerning:

a. the circumstances of the offence;
b. the action taken pursuant to Article 9;
c. the measures taken in relation to the offender or the alleged offender, and, in particular, the results of any extradition proceedings or other legal proceedings.

Article 12

1. Any dispute between two or more Contracting States concerning the interpretation or application of this Convention which cannot be settled through negotiation, shall, at the request of one of them, be submitted to arbitration. If within six months from the date of the request for arbitration the Parties are unable to agree on the organization of the arbitration, any one of those Parties may refer the dispute to the International Court of Justice by request in conformity with the Statute of the Court.

2. Each State may at the time of signature or ratification of this Convention or accession thereto, declare that it does not consider itself bound by the preceding paragraph. The other Contracting States shall not be bound by the preceding paragraph with respect to any Contracting State having made such a reservation.

3. Any Contracting State having made a reservation in accordance with the preceding paragraph may at any time withdraw this reservation by notification to the Depositary Governments.

Article 13

1. This Convention shall be open for signature at The Hague on 16 December 1970, by States participating in the International Conference on Air Law held at The Hague from 1 to 16 December 1970 (hereinafter referred to as The Hague Conference). After 31 December 1970, the Convention shall be open to all States for signature in Moscow, London and Washington. Any State which does not sign this Convention before its entry into force in accordance with paragraph 3 of this Article may accede to it at any time.

2. This Convention shall be subject to ratification by the signatory States. Instruments of ratification and instruments of accession shall be

deposited with the Governments of the Union of Soviet Socialist Republics, the United Kingdom of Great Britain and Northern Ireland, and the United States of America, which are hereby designated the Depositary Governments.

3. This Convention shall enter into force thirty days following the date of the deposit of instruments of ratification by ten States signatory to this Convention which participated in The Hague Conference.

4. For other States, this Convention shall enter into force on the date of entry into force of this Convention in accordance with paragraph 3 of this Article, or thirty days following the date of deposit of their instruments of ratification or accession, whichever is later.

5. The Depositary Governments shall promptly inform all signatory and acceding States of the date of each signature, the date of deposit of each instrument of ratification or accession, the date of entry into force of this Convention, and other notices.

6. As soon as this Convention comes into force, it shall be registered by the Depositary Governments pursuant to Article 102 of the Charter of the United Nations and pursuant to Article 83 of the Convention on International Civil Aviation (Chicago, 1944).

Article 14

1. Any Contracting State may denounce this Convention by written notification to the Depositary Governments.

2. Denunciation shall take effect six months following the date on which notification is received by the Depositary Governments.

IN WITNESS WHEREOF the undersigned Plenipotentiaries, being duly authorised thereto by their Governments, have signed this Convention.

DONE at The Hague, this sixteenth day of December, one thousand nine hundred and seventy, in three originals, each being drawn up in four authentic texts in the English, French, Russian and Spanish languages.

Disclaimer

The present version of the Conventions and Protocols might differ slightly from the consolidated official English versions which were—by end of November 2000—not available to TPB in electronic form. Please contact the Codification Division of the UN Office of Legal Affairs (United Nations, Room S-3450 A, New York, N.Y. 10017, USA) for the official versions in English and other official UN languages.

G. CONVENTION FOR THE SUPPRESSION OF UNLAWFUL ACTS AGAINST THE SAFETY OF CIVIL AVIATION

UNTS No. 14118, vol. 974, pp. 178-84
(Montreal Convention 1971)

ENTRY INTO FORCE: 26 January 1973

THE STATES PARTIES to the Convention

CONSIDERING that unlawful acts against the safety of civil aviation jeopardize the safety of persons and property, seriously affect the operation of air services, and undermine the confidence of the peoples of the world in the safety of civil aviation;

CONSIDERING that the occurrence of such acts is a matter of grave concern;

CONSIDERING that for the purpose of deterring such acts, there is an urgent need to provide appropriate measures for punishment of offenders;

HAVE agreed as follows:

Article 1

1. Any person commits an offence if he unlawfully and intentionally:

   a. performs an act of violence against a person on board an aircraft in flight if that act is likely to endanger the safety of that aircraft; or
   b. destroys an aircraft in service or causes damage to such an aircraft which renders it incapable of flight or which is likely to endanger its safety in flight; or
   c. places or causes to be placed on an aircraft in service, by any means whatsoever, a device or substance which is likely to destroy that aircraft, or to cause damage to it which renders it incapable of flight, or to cause damage to it which is likely to endanger its safety in flight; or
   d. destroys or damages air navigation facilities or interferes with their operation, if any such act is likely to endanger the safety of aircraft in flight; or

e. communicates information which he knows to be false, thereby endangering the safety of an aircraft in flight.

2. Any person also commits an offence if he:

a. attempts to commit any of the offences mentioned in paragraph 1 of this Article; or
b. is an accomplice of a person who commits or attempts to commit any such offence.

Article 2

For the purposes of this Convention:

a. an aircraft is considered to be in flight at any time from the moment when all its external doors are closed following embarkation until the moment when any such door is opened for disembarkation; in the case of a forced landing, the flight shall be deemed to continue until the competent authorities take over the responsibility for the aircraft and for persons and property on board;
b. an aircraft is considered to be in service from the beginning of the preflight preparation of the aircraft by ground personnel or by the crew for a specific flight until twenty-four hours after any landing; the period of service shall, in any event, extend for the entire period during which the aircraft is in flight as defined in paragraph (a) of this Article.

Article 3

Each Contracting State undertakes to make the offences mentioned in Article 1 punishable by severe penalties.

Article 4

1. This Convention shall not apply to aircraft used in military, customs or police services.

2. In the cases contemplated in subparagraphs (a), (b), (c) and (e) of paragraph 1 of Article 1, this Convention shall apply, irrespective of whether the aircraft is engaged in an international or domestic flight, only if:

a. the place of take-off or landing, actual or intended, of the aircraft is situated outside the territory of the State of registration of that aircraft; or

b. the offence is committed in the territory of a State other than the State of registration of the aircraft.

3. Notwithstanding paragraph 2 of this Article, in the cases contemplated in subparagraphs (a), (b), (c) and (e) of paragraph 1 of Article 1, this Convention shall also apply if the offender or the alleged offender is found in the territory of a State other than the State of registration of the aircraft.

4. With respect to the States mentioned in Article 9 and in the cases mentioned in subparagraphs (a), (b), (c) and (e) of paragraph 1 of Article 1, this Convention shall not apply if the places referred to in subparagraph (a) of paragraph 2 of this Article are situated within the territory of the same State where that State is one of those referred to in Article 9, unless the offence is committed or the offender or alleged offender is found in the territory of a State other than that State.

5. In the cases contemplated in subparagraph (d) of paragraph 1 of Article 1, this Convention shall apply only if the air navigation facilities are used in international air navigation.

6. The provisions of paragraphs 2, 3, 4 and 5 of this Article shall also apply in the cases contemplated in paragraph 2 of Article 1.

Article 5

1. Each Contracting State shall take such measures as may be necessary to establish its jurisdiction over the offences in the following cases:

a. when the offence is committed in the territory of that State;
b. when the offence is committed against or on board an aircraft registered in that State;
c. when the aircraft on board which the offence is committed lands in its territory with the alleged offender still on board;
d. when the offence is committed against or on board an aircraft leased without crew to a lessee who has his principal place of business or, if the lessee has no such place of business, his permanent residence, in that State.

2. Each Contracting State shall likewise take such measures as may be necessary to establish its jurisdiction over the offences mentioned in Article 1, paragraph 1 (a), (b) and (c), and in Article 1, paragraph 2, in so far as that paragraph relates to those offences, in the case where the alleged offender is present in its territory and it does not extradite him pursuant to Article 8 to any of the States mentioned in paragraph 1 of this Article.

3. This Convention does not exclude any criminal jurisdiction exercised in accordance with national law.

Article 6

1. Upon being satisfied that the circumstances so warrant, any Contracting State in the territory of which the offender or the alleged offender is present, shall take him into custody or take other measures to ensure his presence. The custody and other measures shall be as provided in the law of that State but may only be continued for such time as is necessary to enable any criminal or extradition proceedings to be instituted.

2. Such State shall immediately make a preliminary enquiry into the facts.

3. Any person in custody pursuant to paragraph 1 of this Article shall be assisted in communicating immediately with the nearest appropriate representative of the State of which he is a national.

4. When a State, pursuant to this Article, has taken a person into custody, it shall immediately notify the States mentioned in Article 5, paragraph 1, the State of nationality of the detained person and, if it considers it advisable, any other interested State of the fact that such person is in custody and of the circumstances which warrant his detention. The State which makes the preliminary enquiry contemplated in paragraph 2 of this Article shall promptly report its findings to the said States and shall indicate whether it intends to exercise jurisdiction.

Article 7

The Contracting State in the territory of which the alleged offender is found shall, if it does not extradite him, be obliged, without exception whatsoever and whether or not the offence was committed in its territory, to submit the case to its competent authorities for the purpose of prosecution. Those authorities shall take their decision in the same manner as in the case of any ordinary offence of a serious nature under the law of that State.

Article 8

1. The offences shall be deemed to be included as extraditable offences in any extradition treaty existing between Contracting States. Contracting States undertake to include the offences as extraditable offences in every etradition treaty to be concluded between them.

2. If a Contracting State which makes extradition conditional on the

existence of a treaty receives a request for extradition from another Contracting State with which it has no extradition treaty, it may at its option consider this Convention as the legal basis for extradition in respect of the offences. Extradition shall be subject to the other conditions provided by the law of the requested State.

3. Contracting States which do not make extradition conditional on the existence of a treaty shall recognize the offences as extraditable offences between themselves subject to the conditions provided by the law of the requested State.

4. Each of the offences shall be treated, for the purpose of extradition between Contracting States, as if it had been committed not only in the place in which it occurred but also in the territories of the States required to establish their jurisdiction in accordance with Article 5, paragraph 1 (b), (c) and (d).

Article 9

The Contracting States which establish joint air transport operating organizations or international operating agencies, which operate aircraft which are subject to joint or international registration shall, by appropriate means, designate for each aircraft the State among them which shall exercise the jurisdiction and have the attributes of the State of registration for the purpose of this Convention and shall give notice thereof to the International Civil Aviation Organization which shall communicate the notice to all States Parties to this Convention.

Article 10

1. Contracting States shall, in accordance with international and national law, endeavour to take all practicable measure for the purpose of preventing the offences mentioned in Article 1.

2. When, due to the commission of one of the offences mentioned in Article 1, a flight has been delayed or interrupted, any Contracting State in whose territory the aircraft or passengers or crew are present shall facilitate the continuation of the journey of the passengers and crew as soon as practicable, and shall without delay return the aircraft and its cargo to the persons lawfully entitled to possession.

Article 11

1. Contracting States shall afford one another the greatest measure of assistance in connection with criminal proceedings brought in respect of

the offences. The law of the State requested shall apply in all cases.

2. The provisions of paragraph 1 of this Article shall not affect obligations under any other treaty, bilateral or multilateral, which governs or will govern, in whole or in part, mutual assistance in criminal matters.

Article 12

Any Contracting State having reason to believe that one of the offences mentioned in Article 1 will be committed shall, in accordance with its national law, furnish any relevant information in its possession to those States which it believes would be the States mentioned in Article 5, paragraph 1.

Article 13

Each Contracting State shall in accordance with its national law report to the Council of the International Civil Aviation Organization as promptly as possible any relevant information in its possession concerning:

a. the circumstances of the offence;
b. the action taken pursuant to Article 10, paragraph 2;
c. the measures taken in relation to the offender or the alleged offender and, in particular, the results of any extradition proceedings or other legal proceedings.

Article 14

1. Any dispute between two or more Contracting States concerning the interpretation or application of this Convention which cannot be settled through negotiation, shall, at the request of one of them, be submitted to arbitration. If within six months from the date of the request for arbitration the Parties are unable to agree on the organization of the arbitration, any one of those Parties may refer the dispute to the International Court of Justice by request in conformity with the Statute of the Court.

2. Each State may at the time of signature or ratification of this Convention or accession thereto, declare that it does not consider itself bound by the preceding paragraph. The other Contracting States shall not be bound by the preceding paragraph with respect to any Contracting State having made such a reservation.

3. Any Contracting State having made a reservation in accordance with the preceding paragraph may at any time withdraw this reservation by notification to the Depositary Governments.

Article 15

1. This Convention shall be open for signature at Montreal on 23 September 1971, by States participating in the International Conference on Air Law held at Montreal from 8 to 23 September 1971 (hereinafter referred to as the Montreal Conference). After 10 October 1971, the Convention shall be open to all States for signature in Moscow, London and Washington. Any State which does not sign this Convention before its entry into force in accordance with paragraph 3 of this Article may accede to it at any time.

2. This Convention shall be subject to ratification by the signatory States. Instruments of ratification and instruments of accession shall be deposited with the Governments of the Union of Soviet Socialist Republics, the United Kingdom of Great Britain and Northern Ireland, and the United States of America, which are hereby designated the Depositary Governments.

3. This Convention shall enter into force thirty days following the date of the deposit of instruments of ratification by ten States signatory to this Convention which participated in the Montreal Conference.

4. For other States, this Convention shall enter into force on the date of entry into force of this Convention in accordance with paragraph 3 of this Article, or thirty days following the date of deposit of their instruments of ratification or accession, whichever is later.

5. The Depositary Governments shall promptly inform all signatory and acceding States of the date of each signature, the date of deposit of each instrument of ratification or accession, the date of entry into force of this Convention, and other notices.

6. As soon as this Convention comes into force, it shall be registered by the Depositary Governments pursuant to Article 102 of the Convention on International Civil Aviation (Chicago, 1944).

Article 16

1. Any Contracting State may denounce this Convention by written notification to the Depositary Governments.

2. Denunciation shall take effect six months following the date on which notification is received by the Depositary Governments.

IN WITNESS WHEREOF the undersigned Plenipotentiaries, being duly authorized thereto by their Governments, have signed this Convention.

DONE at Montreal, this twenty-third day of September, one thousand nine hundred and seventy-one, in three originals, each being drawn up in four authentic texts in the English, French, Russian and Spanish languages.

Disclaimer

The present version of the Conventions and Protocols might differ slightly from the consolidated official English versions which were—by end of November 2000—not available to TPB in electronic form. Please contact the Codification Division of the UN Office of Legal Affairs (United Nations, Room S-3450 A, New York, N.Y. 10017, USA) for the official versions in English and other official UN languages.

H. CONVENTION ON THE PREVENTION AND PUNISHMENT OF CRIMES AGAINST INTERNATIONALLY PROTECTED PERSONS

Opened for signature at New York on 14 December 1973

THE STATES PARTIES to this Convention,

HAVING in mind the purposes and principles of the Charter of the United Nations concerning the maintenance of international peace and the promotion of friendly relations and co-operation among States,

CONSIDERING that crimes against diplomatic agents and other internationally protected persons jeopardizing the safety of these persons create a serious threat to the maintenance of normal international relations which are necessary for co-operation among States,

BELIEVING that the commission of such crimes is a matter of grave concern to the international community,

CONVINCED that there is an urgent need to adopt appropriate and effective measures for the prevention and punishment of such crimes,

HAVE agreed as follows:

Article 1

For the purposes of this Convention:

1. "internationally protected person" means:

a. a Head of State, including any member of a collegial body performing the functions of a Head of State under the constitution of the State concerned, a Head of Government or a Minister for Foreign Affairs, whenever any such person is in a foreign State, as well as members of his family who accompany him;

b. any representative or official of a State or any official or other agent of an international organization of an intergovernmental character who, at the time when and in the place where a crime against him, his official premises, his private accommodation or his means of transport is committed, is entitled pursuant to international law to special protection from any attack on his person, freedom or dignity, as well as members of his family forming part of his household;

2. "alleged offender" means a person as to whom there is sufficient evidence to determine prima facie that he has committed or participated in one or more of the crimes set forth in Article 2.

Article 2

1. The intentional commission of:

a. a murder, kidnapping or other attack upon the person or liberty of an internationally protected person;
b. a violent attack upon the official premises, the private accommodation or the means of transport of an internationally protected person likely to endanger his person or liberty;
c. a threat to commit any such attack;
d. an attempt to commit any such attack; and
e. an act constituting participation as an accomplice in any such attack shall be made by each State Party a crime under its internal law.

2. Each State Party shall make these crimes punishable by appropriate penalties which take into account their grave nature.

3. Paragraphs 1 and 2 of this article in no way derogate from the obligations of States Parties under international law to take all appropriate measures to prevent other attacks on the person, freedom or dignity of an internationally protected person.

Article 3

1. Each State Party shall take such measures as may be necessary to establish its jurisdiction over the crimes set forth in Article 2 in the following cases:

a. when the crime is committed in the territory of that State or on board a ship or aircraft registered in that State;
b. when the alleged offender is a national of that State;
c. when the crime is committed against an internationally protected person as defined in Article 1 who enjoys his status as such by virtue of functions which he exercises on behalf of that State.

2. Each State Party shall likewise take such measures as may be necessary to establish its jurisdiction over these crimes in cases where the alleged offender is present in its territory and it does not extradite him pursuant to Article 8 to any of the States mentioned in paragraph 1 of this article.

3. This Convention does not exclude any criminal jurisdiction exercised in accordance with internal law.

Article 4

States Parties shall co-operate in the prevention of the crimes set forth in Article 2, particularly by:

a. taking all practicable measures to prevent preparations in their respective territories for the commission of those crimes within or outside their territories;
b. exchanging information and co-ordinating the taking of administrative and other measures as appropriate to prevent the commission of those crimes.

Article 5

1. The State Party in which any of the crimes set forth in Article 2 has been committed shall, if it has reason to believe that an alleged offender has fled from its territory, communicate to all other States concerned, directly or through the Secretary-General of the United Nations, all the pertinent facts regarding the crime committed and all available information regarding the identity of the alleged offender.

2. Whenever any of the crimes set forth in Article 2 has been committed against an internationally protected person, any State Party which has information concerning the victim and the circumstances of the crime shall endeavour to transmit it, under the conditions provided for in its internal law, fully and promptly to the State Party on whose behalf he was exercising his functions.

Article 6

1. Upon being satisfied that the circumstances so warrant, the State Party in whose territory the alleged offender is present shall take the appropriate measures under its internal law so as to ensure his presence for the purpose of prosecution or extradition. Such measures shall be notified without delay directly or through the Secretary-General of the United Nations to:

a. the State where the crime was committed;
b. the State or States of which the alleged offender is a national or, if he is a stateless person, in whose territory he permanently resides;

c. the State or States of which the internationally protected person concerned is a national or on whose behalf he was exercising his functions;
d. all other States concerned; and
e. the international organization of which the internationally protected person concerned is an official or an agent.

2. Any person regarding whom the measures referred to in paragraph 1 of this article are being taken shall be entitled:

a. to communicate without delay with the nearest appropriate representative of the State of which he is a national or which is otherwise entitled to protect his rights or, if he is a stateless person, which he requests and which is willing to protect his rights, and
b. to be visited by a representative of that State.

Article 7

The State Party in whose territory the alleged offender is present shall, if it does not extradite him, submit, without exception whatsoever and without undue delay, the case to its competent authorities for the purpose of prosecution, through proceedings in accordance with the laws of that State.

Article 8

1. To the extent that the crimes set forth in Article 2 are not listed as extraditable offences in any extradition treaty existing between States Parties, they shall be deemed to be included as such therein. States Parties undertake to include those crimes as extraditable offences in every future extradition treaty to be concluded between them.

2. If a State Party which makes extradition conditional on the existence of a treaty receives a request for extradition from another State Party with which it has no extradition treaty, it may, if it decides to extradite, consider this Convention as the legal basis for extradition in respect of those crimes. Extradition shall be subject to the procedural provisions and the other conditions of the law of the requested State.

3. States Parties which do not make extradition conditional on the existence of a treaty shall recognize those crimes as extraditable offences between themselves subject to the procedural provisions and the other conditions of the law of the requested State.

4. Each of the crimes shall be treated, for the purpose of extradition between States Parties, as if it had been committed not only in the place in

which it occurred but also in the territories of the States required to establish their jurisdiction in accordance with paragraph 1 of article 3.

Article 9

Any person regarding whom proceedings are being carried out in connexion with any of the crimes set forth in Article 2 shall be guaranteed fair treatment at all stages of the proceedings.

Article 10

1. States Parties shall afford one another the greatest measure of assistance in connexion with criminal proceedings brought in respect of the crimes set forth in Article 2, including the supply of all evidence at their disposal necessary for the proceedings.

2. The provisions of paragraph 1 of this article shall not affect obligations concerning mutual judicial assistance embodied in any other treaty.

Article 11

The State Party where an alleged offender is prosecuted shall communicate the final outcome of the proceedings to the Secretary-General of the United Nations, who shall transmit the information to the other States Parties.

Article 12

The provisions of this Convention shall not affect the application of the Treaties on Asylum, in force at the date of the adoption of this Convention, as between the States which are parties to those Treaties; but a State Party to this Convention may not invoke those Treaties with respect to another State Party to this Convention which is not a party to those Treaties.

Article 13

1. Any dispute between two or more States Parties concerning the interpretation or application of this Convention which is not settled by negotiation shall, at the request of one of them, be submitted to arbitration. If within six months from the date of the request for arbitration the parties are unable to agree on the organization of the arbitration, any one of those parties may refer the dispute to the International Court of Justice by request in conformity with the Statute of the Court.

2. Each State Party may at the time of signature or ratification of this Convention or accession thereto declare that it does not consider itself bound by paragraph 1 of this article. The other States Parties shall not be bound by paragraph 1 of this article with respect to any State Party which has made such a reservation.

3. Any State Party which has made a reservation in accordance with paragraph 2 of this article may at any time withdraw that reservation by notification to the Secretary-General of the United Nations.

Article 14

This Convention shall be open for signature by all States, until 31 December 1974 at United Nations Headquarters in New York.

Article 15

This Convention is subject to ratification. The instruments of ratification shall be deposited with the Secretary-General of the United Nations.

Article 16

This Convention shall remain open for accession by any State. The instruments of accession shall be deposited with the Secretary-General of the United Nations.

Article 17

1. This Convention shall enter into force on the thirtieth day following the date of deposit of the twenty-second instrument of ratification or accession with the Secretary-General of the United Nations.

2. For each State ratifying or acceding to the Convention after the deposit of the twenty-second instrument of ratification or accession, the Convention shall enter into force on the thirtieth day after deposit by such State of its instrument of ratification or accession.

Article 18

1. Any State Party may denounce this Convention by written notification to the Secretary-General of the United Nations.

2. Denunciation shall take effect six months following the date on which notification is received by the Secretary-General of the United Nations.

Article 19

The Secretary-General of the United Nations shall inform all States, inter alia:

a. of signatures to this Convention, of the deposit of instruments of ratification or accession in accordance with Articles 14, 15 and 16 and of notifications made under Article 18.
b. of the date on which this Convention will enter into force in accordance with Article 17.

Article 20

The original of this Convention, of which the Chinese, English, French, Russian and Spanish texts are equally authentic, shall be deposited with the Secretary-General of the United Nations, who shall send certified copies thereof to all States.

IN WITNESS WHEREOF the undersigned, being duly authorized thereto by their respective Governments, have signed this Convention, opened for signature at New York on 14 December 1973.

Disclaimer

The present version of the Conventions and Protocols might differ slightly from the consolidated official English versions which were—by end of November 2000—not available to TPB in electronic form. Please contact the Codification Division of the UN Office of Legal Affairs (United Nations, Room S-3450 A, New York, N.Y. 10017, USA) for the official versions in English and other official UN languages.

I. INTERNATIONAL CONVENTION AGAINST THE TAKING OF HOSTAGES

Signed at New York on 18 December 1979

THE STATES PARTIES to this Convention,

HAVING in mind the purposes and principles of the Charter of the United Nations concerning the maintenance of international peace and security and the promotion of friendly relations and co-operation among States,

RECOGNIZING in particular that everyone has the right to life, liberty and security of person, as set out in the Universal Declaration of Human Rights and the International Covenant on Civil and Political Rights,

REAFFIRMING the principle of equal rights and self-determination of peoples as enshrined in the Charter of the United Nations and the Declaration on Principles of International Law concerning Friendly Relations and Co-operation among States in accordance with the Charter of the United Nations, as well as in other relevant resolutions of the General Assembly,

CONSIDERING that the taking of hostages is an offence of grave concern to the international community and that, in accordance with the provisions of this Convention, any person committing an act of hostage taking shall either be prosecuted or extradited,

BEING CONVINCED that it is urgently necessary to develop international co-operation between States in devising and adopting effective measures for the prevention, prosecution and punishment of all acts of taking of hostages as manifestations of international terrorism,

HAVE agreed as follows:

Article 1

1. Any person who seizes or detains and threatens to kill, to injure or to continue to detain another person (hereinafter referred to as the "hostage") in order to compel a third party, namely, a State, an international intergovernmental organization, a natural or juridical person, or a group of persons, to do or abstain from doing any act as an explicit or implicit condition for the release of the hostage commits the offence of taking of hostages ("hostage-taking") within the meaning of this Convention.

2. Any person who:

a. attempts to commit an act of hostage-taking, or
b. participates as an accomplice of anyone who commits or attempts to commit an act of hostage-taking likewise commits an offence for the purposes of this Convention.

Article 2

Each State Party shall make the offences set forth in Article 1 punishable by appropriate penalties which take into account the grave nature of those offences.

Article 3

1. The State Party in the territory of which the hostage is held by the offender shall take all measures it considers appropriate to ease the situation of the hostage, in particular, to secure his release and, after his release, to facilitate, when relevant, his departure.

2. If any object which the offender has obtained as a result of the taking of hostages comes into the custody of a State Party, that State Party shall return it as soon as possible to the hostage or the third party referred to in Article 1, as the case may be, or to the appropriate authorities thereof.

Article 4

States Parties shall co-operate in the prevention of the offences set forth in Article 1, particularly by:

a. taking all practicable measures to prevent preparations in their respective territories for the commission of those offences within or outside their territories, including measures to prohibit in their territories illegal activities of persons, groups and organizations that encourage, instigate, organize or engage in the perpetration of acts of taking of hostages;
b. exchanging information and co-ordinating the taking of administrative and other measures as appropriate to prevent the commission of those offences.

Article 5

1. Each State Party shall take such measures as may be necessary to establish its jurisdiction over any of the offences set forth in Article 1 which are committed:

a. in its territory or on board a ship or aircraft registered in that State;
b. by any of its nationals or, if that State considers it appropriate, by those stateless persons who have their habitual residence in its territory;
c. in order to compel that State to do or abstain from doing any act; or
d. with respect to a hostage who is a national of that State, if that State considers it appropriate.

2. Each State Party shall likewise take such measures as may be necessary to establish its jurisdiction over the offences set forth in Article 1 in cases where the alleged offender is present in its territory and it does not extradite him to any of the States mentioned in paragraph 1 of this article.

3. This Convention does not exclude any criminal jurisdiction exercised in accordance with internal law.

Article 6

1. Upon being satisfied that the circumstances so warrant, any State Party in the territory of which the alleged offender is present shall, in accordance with its laws, take him into custody or take other measures to ensure his presence for such time as is necessary to enable any criminal or extradition proceedings to be instituted. That State Party shall immediately make a preliminary inquiry into the facts.

2. The custody or other measures referred to in paragraph 1 of this article shall be notified without delay directly or through the Secretary-General of the United Nations to:

a. the State where the offence was committed;
b. the State against which compulsion has been directed or attempted;
c. the State of which the natural or juridical person against whom compulsion has been directed or attempted is a national;
d. the State of which the hostage is a national or in the territory of which he has his habitual residence;
e. the State of which the alleged offender is a national or, if he is a stateless person, in the territory of which he has his habitual residence;
f. the international intergovernmental organization against which compulsion has been directed or attempted;
g. all other States concerned.

3. Any person regarding whom the measures referred to in paragraph 1 of this article are being taken shall be entitled:

a. to communicate without delay with the nearest appropriate representative of the State of which he is a national or which is otherwise entitled to establish such communication or, if he is a stateless person, the State in the territory of which he has his habitual residence;

b. to be visited by a representative of that State.

4. The rights referred to in paragraph 3 of this article shall be exercised in conformity with the laws and regulations of the State in the territory of which the alleged offender is present subject to the proviso, however, that the said laws and regulations must enable full effect to be given to the purposes for which the rights accorded under paragraph 3 of this article are intended.

5. The provisions of paragraphs 3 and 4 of this article shall be without prejudice to the right of any State Party having a claim to jurisdiction in accordance with paragraph 1(b) of Article 5 to invite the International Committee of the Red Cross to communicate with and visit the alleged offender.

6. The State which makes the preliminary inquiry contemplated in paragraph 1 of this article shall promptly report its findings to the States or organization referred to in paragraph 2 of this article and indicate whether it intends to exercise jurisdiction.

Article 7

The State Party where the alleged offender is prosecuted shall in accordance with its laws communicate the final outcome of the proceedings to the Secretary-General of the United Nations, who shall transmit the information to the other States concerned and the international intergovernmental organizations concerned.

Article 8

1. The State Party in the territory of which the alleged offender is found shall, if it does not extradite him, be obliged, without exception whatsoever and whether or not the offence was committed in its territory, to submit the case to its competent authorities for the purpose of prosecution, through proceedings in accordance with the laws of that State. Those authorities shall take their decision in the same manner as in the case of any ordinary offence of a grave nature under the law of that State.

2. Any person regarding whom proceedings are being carried out in connexion with any of the offences set forth in Article 1 shall be guara-

nteed fair treatment at all stages of the proceedings, including enjoyment of all the rights and guarantees provided by the law of the State in the territory of which he is present.

Article 9

1. A request for the extradition of an alleged offender, pursuant to this Convention, shall not be granted if the requested State Party has substantial grounds for believing:

a. that the request for extradition for an offence set forth in Article 1 has been made for the purpose of prosecuting or punishing a person on account of his race, religion, nationality, ethnic origin or political opinion; or
b. that the person's position may be prejudiced:
    i. for any of the reasons mentioned in subparagraph (a) of this paragraph, or
    ii. for the reason that communication with him by the appropriate authorities of the State entitled to exercise rights of protection cannot be effected.

2. With respect to the offences as defined in this Convention, the provisions of all extradition treaties and arrangements applicable between States Parties are modified as between States Parties to the extent that they are incompatible with this Convention.

Article 10

1. The offences set forth in Article 1 shall be deemed to be included as extraditable offences in any extradition treaty existing between States Parties. States Parties undertake to include such offences as extraditable offences in every extradition treaty to be concluded between them.

2. If a State Party which makes extradition conditional on the existence of a treaty receives a request for extradition from another State Party with which it has no extradition treaty, the requested State may at its option consider this Convention as the legal basis for extradition in respect of the offences set forth in Article 1. Extradition shall be subject to the other conditions provided by the law of the requested State.

3. States Parties which do not make extradition conditional on the existence of a treaty shall recognize the offences set forth in Article 1 as extraditable offences between themselves subject to the conditions provided by the law of the requested State.

4. The offences set forth in Article 1 shall be treated, for the purpose of extradition between States Parties, as if they had been committed not only in the place in which they occurred but also in the territories of the States required to establish their jurisdiction in accordance with paragraph 1 of Article 5.

Article 11

1. States Parties shall afford one another the greatest measure of assistance in connexion with criminal proceedings brought in respect of the offences set forth in Article 1, including the supply of all evidence at their disposal necessary for the proceedings.

2. The provisions of paragraph 1 of this article shall not affect obligations concerning mutual judicial assistance embodied in any other treaty.

Article 12

In so far as the Geneva Conventions of 1949 for the protection of war victims or the Additional Protocols to those Conventions are applicable to a particular act of hostage-taking, and in so far as States Parties to this Convention are bound under those conventions to prosecute or hand over the hostage-taker, the present Convention shall not apply to an act of hostage-taking committed in the course of armed conflicts as defined in the Geneva Conventions of 1949 and the Protocols thereto, including armed conflicts mentioned in Article 1, paragraph 4, of Additional Protocol I of 1977, in which peoples are fighting against colonial domination and alien occupation and against racist regimes in the exercise of their right of self-determination, as enshrined in the Charter of the United Nations and the Declaration on Principles of International Law concerning Friendly Relations and Co-operation among States in accordance with the Charter of the United Nations.

Article 13

This Convention shall not apply where the offence is committed within a single State, the hostage and the alleged offender are nationals of that State and the alleged offender is found in the territory of that State.

Article 14

Nothing in this Convention shall be construed as justifying the violation of the territorial integrity or political independence of a State in contravention of the Charter of the United Nations.

Article 15

The provisions of this Convention shall not affect the application of the Treaties on Asylum, in force at the date of the adoption of this Convention, as between the States which are parties to those Treaties; but a State Party to this convention may not invoke those Treaties with respect to another State Party to this Convention which is not a party to those treaties.

Article 16

1. Any dispute between two or more States Parties concerning the interpretation or application of this Convention which is not settled by negotiation shall, at the request of one of them, be submitted to arbitration. If within six months from the date of the request for arbitration the parties are unable to agree on the organization of the arbitration, any one of those parties may refer the dispute to the International Court of Justice by request in conformity with the Statute of the Court.

2. Each State may at the time of signature or ratification of this Convention or accession thereto declare that it does not consider itself bound by paragraph 1 of this article. The other States Parties shall not be bound by paragraph 1 of this article with respect to any State Party which has made such a reservation.

3. Any State Party which has made a reservation in accordance with paragraph 2 of this article may at any time withdraw that reservation by notification to the Secretary-General in the United Nations.

Article 17

1. This Convention is open for signature by all States until 31 December 1980 at United Nations Headquarters in New York.

2. This Convention is subject to ratification. The instruments of ratification shall be deposited with the Secretary-General of the United Nations.

3. This Convention is open for accession by any State. The instruments of accession shall be deposited with the Secretary-General of the United Nations.

Article 18

1. This Convention shall enter into force on the thirtieth day following the date of deposit of the twenty-second instrument of ratification or accession with the Secretary-General of the United Nations.

2. For each State ratifying or acceding to the Convention after the deposit of the twenty-second instrument of ratification or accession, the Convention shall enter into force on the thirtieth day after deposit by such State of its instrument of ratification or accession.

Article 19

1. Any State Party may denounce this Convention by written notification to the Secretary-General of the United Nations.

2. Denunciation shall take effect one year following the date on which notification is received by the Secretary-General of the United Nations.

Article 20

The original of this Convention, of which the Arabic, Chinese, English, French, Russian and Spanish texts are equally authentic, shall be deposited with the Secretary General of the United Nations, who shall send certified copies thereof to all States.

IN WITNESS WHEREOF, the undersigned, being duly authorized thereto by their respective Governments, have signed this Convention, opened for signature at New York on 18 December 1979.

Disclaimer

The present version of the Conventions and Protocols might differ slightly from the consolidated official English versions which were—by end of November 2000—not available to TPB in electronic form. Please contact the Codification Division of the UN Office of Legal Affairs (United Nations, Room S-3450 A, New York, N.Y. 10017, USA) for the official versions in English and other official UN languages.

J. CONVENTION ON THE PHYSICAL PROTECTION OF NUCLEAR MATERIAL

Signed at New York and Vienna, 3 March 1980

THE STATES PARTIES to this Convention,

RECOGNIZING the right of all States to develop and apply nuclear energy for peaceful purposes and their legitimate interests in the potential benefits to be derived from the peaceful application of nuclear energy,

CONVINCED of the need for facilitating international co-operation in the peaceful application of nuclear energy,

DESIRING to avert the potential dangers posed by the unlawful taking and use of nuclear material.

CONVINCED that offences relating to nuclear material are a matter of grave concern and that there is an urgent need to adopt appropriate and effective measures to ensure the prevention, detection and punishment of such offences,

AWARE of the need for international co-operation to establish, in conformity with the national law of each State Party and with this Convention, effective measures for the physical protection of nuclear material,

CONVINCED that this Convention should facilitate the safe transfer of nuclear material.

STRESSING also the importance of the physical protection of nuclear material in domestic use, storage and transport,

RECOGNIZING the importance of effective physical protection of nuclear material used for military purposes, and understanding that such material is and will continue to be accorded stringent physical protection.

HAVE agreed as follows:

Article 1

For the purposes of this Convention:

a. "nuclear material" means plutonium except that with isotopic concentration exceeding 80% in plutonium-238; uranium-233; uranium enriched in the isotopes 235 or 233; uranium containing the mixture of isotopes as occurring in nature other than in the form of ore or ore-residue; any material containing one or more of the foregoing;

b. "uranium enriched in the isotope 235 or 233" means uranium containing the isotopes 235 or 233 or both in an amount such that the abundance ratio of the sum of these isotopes to the isotope 238 is greater than the ratio of the isotope 235 to the isotope 238 occurring in nature;

c. "international nuclear transport" means the carriage of a consignment of nuclear material by any means of transportation intended to go beyond the territory of the State where the shipment originates beginning with the departure from a facility of the shipper in that State and ending with the arrival at a facility of the receiver within the State of ultimate destination.

Article 2

1. This Convention shall apply to nuclear material used for peaceful purposes while in international nuclear transport.

2. With the exception of Articles 3 and 4 and paragraph 3 of Article 5, this Convention shall also apply to nuclear material used for peaceful purposes while in domestic use, storage and transport.

3. Apart from the commitments expressly undertaken by States Parties in the articles covered by paragraph 2 with respect to nuclear material used for peaceful purposes while in domestic use, storage and transport, nothing in this Convention shall be interpreted as affecting the sovereign rights of a State regarding the domestic use, storage and transport of such nuclear material.

Article 3

Each State Party shall take appropriate steps within the framework of its national law and consistent with international law to ensure as far as practicable that, during international nuclear transport, nuclear material within its territory, or on board a ship or aircraft under its jurisdiction insofar as such ship or aircraft is engaged in the transport to or from that State, is protected at the levels described in Annex 1.

Article 4

1. Each State Party shall not export or authorize the export of nuclear

material unless the State Party has received assurances that such material will be protected during the international nuclear transport at the levels described in Annex 1.

2. Each State Party shall not import or authorize the import of nuclear material from a State not party to this Convention unless the State Party has received assurances that such material will during the international nuclear transport be protected at the levels described in Annex 1.

3. A State Party shall not allow the transit of its territory by land or internal waterways or through its airports or seaports of nuclear material between States that are not parties to this Convention unless the State Party has received assurances as far as practicable that this nuclear material will be protected during international nuclear transport at the levels described in Annex 1.

4. Each State Party shall apply within the framework of its national law the levels of physical protection described in Annex 1 to nuclear material being transported from a part of that State to another part of the same State through international waters or airspace.

5. The State Party responsible for receiving assurances that the nuclear material will be protected at the levels described in Annex 1 according to paragraphs 1 to 3 shall identify and inform in advance States which the nuclear material is expected to transit by land or internal waterways, or whose airports or seaports it is expected to enter.

6. The responsibility for obtaining assurances referred to in paragraph 1 may be transferred, by mutual agreement, to the State Party involved in the transport as the importing State.

7. Nothing in this article shall be interpreted as in any way affecting the territorial sovereignty and jurisdiction of a State, including that over its airspace and territorial sea.

Article 5

1. States Parties shall identify and make known to each other directly or through the International Atomic Energy Agency their central authority and point of contact having responsibility for physical protection of nuclear material and for co-ordinating recovery and response operations in the event of any unauthorized removal, use or alteration of nuclear material or in the event of credible threat thereof.

2. In the case of theft, robbery or any other unlawful taking of nuclear material or of credible threat thereof, States Parties shall, in accordance with their national law, provide co-operation and assistance to the maximum feasible extent in the recovery and protection of such material to any State that so requests. In particular:

a. each State Party shall take appropriate steps to inform as soon as possible other States, which appear to it to be concerned, of any theft, robbery or other unlawful taking of nuclear material or credible threat thereof and to inform, where appropriate, international organizations;
b. as appropriate, the States Parties concerned shall exchange information with each other or international organizations with a view to protecting threatened nuclear material, verifying the integrity of the shipping container, or recovering unlawfully taken nuclear material and shall:

   i. co-ordinate their efforts through diplomatic and other agreed channels:
   ii. render assistance, if requested;
   iii. ensure the return of nuclear material stolen or missing as a consequence of the above-mentioned events.

The means of implementation of this co-operation shall be determined by the States Parties concerned.

3. States Parties shall co-operate and consult as appropriate, with each other directly or through international organizations, with a view to obtaining guidance on the design, maintenance and improvement of systems of physical protection of nuclear material in international transport.

Article 6

1. States Parties shall take appropriate measures consistent with their national law to protect the confidentiality of any information which they receive in confidence by virtue of the provisions of this Convention from another State Party or through participation in an activity carried out for the implementation of this Convention. If States Parties provide information to international organizations in confidence, steps shall be taken to ensure that the confidentiality of such information is protected.

2. States Parties shall not be required by this Convention to provide any information which they are not permitted to communicate pursuant to national law or which would jeopardize the security of the State concerned or the physical protection of nuclear material.

Article 7

1. The intentional commission of:

a. an act without lawful authority which constitutes the receipt, possession, use, transfer, alteration, disposal or dispersal of nuclear material and which causes or is likely to cause death or serious injury to any person or substantial damage to property;

b. a theft or robbery of nuclear material;

c. an embezzlement or fraudulent obtaining of nuclear material;

d. an act constituting a demand for nuclear material by threat or use of force or by any other form of intimidation;

e. a threat:

   i. to use nuclear material to cause death or serious injury to any person or substantial property damage, or

   ii. to commit an offence described in sub-paragraph (b) in order to compel a natural or legal person, international organization or State to do or to refrain from doing any act;

f. an attempt to commit any offence described in paragraphs (a), (b) or (c); and

g. an act which constitutes participation in any offence described in paragraphs (a) to (f) shall be made a punishable offence by each State Party under its national law.

2. Each State Party shall make the offences described in this article punishable by appropriate penalties which take into account their grave nature.

Article 8

1. Each State Party shall take such measures as may be necessary to establish its jurisdiction over the offences set forth in Article 7 in the following cases:

a. when the offence is committed in the territory of that State or on board a ship or aircraft registered in that State;

b. when the alleged offender is a national of that State.

2. Each State Party shall likewise take such measures as may be necessary to establish its jurisdiction over these offences in cases where the alleged offender is present in its territory and it does not extradite him pursuant to Article 11 to any of the States mentioned in paragraph 1.

3. This Convention does not exclude any criminal jurisdiction exercised in accordance with national law.

4. In addition to the States Parties mentioned in paragraphs 1 and 2, each State Party may, consistent with international law, establish its

jurisdiction over the offences set forth in Article 7 when it is involved in international nuclear transport as the exporting or importing State.

Article 9

Upon being satisfied that the circumstances so warrant, the State Party in whose territory the alleged offender is present shall take appropriate measures, including detention, under its national law to ensure his presence for the purpose of prosecution or extradition. Measures taken according to this article shall be notified without delay to the States required to establish jurisdiction pursuant to Article 8 and, where appropriate, all other States concerned.

Article 10

The State Party in whose territory the alleged offender is present shall, if it does not extradite him, submit, without exception whatsoever and without undue delay, the case to its competent authorities for the purpose of prosecution, through proceedings in accordance with the laws of that State.

Article 11

1. The offences in Article 7 shall be deemed to be included as extraditable offences in any extradition treaty existing between States Parties. States Parties undertake to include those offences as extraditable offences in every future extradition treaty to be concluded between them.

2. If a State Party which makes extradition conditional on the existence of a treaty receives a request for extradition from another State Party with which it has no extradition treaty, it may at its option consider this Convention as the legal basis for extradition in respect of those offences. Extradition shall be subject to the other conditions provided by the law of the requested State.

3. States Parties which do not make extradition conditional on the existence of a treaty shall recognize those offences as extraditable offences between themselves subject to the conditions provided by the law of the requested State.

4. Each of the offences shall be treated, for the purpose of extradition between States Parties, as if it had been committed not only in the place in which it occurred but also in the territories of the States Parties required to establish their jurisdiction in accordance with paragraph 1 of Article 8.

Article 12

Any person regarding whom proceedings are being carried out in connection with any of the offences set forth in Article 7 shall be guaranteed fair treatment at all stages of the proceedings.

Article 13

1. States Parties shall afford one another the greatest measure of assistance in connection with criminal proceedings brought in respect of the offences set forth in Article 7, including the supply of evidence at their disposal necessary for the proceedings. The law of the State requested shall apply in all cases.

2. The provisions of paragraph 1 shall not affect obligations under any other treaty, bilateral or multilateral, which governs or will govern, in whole or in part, mutual assistance in criminal matters.

Article 14

1. Each State Party shall inform the depositary of its laws and regulations which give effect to this Convention. The depositary shall communicate such information periodically to all States Parties.

2. The State Party where an alleged offender is prosecuted shall, wherever practicable, first communicate the final outcome of the proceedings to the States directly concerned. The State Party shall also communicate the final outcome to the depositary who shall inform all States.

3. Where an offence involves nuclear material used for peaceful purposes in domestic use, storage or transport, and both the alleged offender and the nuclear material remain in the territory of the State Party in which the offence was committed, nothing in this Convention shall be interpreted as requiring that State Party to provide information concerning criminal proceeding arising out of such an offence.

Article 15

The Annexes constitute an integral part of this Convention.

Article 16

1. A conference of States Parties shall be convened by the depositary five years after the entry into force of this Convention to review the

implementation of the Convention and its adequacy as concerns the preamble, the whole of the operative part and the annexes in the light of the then prevailing situation.

2. At intervals of not less than five years thereafter, the majority of States Parties may obtain, by submitting a proposal to this effect to the depositary, the convening of further conferences with the same objective.

Article 17

1. In the event of a dispute between two or more States Parties concerning the interpretation or application of this Convention, such States Parties shall consult with a view to the settlement of the dispute by negotiation, or by any other peaceful means of settling disputes acceptable to all parties to the dispute.

2. Any dispute of this character which cannot be settled in the manner prescribed in paragraph 1 shall, at the request of any party to such dispute, be submitted to arbitration or referred to the International Court of Justice for decision. Where a dispute is submitted to arbitration, if, within six months from the date of the request, the parties to the dispute are unable to agree on the organization of the arbitration, a party may request the President of the International Court of Justice or the Secretary-General of the United Nations to appoint one or more arbitrators. In case of conflicting requests by the parties to the dispute, the request to the Secretary-General of the United Nations shall have priority.

3. Each State Party may at the time of signature, ratification, acceptance or approval of this Convention or accession thereto declare that it does not consider itself bound by either or both of the dispute settlement procedures provided for in paragraph 2. The other States Parties shall not be bound by a dispute settlement procedure provided for in paragraph 2, with respect to a State Party which has made a reservation to that procedure.

4. Any State Party which has made a reservation in accordance with paragraph 3 may at any time withdraw that reservation by notification to the depositary.

Article 18

1. This Convention shall be open for signature by all States at the Headquarters of the International Atomic Energy Agency in Vienna and at the Headquarters of the United Nations in New York from 3 March 1980 until its entry into force.

2. This Convention is subject to ratification, acceptance or approval by the signatory States.

3. After its entry into force, this Convention will be open for accession by all States.

4. a. This Convention shall be open for signature or accession by international organizations and regional organizations of an integration or other nature, provided that any such organization is constituted by sovereign States and has competence in respect of the negotiaion, conclusion and application of international agreement in matters covered by this Convention.

b. In matters within their competence, such organizations shall, on their own behalf, exercise the rights and fulfil the responsibilities which this Convention attributes to States Parties.

c. When becoming party to this Convention such an organization shall communicate to the depositary a declaration indicating which States are members thereof and which articles of this Convention do not apply to it.

d. Such an organization shall not hold any vote additional to those of its Member States.

5. Instruments of ratification, acceptance, approval or accession shall be deposited with the depositary.

Article 19

1. This Convention shall enter into force on the thirtieth day following the date of deposit of the twenty-first instrument of ratification, acceptance or approval with the depositary.

2. For each State ratifying, accepting, approving or acceding to the Convention after the date of deposit of the twenty-first instrument of ratification, acceptance or approval, the Convention shall enter into force on the thirtieth day after the deposit by such State of its instrument of ratification, acceptance, approval or accession.

Article 20

1. Without prejudice to Article 16 a State Party may propose amendments to this Convention. The proposed amendment shall be submitted to the depositary who shall circulate it immediately to all States Parties. If a majority of States Parties request the depositary to convene a conference to consider the proposed amendments, the depositary shall invite all States Parties to attend such a conference to begin not sooner than thirty days after the invitations are issued. Any amendment adopted at the conference by a two-thirds majority of all States Parties shall be promptly circulated by the depositary to all States Parties.

2. The amendment shall enter into force for each State Party that deposits its instrument of ratification, acceptance or approval of the amendment on the thirtieth day after the date on which two thirds of the States Parties have deposited their instruments of ratification, acceptance or approval with the depositary. Thereafter, the amendment shall enter into force for any other State Party on the day on which that State Party deposits its instrument of ratification, acceptance or approval of the amendment.

Article 21

1. Any State Party may denounce this Convention by written notification to the depositary.

2. Denunciation shall take effect one hundred and eighty days following the date on which notification is received by the depositary.

Article 22

The depositary shall promptly notify all States of:

a. each signature of this Convention;
b. each deposit of an instrument of ratification, acceptance, approval or accession;
c. any reservation or withdrawal in accordance with Article 17;
d. any communication made by an organization in accordance with paragraph 4(c) of Article 18;
e. the entry into force of this Convention;
f. the entry into force of any amendment to this Convention; and
g. any denunciation made under Article 21.

Article 23

The original of this Convention, of which the Arabic, Chinese, English, French, Russian and Spanish texts are equally authentic, shall be deposited with the Director General of the International Atomic Energy Agency who shall send certified copies thereof to all States.

IN WITNESS WHEREOF, the undersigned, being duly authorized, have signed this Convention, opened for signature at Vienna and at New York on 3 March 1980.

ANNEX 1

Levels of Physical Protection to be Applied in International Transport of Nuclear Material as Categorized in Annex 2.

1. Levels of physical protection for nuclear material during storage incidental to international nuclear transport include:

   a. For Category III materials, storage within an area to which access is controlled;
   b. For Category II materials, storage within an area under constant surveillance by guards or electronic devices, surrounded by a physical barrier with a limited number of points of entry under appropriate control or any area with an equivalent level of physical protection;

2. For Category I material, storage within a protected area as defined for Category II above, to which, in addition, access is restricted to persons whose trustworthiness has been determined, and which is under surveillance by guards who are in close communication with appropriate response forces. Specific measures taken in this context should have as their object the detection and prevention of any assault, unauthorized access or unauthorized removal of material.

3. Levels of physical protection for nuclear material during international transport include:

   a. For Category II and III materials, transportation shall take place under special precautions including prior arrangements among sender, receiver, and carrier, and prior agreement between natural or legal persons subject to the jurisdiction and regulation of exporting and importing States, specifying time, place and procedures for transferring transport responsibility;
   b. For Category I materials, transportation shall take place under special precautions identified above for transportation of Category II and III materials, and in addition, under constant surveillance by escorts and under conditions which assure close communication with appropriate response forces;
   c. For natural uranium other than in the form of ore or ore-residue transportation protection for quantities exceeding 500 kilograms U shall include advance notification of shipment specifying mode of transport, expected time of arrival and confirmation of receipt of shipment.

ANNEX 2

a. All plutonium except that with isotopic concentration exceeding 80% in plutonium-238.
b. Material not irradiated in a reactor or material irradiated in a reactor but with a radiation level equal to or less than 100 reds/hour at one metre unshielded.
c. Quantities not falling in Category III and natural uranium should be protected in accordance with prudent management practice,
d. Although this level of protection is recommended, it would be open to States, upon evaluation of the specific circumstances, to assign a different category of physical protection.
e. Other fuel which by virtue of its original fissile material content is classified as Category I and II before irradiation may be reduced one category level while the radiation level from the fuel exceeds 100 reds/hour at one metre unshielded.

Disclaimer

The present version of the Conventions and Protocols might differ slightly from the consolidated official English versions which were—by end of November 2000—not available to TPB in electronic form. Please contact the Codification Division of the UN Office of Legal Affairs (United Nations, Room S-3450 A, New York, N.Y. 10017, USA) for the official versions in English and other official UN languages.

K. CONVENTION FOR THE SUPPRESSION OF UNLAWFUL ACTS AGAINST THE SAFETY OF MARITIME NAVIGATION

Signed at Rome, 10 March 1988

THE STATES PARTIES to this Convention,

HAVING in mind the purposes and principles of the Charter of the United Nations concerning the maintenance of international peace and security and the promotion of friendly relations and co-operation among States,

RECOGNIZING in particular that everyone has the right to life, liberty and security of person, as set out in the Universal Declaration of Human Rights and the International Covenant on Civil and Political Rights,

DEEPLY concerned about the worldwide escalation of acts of terrorism in all its forms, which endanger or take innocent human lives, jeopardize fundamental freedoms and seriously impair the dignity of human beings,

CONSIDERING that unlawful acts against the safety of maritime navigation jeopardize the safety of persons and property, seriously affect the operation of maritime services, and undermine the confidence of the peoples of the world in the safety of maritime navigation,

CONSIDERING that the occurrence of such acts is a matter of grave concern to the international community as a whole,

BEING convinced of the urgent need to develop international co-operation between States in devising and adopting effective and practical measures for the prevention of all unlawful acts against the safety of maritime navigation, and the prosecution and punishment of their perpetrators,

RECALLING Resolution 40/61 of the General Assembly of the United Nations of 9 December 1985 which, inter alia, "urges all States unilaterally and in co-operation with other States, as well as relevant United Nations organs, to contribute to the progressive elimination of causes underlying international terrorism and to pay special attention to all situations, including colonialism, racism and situations involving mass and flagrant violations of human rights and fundamental freedoms and those involving alien occupation, that may give rise to international terrorism and may endanger international peace and security",

RECALLING FURTHER that Resolution 40/61 "unequivocally condemns, as criminal) all acts, methods and practices of terrorism wherever and by whomever committed, including those which jeopardize friendly relations among States and their security",

RECALLING ALSO that by Resolution 40/61, the International Maritime Organization was invited to "study the problem of terrorism aboard or against ships with a view to making recommendations on appropriate measures",

HAVING IN MIND Resolution A.584(14) of 20 November 1985, of the Assembly of the International Maritime Organization, which called for development of measures to prevent unlawful acts which threaten the safety of ships and the security of their passengers and crews,

NOTING that acts of the crew which are subject to normal shipboard discipline are outside the purview of this Convention,

AFFIRMING the desirability of monitoring rules and standards relating to the prevention and control of unlawful acts against ships and persons on board ships, with a view to updating them as necessary, and, to this effect, taking note with satisfaction of the Measures to Prevent Unlawful Acts against Passengers and Crews on Board Ships, recommended by the Maritime Safety Committee of the International Maritime Organization,

AFFIRMING further that matters not regulated by this Convention continue to be governed by the rules and principles of general international law,

RECOGNIZING the need for all States, in combating unlawful acts against the safety of maritime navigation, strictly to comply with rules and principles of general international law,

HAVE agreed as follows:

Article 1

For the purposes of this Convention, "ship" means a vessel of any type whatsoever not permanently attached to the sea-bed, including dynamically supported craft, submersibles, or any other floating craft.

Article 2

1. This Convention does not apply to:

   a. a warship; or

b. a ship owned or operated by a State when being used as a naval auxiliary or for customs or police purposes; or
c. a ship which has been withdrawn from navigation or laid up.

2. Nothing in this Convention affects the immunities of warships and other government ships operated for non-commercial purposes.

Article 3

1. Any person commits an offence if that person unlawfully and intentionally:

a. seizes or exercises control over a ship by force or threat thereof or any other form of intimidation; or
b. performs an act of violence against a person on board a ship if that act is likely to endanger the safe navigation of that ship; or
c. destroys a ship or causes damage to a ship or to its cargo which is likely to endanger the safe navigation of that ship; or
d. places or causes to be placed on a ship, by any means whatsoever, a device or substance which is likely to destroy that ship, or cause damage to that ship or its cargo which endangers or is likely to endanger the safe navigation of that ship; or
e. destroys or seriously damages maritime navigational facilities or seriously interferes with their operation, if any such act is likely to endanger the safe navigation of a ship; or
f. communicates information which he knows to be false, thereby endangering the safe navigation of a ship; or
g. injures or kills any person, in connection with the commission or the attempted commission of any of the offences set forth in sub-paragraphs (a) to (f).

2. Any person also commits an offence if that person:

a. attempts to commit any of the offences set forth in paragraph 1; or
b. abets the commission of any of the offences set forth in paragraph 1 perpetrated by any person or is otherwise an accomplice of a person who commits such an offence; or
c. threatens, with or without a condition, as is provided for under national law, aimed at compelling a physical or juridical person to do or refrain from doing any act, to commit any of the of fences set forth in paragraph 1, subparagraphs (b), (c) and (e), if that threat is likely to endanger the safe navigation of the ship in question.

Article 4

1. This Convention applies if the ship is navigating or is scheduled to navigate into, through or from waters beyond the outer limit of the territorial sea of a single State, or the lateral limits of its territorial sea with adjacent States.

2. In cases where the Convention does not apply pursuant to paragraph 1, it nevertheless applies when the offender or the alleged offender is found in the territory of a State Party other than the State referred to in paragraph 1.

Article 5

Each State Party shall make the offences set forth in Article 3 punishable by appropriate penalties which take into account the grave nature of those offences.

Article 6

1. Each State Party shall take such measures as may be necessary to establish its jurisdiction over the offences set forth in Article 3 when the offence is committed:

a. against or on board a ship flying the flag of the State at the time the offence is committed; or
b. in the territory of that State, including its territorial sea; or
c. by a national of that State.

2. A State Party may also establish its jurisdiction over any such offence when:

a. it is committed by a stateless person whose habitual residence is in that State; or
b. during its commission a national of that State is seized, threatened, injured or killed; or
c. it is committed in an attempt to compel that State to do or abstain from doing any act.

3. Any State Party which has established jurisdiction mentioned in paragraph 2 shall notify the Secretary-General of the International Maritime Organization (hereinafter referred to as "the Secretary-General"). If such State Party subsequently rescinds that jurisdiction, it shall notify the Secretary-General.

4. Each State Party shall take such measures as may be necessary to establish its jurisdiction over the offences set forth in Article 3 in cases where the alleged offender is present in its territory and it does not extradite him to any of the States Parties which have established their jurisdiction in accordance with paragraphs 1 and 2 of this article.

5. This Convention does not exclude any criminal jurisdiction exercised in accordance with national law.

Article 7

1. Upon being satisfied that the circumstances so warrant, any State Party in the territory of which the offender or the alleged offender is present shall, in accordance with its law, take him into custody or take other measures to ensure his presence for such time as is necessary to enable any criminal or extradition proceedings to be instituted.

2. Such State shall immediately make a preliminary inquiry into the facts, in accordance with its own legislation.

3. Any person regarding whom the measures referred to in paragraph 1 are being taken shall be entitled to:

a. communicate without delay with the nearest appropriate representative of the State of which he is a national or which is otherwise entitled to establish such communication or, if he is a stateless person, the State in the territory of which he has his habitual residence;
b. be visited by a representative of that State.

4. The rights referred to in paragraph 3 shall be exercised in conformity with the laws and regulations of the State in the territory of which the offender or the alleged offender is present, subject to the proviso that the said laws and regulations must enable full effect to be given to the purposes for which the rights accorded under paragraph 3 are intended.

5. When a State Party, pursuant to this article, has taken a person into custody, it shall immediately notify the States which have established jurisdiction in accordance with article 6, paragraph 1 and, if it considers it advisable, any other interested States, of the fact that such person is in custody and of the circumstances which warrant his detention. The State which makes the preliminary inquiry contemplated in paragraph 2 of this article shall promptly report its findings to the said States and shall indicate whether it intends to exercise jurisdiction.

Article 8

1. The master of a ship of a State Party (the "flag State") may deliver to the authorities of any other State Party (the "receiving State") any person who he has reasonable grounds to believe has committed one of the offences set forth in Article 3.

2. The flag State shall ensure that the master of its ship is obliged, whenever practicable, and if possible before entering the territorial sea of the receiving State carrying on board any person whom the master intends to deliver in accordance with paragraph 1, to give notification to the authorities of the receiving State of his intention to deliver such person and the reasons therefor.

3. The receiving State shall accept the delivery, except where it has grounds to consider that the Convention is not applicable to the acts giving rise to the delivery, and shall proceed in accordance with the provisions of Article 1. Any refusal to accept a delivery shall be accompanied by a statement of the reasons for refusal.

4. The flag State shall ensure that the master of its ship is obliged to furnish the authorities of the receiving State with the evidence in the master's possession which pertains to the alleged offence.

5. A receiving State which has accepted the delivery of a person in accordance with paragraph 3 may, in turn, request the flag State to accept delivery of that person. The flag State shall consider any such request, and if it accedes to the request it shall proceed in accordance with Article 7. If the flag State declines a request, it shall furnish the receiving State with a statement of the reasons therefor.

Article 9

Nothing in this Convention shall affect in any way the rules of international law pertaining to the competence of States to exercise investigative or enforcement jurisdiction on board ships not flying their flag.

Article 10

1. The State Party in the territory of which the offender or the alleged offender is found shall, in cases to which Article 6 applies, if it does not extradite him, be obliged, without exception whatsoever and whether or not the offence was committed in its territory, to submit the case without delay to its competent authorities for the purpose of prosecution, through proceedings in accordance with the laws of that State. Those authorities

shall take their decision in the same manner as in the case of any other offence of a grave nature under the law of that State.

2. Any person regarding whom proceedings are being carried out in connection with any of the offences set forth in Article 3 shall be guaranteed fair treatment at all stages of the proceedings, including enjoyment of all the rights and guarantees provided for such proceedings by the law of the State in the territory of which he is present.

Article 11

1. The offences set forth in Article 3 shall be deemed to be included as extraditable offences in any extradition treaty existing between any of the States Parties. States Parties undertake to include such offences as extraditable offences in every extradition treaty to be concluded between them.

2. If a State Party which makes extradition conditional on the existence of a treaty receives a request for extradition from another State Party with which it has no extradition treaty, the requested State Party may, at its option, consider this Convention as a legal basis for extradition in respect of the offences set forth in Article 3. Extradition shall be subject to the other conditions provided by the law of the requested State Party.

3. States Parties which do not make extradition conditional on the existence of a treaty shall recognize the offences set forth in Article 3 as extraditable offences between themselves, subject to the conditions provided by the law of the requested State.

4. If necessary, the offences set forth in Article 3 shall be treated, for the purposes of extradition between States Parties, as if they had been committed not only in the place in which they occurred but also in a place within the jurisdiction of the State Party requesting extradition.

5. A State Party which receives more than one request for extradition from States which have established jurisdiction in accordance with Article 7 and which decides not to prosecute shall, in selecting the State to which the offender or alleged offender is to be extradited, pay due regard to the interests and responsibilities of the State Party whose flag the ship was flying at the time of the commission of the offence.

6. In considering a request for the extradition of an alleged offender pursuant to this Convention, the requested State shall pay due regard to whether his rights as set forth in Article 7, paragraph 3, can be effected in the requesting State.

7. With respect to the offences as defined in this Convention, the provisions of all extradition treaties and arrangements applicable between

States Parties are modified as between States Parties to the extent that they are incompatible with this Convention.

Article 12

1. State Parties shall afford one another the greatest measure of assistance in connection with criminal proceedings brought in respect of the offences set forth in Article 3, including assistance in obtaining evidence at their disposal necessary for the proceedings.

2. States Parties shall carry out their obligations under paragraph 1 in conformity with any treaties on mutual assistance that may exist between them. In the absence of such treaties, States Parties shall afford each other assistance in accordance with their national law.

Article 13

1. States Parties shall co-operate in the prevention of the offences set forth in Article 3, particularly by:

a. taking all practicable measures to prevent preparations in their respective territories for the commission of those offences within or outside their territories;
b. exchanging information in accordance with their national law, and co-ordinating administrative and other measures taken as appropriate to prevent the commission of offences set forth in Article 3.

2. When, due to the commission of an offence set forth in Article 3, the passage of a ship has been delayed or interrupted, any State Party in whose territory the ship or passengers or crew are present shall be bound to exercise all possible efforts to avoid a ship, its passengers, crew or cargo being unduly detained or delayed.

Article 14

Any State Party having reason to believe that an offence set forth in Article 3 will be committed shall, in accordance with its national law, furnish as promptly as possible any relevant information in its possession to those States which it believes would be the States having established jurisdiction in accordance with Article 6.

Article 15

1. Each State Party shall, in accordance with its national law) provide to

the Secretary-General, as promptly as possible, any relevant information in its possession concerning:

a. the circumstances of the offence;
b. the action taken pursuant to Article 13, paragraph 2;
c. the measures taken in relation to the offender or the alleged offender and, in particular, the results of any extradition proceedings or other legal proceedings.

2. The State Party where the alleged offender is prosecuted shall, in accordance with its national law, communicate the final outcome of the proceedings to the Secretary-General.

3. The information transmitted in accordance with paragraphs 1 and 2 shall be communicated by the Secretary-General to all States Parties, to Members of the International Maritime Organization (hereinafter referred to as "the Organization"), to the other States concerned, and to the appropriate international intergovernmental organizations.

Article 16

1. Any dispute between two or more States Parties concerning the interpretation or application of this Convention which cannot be settled through negotiation within a reasonable time shall, at the request of one of them, be submitted to arbitration. If, within six months from the date of the request for arbitration, the parties are unable to agree on the organization of the arbitration any one of those parties may refer the dispute to the International Court of Justice by request in conformity with the Statute of the Court.

2. Each State may at the time of signature or ratification, acceptance or approval of this Convention or accession thereto, declare that it does not consider itself bound by any or all of the provisions of paragraph 1. The other States Parties shall not be bound by those provisions with respect to any State Party which has made such a reservation.

3. Any State which has made a reservation in accordance with paragraph 2 may, at any time, withdraw that reservation by notification to the Secretary-General.

Article 17

1. This Convention shall be open for signature at Rome on 10 March 1988 by States participating in the International Conference on the Suppression of Unlawful Acts against the Safety of Maritime Navigation and at the

Headquarters of the Organization by all States from 14 March 1988 to 9 March 1989. It shall thereafter remain open for accession.

2. States may express their consent to be bound by this Convention by:

a. signature without reservation as to ratification, acceptance or approval; or
b. signature subject to ratification, acceptance or approval, followed by ratification, acceptance or approval; or
c. accession.

3. Ratification, acceptance, approval or accession shall be effected by the deposit of an instrument to that effect with the Secretary-General.

Article 18

1. This Convention shall enter into force ninety days following the date on which fifteen States have either signed it without reservation as to ratification, acceptance or approval, or have deposited an instrument of ratification, acceptance, approval or accession in respect thereof.

2. For a State which deposits an instrument of ratification, acceptance, approval or accession in respect of this Convention after the conditions for entry into force thereof have been met, the ratification, acceptance, approval or accession shall take effect ninety days after the date of such deposit.

Article 19

1. This Convention may be denounced by any State Party at any time after the expiry of one year from the date on which this Convention enters into force for that State.

2. Denunciation shall be effected by the deposit of an instrument of denunciation with the Secretary-General.

3. A denunciation shall take effect one year, or such longer period as may be specified in the instrument of denunciation, after the receipt of the instrument of denunciation by the Secretary-General.

Article 20

1. A conference for the purpose of revising or amending this Convention may be convened by the Organization.

2. The Secretary-General shall convene a conference of the States Parties to this Convention for revising or amending the Convention, at the request of one-third of the States Parties, or ten States Parties, whichever is the higher figure.

3. Any instrument of ratification, acceptance, approval or accession deposited after the date of entry into force of an amendment to this Convention shall be deemed to apply to the Convention as amended.

Article 21

1. This Convention shall be deposited with the Secretary-General.

2. The Secretary-General shall:

a. inform all States which have signed this Convention or acceded thereto, and all Members of the Organization, of:

   i. each new signature or deposit of an instrument of ratification, acceptance, approval or accession together with the date thereof;
   ii. the date of the entry into force of this Convention;
   iii. the deposit of any instrument of denunciation of this Convention together with the date on which it is received and the date on which the denunciation takes effect;
   iv. the receipt of any declaration or notification made under this Convention;

b. transmit certified true copies of this Convention to all States which have signed this Convention or acceded thereto.

3. As soon as this Convention enters into force, a certified true copy thereof shall be transmitted by the Depositary to the Secretary-General of the United Nations for registration and publication in accordance with Article 102 of the Charter of the United Nations.

Article 22

This Convention is established in a single original in the Arabic, Chinese, English, French, Russian and Spanish languages, each text being equally authentic.

IN WITNESS WHEREOF the undersigned being duly authorized by their respective Governments for that purpose have signed this Convention.

DONE at Rome this tenth day of March one thousand nine hundred and eighty-eight.

Disclaimer

The present version of the Conventions and Protocols might differ slightly from the consolidated official English versions which were—by end of November 2000—not available to TPB in electronic form. Please contact the Codification Division of the UN Office of Legal Affairs (United Nations, Room S-3450 A, New York, N.Y. 10017, USA) for the official versions in English and other official UN languages.

L. PROTOCOL FOR THE SUPPRESSION OF UNLAWFUL ACTS OF VIOLENCE AT AIRPORTS SERVING INTERNATIONAL CIVIL AVIATION (1971)

(Supplementary to the Convention for the Suppression of Unlawful Acts against the Safety of Civil Aviation)

Done at Montreal on 23 September 1971

THE STATES PARTIES to this Convention,

CONSIDERING that unlawful acts of violence which endanger or are likely to endanger the safety of persons at airports serving international civil aviation or which jeopardize the safe operation of such airports undermine the confidence of the peoples of the world in safety at such airports and disturb the safe and orderly conduct of civil aviation for all States;

CONSIDERING that the occurrence of such acts is a matter of grave concern to the international community and that, for the purpose of deterring such acts, there is an urgent need to provide appropriate measures for punishment of offenders;

CONSIDERING that it is necessary to adopt provisions supplementary to those of the Convention for the Suppression of Unlawful Acts against the Safety of Civil Aviation, done at Montreal on 23 September 1971, to deal with such unlawful acts of violence at airports serving international civil aviation;

HAVE agreed as follows:

Article 1

This Protocol supplements the Convention for the Suppression of Unlawful Acts against the Safety of Civil Aviation, done at Montreal on 23 September 1971 (hereinafter referred to as "the Convention"), and, as between the Parties to this Protocol, the Convention and the Protocol shall be read and interpreted together as one single instrument.

Article 2

1. In Article 1 of the Convention, the following shall be added as new paragraph 1 bis:

"1 bis: Any person commits an offence if he unlawfully and intentionally, using any device, substance or weapon:

a. performs an act of violence against a person at an airport serving international civil aviation which causes or is likely to cause serious injury or death; or
b. destroys or seriously damages the facilities of an airport serving international civil aviation or aircraft not in service located thereon or disrupts the services of the airport, if such an act endangers or is likely to endanger safety at that airport."

2. In paragraph 2 (a) of Article 1 of the Convention, the following words shall be inserted after the words "paragraph 1": or "paragraph 1 bis".

Article 3

In Article 5 of the Convention, the following shall be added as paragraph 2 bis:

"2 bis: Each Contracting State shall likewise take such measures as may be necessary to establish its jurisdiction over the offences mentioned in Article 1, paragraph 1 bis, and in Article 1, paragraph 2, in so far as that paragraph relates to those offences, in the case where the alleged offender is present in its territory and it does not extradite him pursuant to Article 8 to the State mentioned in paragraph 1(a) of this Article."

Article 4

This Protocol shall be open for signature at Montreal on 24 February 1988 by States participating in the International Conference on Air Law held at Montreal from 9 to 24 February 1988. After 1 March 1988, the Protocol shall be open for signature to all States in London, Moscow, Washington and Montreal, until it enters into force in accordance with Article 6.

Article 5

1. This Protocol shall be subject to ratification by the signatory States.

2. Any State which is not a Contracting State to the Convention may ratify this Protocol if at the same lime it ratifies or accedes to the Convention in accordance with Article 15 thereof.

3. Instruments of ratification shall be deposited with the Governments of the Union of Soviet Socialist Republics, the United Kingdom of Great Britain and Northern Ireland and the United States of America or with the

International Civil Aviation Organization, which are hereby designated the Depositaries.

Article 6

1. As soon as ten of the signatory States have deposited their instruments of ratification of this Protocol, it shall enter into force between them on the thirtieth day after the date of the deposit of the tenth instrument of ratification. It shall enter into force for each State which deposits its instrument of ratification after that date on the thirtieth day after deposit of its instrument of ratification

2. As soon as this Protocol enters into force, it shall be registered by the Depositaries pursuant to Article 102 of the Charter of the United Nations and pursuant to Article 83 of the Convention on International Civil Aviation (Chicago, 1944).

Article 7

1. This Protocol shall, after it has entered into force, be open for accession by any nonsignatory State.

2. Any State which is not a Contracting State to the Convention may accede to this Protocol if at the same time it ratifies or accedes to the Convention in accordance with Article 15 thereof.

3. Instruments of accession shall be deposited with the Depositaries and accession shall take effect on the thirtieth day after the deposit.

Article 8

1. Any Party to this Protocol may denounce it by written notification addressed to the Depositaries.

2. Denunciation shall take effect six months following the date on which notification is received by the Depositaries.

3. Denunciation of this Protocol shall not of itself have the effect of denunciation of the Convention.

4. Denunciation of the Convention by a Contracting State to the Convention as supplemented by this Protocol shall also have the effect of denunciation of this Protocol.

Article 9

1. The Depositaries shall promptly inform all signatory and acceding States to this Protocol and all signatory and acceding States to the Convention:

a. of the date of each signature and the date of deposit of each instrument of ratification of, or accession to, this Protocol, and
b. of the receipt of any notification of denunciation of this Protocol and the date thereof.

2. The Depositaries shall also notify the States referred to in paragraph 1 of the date on which this Protocol enters into force in accordance with Article 6.

IN WITNESS WHEREOF the undersigned Plenipotentiaries, being duly authorized thereto by their Governments, have signed this Protocol.

DONE at Montreal on the twenty-fourth day of February of the year one thousand nine hundred and eighty-eight, in four originals, each being drawn up in four authentic texts in the English, French, Russian and Spanish languages.

Disclaimer

The present version of the Conventions and Protocols might differ slightly from the consolidated official English versions which were—by end of November 2000—not available to TPB in electronic form. Please contact the Codification Division of the UN Office of Legal Affairs (United Nations, Room S-3450 A, New York, N.Y. 10017, USA) for the official versions in English and other official UN languages.

M. INTERNATIONAL CONVENTION FOR THE SUPPRESSION OF TERRORIST BOMBING

New York: 12 January 1998

THE STATES PARTIES to this Convention,

HAVING in mind the purposes and principles of the Charter of the United Nations concerning the maintenance of international peace and security and the promotion of good-neighbourliness and friendly relations and cooperation among States,

DEEPLY concerned about the worldwide escalation of acts of terrorism in all its forms and manifestations,

RECALLING the Declaration on the Occasion of the Fiftieth Anniversary of the United Nations of 24 October 1995,

RECALLING also the Declaration on Measures to Eliminate International Terrorism, annexed to General Assembly Resolution 49/60 of 9 December 1994, in which, inter alia, "the States Members of the United Nations solemnly reaffirm their unequivocal condemnation of all acts, methods and practices of terrorism as criminal and unjustifiable, wherever and by whomever committed, including those which jeopardize the friendly relations among States and peoples and threaten the territorial integrity and security of States",

NOTING that the Declaration also encouraged States "to review urgently the scope of the existing international legal provisions on the prevention, repression and elimination of terrorism in all its forms and manifestations, with the aim of ensuring that there is a comprehensive legal framework covering all aspects of the matter",

RECALLING General Assembly Resolution 51/210 of 17 December 1996 and the Declaration to Supplement the 1994 Declaration on Measures to Eliminate International Terrorism annexed thereto,

NOTING that terrorist attacks by means of explosives or other lethal devices have become increasingly widespread,

NOTING also that existing multilateral legal provisions do not adequately address these attacks,

BEING convinced of the urgent need to enhance international cooperation between States in devising and adopting effective and practical measures for the prevention of such acts of terrorism and for the prosecution and punishment of their perpetrators,

CONSIDERING that the occurrence of such acts is a matter of grave concern to the international community as a whole,

NOTING that the activities of military forces of States are governed by rules of international law outside the framework of this Convention and that the exclusion of certain actions from the coverage of this Convention does not condone or make lawful otherwise unlawful acts, or preclude prosecution under other laws,

HAVE agreed as follows:

Article 1

For the purposes of this Convention

1. "State or government facility" includes any permanent or temporary facility or conveyance that is used or occupied by representatives of a State, members of Government, the legislature or the judiciary or by officials or employees of a State or any other public authority or entity or by employees or officials of an intergovernmental organization in connection with their official duties.

2. "Infrastructure facility" means any publicly or privately owned facility providing or distributing services for the benefit of the public, such as water, sewage, energy, fuel or communications.

3. "Explosive or other lethal device" means:

a. An explosive or incendiary weapon or device that is designed, or has the capability, to cause death, serious bodily injury or substantial material damage; or

b. A weapon or device that is designed, or has the capability, to cause death, serious bodily injury or substantial material damage through the release, dissemination or impact of toxic chemicals, biological agents or toxins or similar substances or radiation or radioactive material.

4. "Military forces of a State" means the armed forces of a State which are organized, trained and equipped under its internal law for the primary purpose of national defence or security and persons acting in support of those armed forces who are under their formal command, control and responsibility.

5. "Place of public use" means those parts of any building, land, street,

waterway or other location that are accessible or open to members of the public, whether continuously, periodically or occasionally, and encompasses any commercial, business, cultural, historical, educational, religious, governmental, entertainment, recreational or similar place that is so accessible or open to the public.

6. "Public transportation system" means all facilities, conveyances and instrumentalities, whether publicly or privately owned, that are used in or for publicly available services for the transportation of persons or cargo.

Article 2

1. Any person commits an offence within the meaning of this Convention if that person unlawfully and intentionally delivers, places, discharges or detonates an explosive or other lethal device in, into or against a place of public use, a State or government facility, a public transportation system or an infrastructure facility:

a. With the intent to cause death or serious bodily injury; or
b. With the intent to cause extensive destruction of such a place, facility or system, where such destruction results in or is likely to result in major economic loss.

2. Any person also commits an offence if that person attempts to commit an offence as set forth in paragraph 1 of the present article.

3. Any person also commits an offence if that person:

a. Participates as an accomplice in an offence as set forth in paragraph 1 or 2 of the present article; or
b. Organizes or directs others to commit an offence as set forth in paragraph 1 or 2 of the present article; or
c. In any other way contributes to the commission of one or more offences as set forth in paragraph 1 or 2 of the present article by a group of persons acting with a common purpose; such contribution shall be intentional and either be made with the aim of furthering the general criminal activity or purpose of the group or be made in the knowledge of the intention of the group to commit the offence or offences concerned.

Article 3

This Convention shall not apply where the offence is committed within a single State, the alleged offender and the victims are nationals of that State, the alleged offender is found in the territory of that State and no other State has a basis under Article 6, paragraph 1 or paragraph 2, of this Convention to exercise jurisdiction, except that the provisions of Articles 10 to 15 shall, as appropriate, apply in those cases.

Article 4

Each State Party shall adopt such measures as may be necessary:

a. To establish as criminal offences under its domestic law the offences set forth in Article 2 of this Convention;
b. To make those offences punishable by appropriate penalties which take into account the grave nature of those offences.

Article 5

Each State Party shall adopt such measures as may be necessary, including, where appropriate, domestic legislation, to ensure that criminal acts within the scope of this Convention, in particular where they are intended or calculated to provoke a state of terror in the general public or in a group of persons or particular persons, are under no circumstances justifiable by considerations of a political, philosophical, ideological, racial, ethnic, religious or other similar nature and are punished by penalties consistent with their grave nature.

Article 6

1. Each State Party shall take such measures as may be necessary to establish its jurisdiction over the offences set forth in Article 2 when:

a. The offence is committed in the territory of that State; or
b. The offence is committed on board a vessel flying the flag of that State or an aircraft which is registered under the laws of that State at the time the offence is committed; or
c. The offence is committed by a national of that State.

2. A State Party may also establish its jurisdiction over any such offence when:

a. The offence is committed against a national of that State; or
b. The offence is committed against a State or government facility of that State abroad, including an embassy or other diplomatic or consular premises of that State; or

c. The offence is committed by a stateless person who has his or her habitual residence in the territory of that State; or
d. The offence is committed in an attempt to compel that State to do or abstain from doing any act; or
e. The offence is committed on board an aircraft which is operated by the Government of that State.

3. Upon ratifying, accepting, approving or acceding to this Convention, each State Party shall notify the Secretary-General of the United Nations of the jurisdiction it has established under its domestic law in accordance with paragraph 2 of the present article. Should any change take place, the State Party concerned shall immediately notify the Secretary-General.

4. Each State Party shall likewise take such measures as may be necessary to establish its jurisdiction over the offences set forth in Article 2 in cases where the alleged offender is present in its territory and it does not extradite that person to any of the States Parties which have established their jurisdiction in accordance with paragraph 1 or 2 of the present article.

5. This Convention does not exclude the exercise of any criminal jurisdiction established by a State Party in accordance with its domestic law.

Article 7

1. Upon receiving information that a person who has committed or who is alleged to have committed an offence as set forth in Article 2 may be present in its territory, the State Party concerned shall take such measures as may be necessary under its domestic law to investigate the facts contained in the information.

2. Upon being satisfied that the circumstances so warrant, the State Party in whose territory the offender or alleged offender is present shall take the appropriate measures under its domestic law so as to ensure that person's presence for the purpose of prosecution or extradition.

3. Any person regarding whom the measures referred to in paragraph 2 of the present article are being taken shall be entitled to:

a. Communicate without delay with the nearest appropriate representative of the State of which that person is a national or which is otherwise entitled to protect that person's rights or, if that person is a stateless person, the State in the territory of which that person habitually resides;
b. Be visited by a representative of that State;

c. Be informed of that person's rights under subparagraphs (a) and (b).

4. The rights referred to in paragraph 3 of the present article shall be exercised in conformity with the laws and regulations of the State in the territory of which the offender or alleged offender is present, subject to the provision that the said laws and regulations must enable full effect to be given to the purposes for which the rights accorded under paragraph 3 are intended.

5. The provisions of paragraphs 3 and 4 of the present article shall be without prejudice to the right of any State Party having a claim to jurisdiction in accordance with article 6, subparagraph 1 (c) or 2 (c), to invite the International Committee of the Red Cross to communicate with and visit the alleged offender.

6. When a State Party, pursuant to the present Article, has taken a person into custody, it shall immediately notify, directly or through the Secretary-General of the United Nations, the States Parties which have established jurisdiction in accordance with Article 6, paragraphs 1 and 2, and, if it considers it advisable, any other interested States Parties, of the fact that that person is in custody and of the circumstances which warrant that person's detention. The State which makes the investigation contemplated in paragraph 1 of the present article shall promptly inform the said States Parties of its findings and shall indicate whether it intends to exercise jurisdiction.

Article 8

1. The State Party in the territory of which the alleged offender is present shall, in cases to which Article 6 applies, if it does not extradite that person, be obliged, without exception whatsoever and whether or not the offence was committed in its territory, to submit the case without undue delay to its competent authorities for the purpose of prosecution, through proceedings in accordance with the laws of that State. Those authorities shall take their decision in the same manner as in the case of any other offence of a grave nature under the law of that State.

2. Whenever a State Party is permitted under its domestic law to extradite or otherwise surrender one of its nationals only upon the condition that the person will be returned to that State to serve the sentence imposed as a result of the trial or proceeding for which the extradition or surrender of the person was sought, and this State and the State seeking the extradition of the person agree with this option and other terms they may deem appropriate, such a conditional extradition or surrender shall be

sufficient to discharge the obligation set forth in paragraph 1 of the present article.

Article 9

1. The offences set forth in Article 2 shall be deemed to be included as extraditable offences in any extradition treaty existing between any of the States Parties before the entry into force of this Convention. States Parties undertake to include such offences as extraditable offences in every extradition treaty to be subsequently concluded between them.

2. When a State Party which makes extradition conditional on the existence of a treaty receives a request for extradition from another State Party with which it has no extradition treaty, the requested State Party may, at its option, consider this Convention as a legal basis for extradition in respect of the offences set forth in Article 2. Extradition shall be subject to the other conditions provided by the law of the requested State.

3. States Parties which do not make extradition conditional on the existence of a treaty shall recognize the offences set forth in Article 2 as extraditable offences between themselves, subject to the conditions provided by the law of the requested State.

4. If necessary, the offences set forth in Article 2 shall be treated, for the purposes of extradition between States Parties, as if they had been committed not only in the place in which they occurred but also in the territory of the States that have established jurisdiction in accordance with Article 6, paragraphs 1 and 2.

5. The provisions of all extradition treaties and arrangements between States Parties with regard to offences set forth in Article 2 shall be deemed to be modified as between State Parties to the extent that they are incompatible with this Convention.

Article 10

1. States Parties shall afford one another the greatest measure of assistance in connection with investigations or criminal or extradition proceedings brought in respect of the offences set forth in Article 2, including assistance in obtaining evidence at their disposal necessary for the proceedings.

2. States Parties shall carry out their obligations under paragraph 1 of the present article in conformity with any treaties or other arrangements on mutual legal assistance that may exist between them. In the absence of such treaties or arrangements, States Parties shall afford one another assistance in accordance with their domestic law.

Article 11

None of the offences set forth in Article 2 shall be regarded, for the purposes of extradition or mutual legal assistance, as a political offence or as an offence connected with a political offence or as an offence inspired by political motives. Accordingly, a request for extradition or for mutual legal assistance based on such an offence may not be refused on the sole ground that it concerns a political offence or an offence connected with a political offence or an offence inspired by political motives.

Article 12

Nothing in this Convention shall be interpreted as imposing an obligation to extradite or to afford mutual legal assistance, if the requested State Party has substantial grounds for believing that the request for extradition for offences set forth in Article 2 or for mutual legal assistance with respect to such offences has been made for the purpose of prosecuting or punishing a person on account of that person's race, religion, nationality, ethnic origin or political opinion or that compliance with the request would cause prejudice to that person's position for any of these reasons.

Article 13

1. A person who is being detained or is serving a sentence in the territory of one State Party whose presence in another State Party is requested for purposes of testimony, identification or otherwise providing assistance in obtaining evidence for the investigation or prosecution of offences under this Convention may be transferred if the following conditions are met:

a. The person freely gives his or her informed consent; and
b. The competent authorities of both States agree, subject to such conditions as those States may deem appropriate.

2. For the purposes of the present article:

a. The State to which the person is transferred shall have the authority and obligation to keep the person transferred in custody, unless otherwise requested or authorized by the State from which the person was transferred;
b. The State to which the person is transferred shall without delay implement its obligation to return the person to the custody of the State from which the person was transferred as agreed beforehand,

or as otherwise agreed, by the competent authorities of both States;

c. The State to which the person is transferred shall not require the State from which the person was transferred to initiate extradition proceedings for the return of the person;
d. The person transferred shall receive credit for service of the sentence being served in the State from which he was transferred for time spent in the custody of the State to which he was transferred.

3. Unless the State Party from which a person is to be transferred in accordance with the present article so agrees, that person, whatever his or her nationality, shall not be prosecuted or detained or subjected to any other restriction of his or her personal liberty in the territory of the State to which that person is transferred in respect of acts or convictions anterior to his or her departure from the territory of the State from which such person was transferred.

Article 14

Any person who is taken into custody or regarding whom any other measures are taken or proceedings are carried out pursuant to this Convention shall be guaranteed fair treatment, including enjoyment of all rights and guarantees in conformity with the law of the State in the territory of which that person is present and applicable provisions of international law, including international law of human rights.

Article 15

States Parties shall cooperate in the prevention of the offences set forth in Article 2, particularly:

a. By taking all practicable measures, including, if necessary, adapting their domestic legislation, to prevent and counter preparations in their respective territories for the commission of those offences within or outside their territories, including measures to prohibit in their territories illegal activities of persons, groups and organizations that encourage, instigate, organize, knowingly finance or engage in the perpetration of offences as set forth in Article 2;
b. By exchanging accurate and verified information in accordance with their national law, and coordinating administrative and other measures taken as appropriate to prevent the commission of offences as set forth in Article 2;

c. Where appropriate, through research and development regarding methods of detection of explosives and other harmful substances that can cause death or bodily injury, consultations on the development of standards for marking explosives in order to identify their origin in post-blast investigations, exchange of information on preventive measures, cooperation and transfer of technology, equipment and related materials.

Article 16

The State Party where the alleged offender is prosecuted shall, in accordance with its domestic law or applicable procedures, communicate the final outcome of the proceedings to the Secretary-General of the United Nations, who shall transmit the information to the other States Parties.

Article 17

The States Parties shall carry out their obligations under this Convention in a manner consistent with the principles of sovereign equality and territorial integrity of States and that of non-intervention in the domestic affairs of other States.

Article 18

Nothing in this Convention entitles a State Party to undertake in the territory of another State Party the exercise of jurisdiction and performance of functions which are exclusively reserved for the authorities of that other State Party by its domestic law.

Article 19

1. Nothing in this Convention shall affect other rights, obligations and responsibilities of States and individuals under international law, in particular the purposes and principles of the Charter of the United Nations and international humanitarian law.

2. The activities of armed forces during an armed conflict, as those terms are understood under international humanitarian law, which are governed by that law, are not governed by this Convention, and the activities undertaken by military forces of a State in the exercise of their official duties, inasmuch as they are governed by other rules of international law, are not governed by this Convention.

Article 20

1. Any dispute between two or more States Parties concerning the interpretation or application of this Convention which cannot be settled through negotiation within a reasonable time shall, at the request of one of them, be submitted to arbitration. If, within six months from the date of the request for arbitration, the parties are unable to agree on the organization of the arbitration, any one of those parties may refer the dispute to the International Court of Justice, by application, in conformity with the Statute of the Court.

2. Each State may at the time of signature, ratification, acceptance or approval of this Convention or accession thereto declare that it does not consider itself bound by paragraph 1 of the present article. The other States Parties shall not be bound by paragraph 1 with respect to any State Party which has made such a reservation.

3. Any State which has made a reservation in accordance with paragraph 2 of the present article may at any time withdraw that reservation by notification to the Secretary-General of the United Nations.

Article 21

1. This Convention shall be open for signature by all States from 12 January 1998 until 31 December 1999 at United Nations Headquarters in New York.

2. This Convention is subject to ratification, acceptance or approval. The instruments of ratification, acceptance or approval shall be deposited with the Secretary-General of the United Nations.

3. This Convention shall be open to accession by any State. The instruments of accession shall be deposited with the Secretary-General of the United Nations.

Article 22

1. This Convention shall enter into force on the thirtieth day following the date of the deposit of the twenty-second instrument of ratification, acceptance, approval or accession with the Secretary-General of the United Nations.

2. For each State ratifying, accepting, approving or acceding to the Convention after the deposit of the twenty-second instrument of ratification, acceptance, approval or accession, the Convention shall enter into force on the thirtieth day after deposit by such State of its instrument of ratification, acceptance, approval or accession.

Article 23

1. Any State Party may denounce this Convention by written notification to the Secretary-General of the United Nations.

2. Denunciation shall take effect one year following the date on which notification is received by the Secretary-General of the United Nations.

Article 24

The original of this Convention, of which the Arabic, Chinese, English, French, Russian and Spanish texts are equally authentic, shall be deposited with the Secretary-General of the United Nations, who shall send certified copies thereof to all States.

Disclaimer

The present version of the Conventions and Protocols might differ slightly from the consolidated official English versions which were—by end of November 2000—not available to TPB in electronic form. Please contact the Codification Division of the UN Office of Legal Affairs (United Nations, Room S-3450 A, New York, N.Y. 10017, USA) for the official versions in English and other official UN languages.

N. INTERNATIONAL CONVENTION FOR THE SUPPRESSION OF THE FINANCING OF TERRORISM

United Nations, 1999

Preamble

THE STATES PARTIES to this Convention,

BEARING in mind the purposes and principles of the Charter of the United Nations concerning the maintenance of international peace and security and the promotion of good-neighbourliness and friendly relations and cooperation among States,

DEEPLY concerned about the worldwide escalation of acts of terrorism in all its forms and manifestations,

RECALLING the Declaration on the Occasion of the Fiftieth Anniversary of the United Nations, contained in General Assembly Resolution 50/6 of 24 October 1995,

RECALLING also all the relevant General Assembly resolutions on the matter, including Resolution 49/60 of 9 December 1994 and its annex on the Declaration on Measures to Eliminate International Terrorism, in which the States Members of the United Nations solemnly reaffirmed their unequivocal condemnation of all acts, methods and practices of terrorism as criminal and unjustifiable, wherever and by whomever committed, including those which jeopardize the friendly relations among States and peoples and threaten the territorial integrity and security of States,

NOTING that the Declaration on Measures to Eliminate International Terrorism also encouraged States to review urgently the scope of the existing international legal provisions on the prevention, repression and elimination of terrorism in all its forms and manifestations, with the aim of ensuring that there is a comprehensive legal framework covering all aspects of the matter,

RECALLING General Assembly Resolution 51/210 of 17 December 1996, paragraph 3, subparagraph (f), in which the Assembly called upon all States to take steps to prevent and counteract, through appropriate domestic measures, the financing of terrorists and terrorist organizations, whether such financing is direct or indirect through organizations which also have or claim to have charitable, social or cultural goals or which are also engaged in unlawful activities such as illicit arms trafficking, drug dealing and racketeering, including the exploitation of persons for purposes of funding terrorist activities, and in particular to consider, where appropriate, adopting regulatory measures to prevent and counteract movements of funds suspected to be intended for terrorist purposes without impeding in any way the freedom of legitimate capital movements and to intensify the exchange of information concerning international movements of such funds,

RECALLING also General Assembly Resolution 52/165 of 15 December 1997, in which the Assembly called upon States to consider, in particular, the implementation. of the measures set out in paragraphs 3 (a) to (f) of its resolution 51/210 of 17 December 1996,

RECALLING further General Assembly Resolution 53/108 of 8 December 1998, in which the Assembly decided that the Ad Hoc Committee established by General Assembly Resolution 51/210 of 17 December 1996 should elaborate a draft international convention for the suppression of terrorist financing to supplement related existing international instruments,

CONSIDERING that the financing of terrorism is a matter of grave concern to the international community as a whole, *Noting* that the number and seriousness of acts of international terrorism depend on the financing that terrorists may obtain,

NOTING also that existing multilateral legal instruments do not expressly address such financing,

BEING convinced of the urgent need to enhance international cooperation among States in devising and adopting effective measures for the prevention of the financing of terrorism, as well as for its suppression through the prosecution and punishment of its perpetrators,

HAVE agreed as follows:

Article 1

For the purposes of this Convention:

1. "Fund' means assets of every kind, whether tangible or intangible, movable or immovable, however acquired, and legal documents or instruments in any form, including electronic or digital, evidencing title to, or interest in, such assets, including, but not limited to, bank credits,

travellers cheques, bank cheques, money orders, shares, securities, bonds, drafts, letters of credit.

2. "A State or governmental facility" means any permanent or temporary facility or conveyance that is used or occupied by representatives of a State, members of Government, the legislature or the judiciary or by officials or employees of a State or any other public authority or entity or by employees or officials of an intergovernmental organization in connection with their official duties.

3. "Proceeds" means any funds derived from or obtained, directly or indirectly, through the commission of an offence set forth in Article 2.

Article 2

1. Any person commits an offence within the meaning of this Convention if that person by any means, directly or indirectly, unlawfully and wilfully, provides or collects funds with the intention that they should be used or in the knowledge that they are to be used, in full or in part, in order to carry out:

(a) An act which constitutes an offence within the scope of and as defined in one of the treaties listed in the annex; or

(b) Any other act intended to cause death or serious bodily injury to a civilian, or to any other person not taking an active part in the hostilities in a situation of armed conflict, when the purpose of such act, by its nature or context, is to intimidate a population, or to compel a government or an international organization to do or to abstain from doing any act.

2. (a) On depositing its instrument of ratification, acceptance, approval or accession, a State Party which is not a party to a treaty listed in the annex may declare that, in the application of this Convention to the State Party, the treaty shall be deemed not to be included in the annex referred to in paragraph 1, subparagraph (a). The declaration shall cease to have effect as soon as the treaty enters into force for the State Party, which shall notify the depositary of this fact;

(b) When a State Party ceases to be a party to a treaty listed in the annex, it may make a declaration as provided for in this article, with respect to that treaty.

3. For an act to constitute an offence set forth in paragraph 1, it shall not be necessary that the funds were actually used to carry out an offence referred to in paragraph 1, subparagraphs (a) or (b).

4. Any person also commits an offence if that person attempts to

commit an offence as set forth in paragraph 1 of this article.

5. Any person also commits an offence if that person:

(a) Participates as an accomplice in an offence as set forth in paragraph 1 or 4 of this article;
(b) Organizes or directs others to commit an offence as set forth in paragraph 1 or 4 of this article;
(c) Contributes to the commission of one or more offences as set forth in paragraphs 1 or 4 of this article by a group of persons acting with a common purpose. Such contribution shall be intentional and shall either:

    (i) Be made with the aim of furthering the criminal activity or criminal purpose of the group, where such activity or purpose involves the commission of an offence as set forth in paragraph 1 of this article; or
    (ii) Be made in the knowledge of the intention of the group to commit an offence as set forth in paragraph 1 of this article.

Article 3

This Convention shall not apply where the offence is committed within a single State, the alleged offender is a national of that State and is present in the territory of that State and no other State has a basis under Article 7, paragraph 1, or Article 7, paragraph 2, to exercise jurisdiction, except that the provisions of Articles 12 to 18 shall, as appropriate, apply in those cases.

Article 4

Each State Party shall adopt such measures as may be necessary:

(a) To establish as criminal offences under its domestic law the offences set forth in Article 2;
(b) To make those offences punishable by appropriate penalties which take into account the grave nature of the offences.

Article 5

1. Each State Party, in accordance with its domestic legal principles, shall take the necessary measures to enable a legal entity located in its territory or organized under its laws to be held liable when a person responsible for the management or control of that legal entity has, in that capacity,

committed an offence set forth in Article 2. Such liability may be criminal, civil or administrative.

2. Such liability is incurred without prejudice to the criminal liability of individuals having committed the offences.

3. Each State Party shall ensure, in particular, that legal entities liable in accordance with paragraph 1 above are subject to effective, proportionate and dissuasive criminal, civil or administrative sanctions. Such sanctions may include monetary sanctions.

Article 6

Each State Party shall adopt such measures as may be necessary, including, where appropriate, domestic legislation, to ensure that criminal acts within the scope of this Convention are under no circumstances justifiable by considerations of a political, philosophical, ideological, racial, ethnic, religious or other similar nature.

Article 7

1. Each State Party shall take such measures as may be necessary to establish its jurisdiction over the offences set forth in Article 2 when:

(a) The offence is committed in the territory of that State;
(b) The offence is committed on board a vessel flying the flag of that State or an aircraft registered under the laws of that State at the time the offence is committed;
(c) The offence is committed by a national of that State.

2. A State Party may also establish its jurisdiction over any such offence when:

(a) The offence was directed towards or resulted in the carrying out of an offence referred to in Article 2, paragraph 1, subparagraph (a) or (b), in the territory of or against a national of that State;
(b) The offence was directed towards or resulted in the carrying out of an offence referred to in Article 2, paragraph 1, subparagraph (a) or (b), against a State or government facility of that State abroad, including diplomatic or consular premises of that State;
(c) The offence was directed towards or resulted in an offence referred to in Article 2, paragraph 1, subparagraph (a) or (b), committed in an attempt to compel that State to do or abstain from doing any act;
(d) The offence is committed by a stateless person who has his or her habitual residence in the territory of that State;

(e) The offence is committed on board an aircraft which is operated by the Government of that State.

3. Upon ratifying, accepting, approving or acceding to this Convention, each State Party shall notify the Secretary-General of the United Nations of the jurisdiction it has established in accordance with paragraph 2. Should any change take place, the State Party concerned shall immediately notify the Secretary-General.

4. Each State Party shall likewise take such measures as may be necessary to establish its jurisdiction over the offences set forth in Article 2 in cases where the alleged offender is present in its territory and it does not extradite that person to any of the States Parties that have established their jurisdiction in accordance with paragraphs 1 or 2.

5. When more than one State Party claims jurisdiction over the offences set forth in Article 2, the relevant States Parties shall strive to coordinate their actions appropriately, in particular concerning the conditions for prosecution and the modalities for mutual legal assistance.

6. Without prejudice to the norms of general international law, this Convention does not exclude the exercise of any criminal jurisdiction established by a State Party in accordance with its domestic law.

Article 8

1. Each State Party shall take appropriate measures, in accordance with its domestic legal principles, for the identification, detection and freezing or seizure of any funds used or allocated for the purpose of committing the offences set forth in Article 2 as well as the proceeds derived from such offences, for purposes of possible forfeiture.

2. Each State Party shall take appropriate measures, in accordance with its domestic legal principles, for the forfeiture of funds used or allocated for the purpose of committing the offences set forth in Article 2 and the proceeds derived from such offences.

3. Each State Party concerned may give consideration to concluding agreements on the sharing with other States Parties, on a regular or case-by-case basis, of the funds derived from the forfeitures referred to in this article.

4. Each State Party shall consider establishing mechanisms whereby the funds derived from the forfeitures referred to in this article are utilized to compensate the victims of offences referred to in Article 2, paragraph 1, subparagraph (a) or (b), or their families.

5. The provisions of this article shall be implemented without prejudice to the rights of third parties acting in good faith.

Article 9

1. Upon receiving information that a person who has committed or who is alleged to have committed an offence set forth in Article 2 may be present in its territory, the State Party concerned shall take such measures as may be necessary under its domestic law to investigate the facts contained in the information.

2. Upon being satisfied that the circumstances so warrant, the State Party in whose territory the offender or alleged offender is present shall take the appropriate measures under its domestic law so as to ensure that person's presence for the purpose of prosecution or extradition.

3. Any person regarding whom the measures referred to in paragraph 2 are being taken shall be entitled to:

(a) Communicate without delay with the nearest appropriate representative of the State of which that person is a national or which is otherwise entitled to protect that person's rights or, if that person is a stateless person, the State in the territory of which that person habitually resides;
(b) Be visited by a representative of that State;
(c) Be informed of that person's rights under subparagraphs (a) and (b).

4. The rights referred to in paragraph 3 shall be exercised in conformity with the laws and regulations of the State in the territory of which the offender or alleged offender is present, subject to the provision that the said laws and regulations must enable full effect to be given to the purposes for which the rights accorded under paragraph 3 are intended.

5. The provisions of paragraphs 3 and 4 shall be without prejudice to the right of any State Party having a claim to jurisdiction in accordance with Article 7, paragraph 1, subparagraph (b), or paragraph 2, subparagraph (b), to invite the International Committee of the Red Cross to communicate with and visit the alleged offender.

6. When a State Party, pursuant to the present article, has taken a person into custody, it shall immediately notify, directly or through the Secretary-General of the United Nations, the States Parties which have established jurisdiction in accordance with Article 7, paragraph 1 or 2, and, if it considers it advisable, any other interested States Parties, of the fact that such person is in custody and of the circumstances which warrant that person's detention. The State which makes the investigation contemplated in paragraph 1 shall promptly inform the said States Parties of its findings and shall indicate whether it intends to exercise jurisdiction.

Article 10

1. The State Party in the territory of which the alleged offender is present shall, in cases to which article 7 applies, if it does not extradite that person, be obliged, without exception whatsoever and whether or not the offence was committed in its territory, to submit the case without undue delay to its competent authorities for the purpose of prosecution, through proceedings in accordance with the laws of that State. Those authorities shall take their decision in the same manner as in the case of any other offence of a grave nature under the law of that State.

2. Whenever a State Party is permitted under its domestic law to extradite or otherwise surrender one of its nationals only upon the condition that the person will be returned to that State to serve the sentence imposed as a result of the trial or proceeding for which the extradition or surrender of the person was sought, and this State and the State seeking the extradition of the person agree with this option and other terms they may deem appropriate, such a conditional extradition or surrender shall be sufficient to discharge the obligation set forth in paragraph 1.

Article 11

1. The offences set forth in Article 2 shall be deemed to be included as extraditable offences in any extradition treaty existing between any of the States Parties before the entry into force of this Convention. States Parties undertake to include such offences as extraditable offences in every extradition treaty to be subsequently concluded between them.

2. When a State Party which makes extradition conditional on the existence of a treaty receives a request for extradition from another State Party with which it has no extradition treaty, the requested State Party may, at its option, consider this Convention as a legal basis for extradition in respect of the offences set forth in Article 2. Extradition shall be subject to the other conditions provided by the law of the requested State.

3. States Parties which do not make extradition conditional on the existence of a treaty shall recognize the offences set forth in Article 2 as extraditable offences between themselves, subject to the conditions provided by the law of the requested State.

4. If necessary, the offences set forth in Article 2 shall be treated, for the purposes of extradition between States Parties, as if they had been committed not only in the place in which they occurred but also in the territory of the States that have established jurisdiction in accordance with Article 7, paragraphs 1 and 2.

5. The provisions of all extradition treaties and arrangements between

States Parties with regard to offences set forth in Article 2 shall be deemed to be modified as between States Parties to the extent that they are incompatible with this Convention.

Article 12

1. States Parties shall afford one another the greatest measure of assistance in connection with criminal investigations or criminal or extradition proceedings in respect of the offences set forth in Article 2, including assistance in obtaining evidence in their possession necessary for the proceedings.

2. States Parties may not refuse a request for mutual legal assistance on the ground of bank secrecy.

3. The requesting Party shall not transmit nor use information or evidence furnished by the requested Party for investigations, prosecutions or proceedings other than those stated in the request without the prior consent of the requested Party.

4. Each State Party may give consideration to establishing mechanisms to share with other States Parties information or evidence needed to establish criminal, civil or administrative liability pursuant to Article 5.

5. States Parties shall carry out their obligations under paragraphs 1 and 2 in conformity with any treaties or other arrangements on mutual legal assistance or information exchange that may exist between them. In the absence of such treaties or arrangements, States Parties shall afford one another assistance in accordance with their domestic law.

Article 13

None of the offences set forth in Article 2 shall be regarded, for the purposes of extradition or mutual legal assistance, as a fiscal offence. Accordingly, States Parties may not refuse a request for extradition or for mutual legal assistance on the sole ground that it concerns a fiscal offence.

Article 14

None of the offences set forth in Article 2 shall be regarded for the purposes of extradition or mutual legal assistance as a political offence or as an offence connected with a political offence or as an offence inspired by political motives. Accordingly, a request for extradition or for mutual legal assistance based on such an offence may not be refused on the sole ground that it concerns a political offence or an offence connected with a political offence or an offence inspired by political motives.

Article 15

Nothing in this Convention shall be interpreted as imposing an obligation to extradite or to afford mutual legal assistance, if the requested State Party has substantial grounds for believing that the request for extradition for offences set forth in Article 2 or for mutual legal assistance with respect to such offences has been made for the purpose of prosecuting or punishing a person on account of that person's race, religion, nationality, ethnic origin or political opinion or that compliance with the request would cause prejudice to that person's position for any of these reasons.

Article 16

1. A person who is being detained or is serving a sentence in the territory of one State Party whose presence in another State Party is requested for purposes of identification, testimony or otherwise providing assistance in obtaining evidence for the investigation or prosecution of offences set forth in Article 2 may be transferred if the following conditions are met:

(a) The person freely gives his or her informed consent;
(b) The competent authorities of both States agree, subject to such conditions as those States may deem appropriate.

2. For the purposes of the present article:

(a) The State to which the person is transferred shall have the authority and obligation to keep the person transferred in custody, unless otherwise requested or authorized by the State from which the person was transferred;
(b) The State to which the person is transferred shall without delay implement its obligation to return the person to the custody of the State from which the person was transferred as agreed beforehand, or as otherwise agreed, by the competent authorities of both States;
(c) The State to which the person is transferred shall not require the State from which the person was transferred to initiate extradition proceedings for the return of the person;
(d) The person transferred shall receive credit for service of the sentence being served in the State from which he or she was transferred for time spent in the custody of the State to which he or she was transferred.

3. Unless the State Party from which a person is to be transferred in accordance with the present article so agrees, that person, whatever his or

her nationality, shall not be prosecuted or detained or subjected to any other restriction of his or her personal liberty in the territory of the State to which that person is transferred in respect of acts or convictions anterior to his or her departure from the territory of the State from which such person was transferred.

Article 17

Any person who is taken into custody or regarding whom any other measures are taken or proceedings are carried out pursuant to this Convention shall be guaranteed fair treatment, including enjoyment of all rights and guarantees in conformity with the law of the State in the territory of which that person is present and applicable provisions of international law, including international human rights law.

Article 18

1. States Parties shall cooperate in the prevention of the offences set forth in Article 2 by taking all practicable measures, inter alia, by adapting their domestic legislation, if necessary, to prevent and counter preparations in their respective territories for the commission of those offences within or outside their territories, including:

(a) Measures to prohibit in their territories illegal activities of persons and organizations that knowingly encourage, instigate, organize or engage in the commission of offences set forth in Article 2;

(b) Measures requiring financial institutions and other professions involved in financial transactions to utilize the most efficient measures available for the identification of their usual or occasional customers, as well as customers in whose interest accounts are opened, and to pay special attention to unusual or suspicious transactions and report transactions suspected of stemming from a criminal activity. For this purpose, States Parties shall consider:

(i) Adopting regulations prohibiting the opening of accounts the holders or beneficiaries of which are unidentified or unidentifiable, and measures to ensure that such institutions verify the identity of the real owners of such transactions;

(ii) With respect to the identification of legal entities, requiring financial institutions, when necessary, to take measures to verify the legal existence and the structure of the customer by obtaining, either from a public register or from the customer or both, proof of incorporation, including information concerning the customer's name, legal form, address, directors and provisions regulating the power to bind the entity;

(iii) Adopting regulations imposing on financial institutions the obligation to report promptly to the competent authorities all complex, unusual large transactions and unusual patterns of transactions, which have no apparent economic or obviously lawful purpose, without fear of assuming criminal or civil liability for breach of any restriction on disclosure of information if they report their suspicions in good faith;

(iv) Requiring financial institutions to maintain, for at least five years, all necessary records on transactions, both domestic or international.

2. States Parties shall further cooperate in the prevention of offences set forth in Article 2 by considering:

(a) Measures for the supervision, including, for example, the licensing, of all money transmission agencies;

(b) Feasible measures to detect or monitor the physical cross-border transportation of cash and bearer negotiable instruments, subject to strict safeguards to ensure proper use of information and without impeding in any way the freedom of capital movements.

3. States Parties shall further cooperate in the prevention of the offences set forth in Article 2 by exchanging accurate and verified information in accordance with their domestic law and coordinating administrative and other measures taken, as appropriate, to prevent the commission of offences set forth in Article 2, in particular by:

(a) Establishing and maintaining channels of communication between their competent agencies and services to facilitate the secure and rapid exchange of information concerning all aspects of offences set forth in Article 2;

(b) Cooperating with one another in conducting inquiries, with respect to the offences set forth in Article 2, concerning:

   (i) The identity, whereabouts and activities of persons in respect of whom reasonable suspicion exists that they are involved in such offences;

   (ii) The movement of funds relating to the commission of such offences.

4. States Parties may exchange information through the International Criminal Police Organization (Interpol).

Article 19

The State Party where the alleged offender is prosecuted shall, in accordance with its domestic law or applicable procedures, communicate the final outcome of the proceedings to the Secretary-General of the United Nations, who shall transmit the information to the other States Parties.

Article 20

The States Parties shall carry out their obligations under this Convention in a manner consistent with the principles of sovereign equality and territorial integrity of States and that of non-intervention in the domestic affairs of other States.

Article 21

Nothing in this Convention shall affect other rights, obligations and responsibilities of States and individuals under international law, in particular the purposes of the Charter of the United Nations, international humanitarian law and other relevant conventions.

Article 22

Nothing in this Convention entitles a State Party to undertake in the territory of another State Party the exercise of jurisdiction or performance of functions which are exclusively reserved for the authorities of that other State Party by its domestic law.

Article 23

1. The annex may be amended by the addition of relevant treaties that:

   (a) Are open to the participation of all States;
   (b) Have entered into force;
   (c) Have been ratified, accepted, approved or acceded to by at least twenty-two States Parties to the present Convention.

2. After the entry into force of this Convention, any State Party may propose such an amendment. Any proposal for an amendment shall be communicated to the depositary in written form. The depositary shall notify proposals that meet the requirements of paragraph 1 to all States Parties and seek their views on whether the proposed amendment should be adopted.

3. The proposed amendment shall be deemed adopted unless one-third of the States Parties object to it by a written notification not later than 180 days after its circulation.

4. The adopted amendment to the annex shall enter into force 30 days after the deposit of the twenty-second instrument of ratification, acceptance or approval of such amendment for all those States Parties having deposited such an instrument. For each State Party ratifying, accepting or approving the amendment after the deposit of the twenty-second instrument, the amendment shall enter into force on the thirtieth day after deposit by such State Party of its instrument of ratification, acceptance or approval.

Article 24

1. Any dispute between two or more States Parties concerning the interpretation or application of this Convention which cannot be settled through negotiation within a reasonable time shall, at the request of one of them, be submitted to arbitration. If, within six months from the date of the request for arbitration, the parties are unable to agree on the organization of the arbitration, any one of those parties may refer the dispute to the International Court of Justice, by application, in conformity with the Statute of the Court.

2. Each State may at the time of signature, ratification, acceptance or approval of this Convention or accession thereto declare that it does not consider itself bound by paragraph 1. The other States Parties shall not be bound by paragraph 1 with respect to any State Party which has made such a reservation.

3. Any State which has made a reservation in accordance with paragraph 2 may at any time withdraw that reservation by notification to the Secretary-General of the United Nations.

Article 25

1. This Convention shall be open for signature by all States from 10 January 2000 to 31 December 2001 at United Nations Headquarters in New York.

2. This Convention is subject to ratification, acceptance or approval. The instruments of ratification, acceptance or approval shall be deposited with the Secretary-General of the United Nations.

3. This Convention shall be open to accession by any State. The instruments of accession shall be deposited with the Secretary-General of the United Nations.

Article 26

1. This Convention shall enter into force on the thirtieth day following the date of the deposit of the twenty-second instrument of ratification, acceptance, approval or accession with the Secretary-General of the United Nations.

2. For each State ratifying, accepting, approving or acceding to the Convention after the deposit of the twenty-second instrument of ratification, acceptance, approval or accession, the Convention shall enter into force on the thirtieth day after deposit by such State of its instrument of ratification, acceptance, approval or accession.

Article 27

1. Any State Party may denounce this Convention by written notification to the Secretary-General of the United Nations.

2. Denunciation shall take effect one year following the date on which notification is received by the Secretary-General of the United Nations.

Article 28

The original of this Convention, of which the Arabic, Chinese, English, French, Russian and Spanish texts are equally authentic, shall be deposited with the Secretary-General of the United Nations who shall send certified copies thereof to all States.

IN WITNESS WHEREOF, the undersigned, being duly authorized thereto by their respective Governments, have signed this Convention, opened for signature at United Nations Headquarters in New York on 10 January 2000.

ANNEX

1. Convention for the Suppression of Unlawful Seizure of Aircraft, done at The Hague on 16 December 1970.
2. Convention for the Suppression of Unlawful Acts against the Safety of Civil Aviation, done at Montreal on 23 September 1971.
3. Convention on the Prevention and Punishment of Crimes against Internationally Protected Persons, including Diplomatic Agents,

adopted by the General Assembly of the United Nations on 14 December 1973.

4. International Convention against the Taking of Hostages, adopted by the General Assembly of the United Nations on 17 December 1979.
5. Convention on the Physical Protection of Nuclear Material, adopted at Vienna on 3 March 1980.
6. Protocol for the Suppression of Unlawful Acts of Violence at Airports Serving International Civil Aviation, supplementary to the Convention for the Suppression of Unlawful Acts against the Safety of Civil Aviation, done at Montreal on 24 February 1988.
7. Convention for the Suppression of Unlawful Acts against the Safety of Maritime Navigation, done at Rome on 10 March 1988.
8. Protocol for the Suppression of Unlawful Acts against the Safety of Fixed Platforms located on the Continental Shelf, done at Rome on 10 March 1988.
9. International Convention for the Suppression of Terrorist Bombings, adopted by the General Assembly of the United Nations on 15 December 1997.